IP Addressing Fundamentals

Mark A. Sportack

Cisco Press

Cisco Press
201 West 103rd Street
Indianapolis, IN 46290 USA

ssing Fundamentals

2003 Cisco Systems, Inc.

logo is a trademark of Cisco Systems, Inc.

by:

ss

103rd Street

olis, IN 46290 USA

nts reserved. No part of this book may be reproduced or transmitted in any form or by any means, electronic
chanical, including photocopying and recording, or by any information storage and retrieval system, without
n permission from the publisher, except for the inclusion of brief quotations in a review.

ted in the United States of America 1 2 3 4 5 6 7 8 9 0

st printing November 2002

brary of Congress Cataloging-in-Publication Number: 2001093680

SBN: 1-58705-067-6

Warning and Disclaimer

This book is designed to provide information about the fundamental concepts and technologies associated with IP
addressing. Every effort has been made to make this book as complete and accurate as possible, but no warranty or
fitness is implied.

The information is provided on an "as is" basis. The author, Cisco Press, and Cisco Systems, Inc. shall have neither
liability nor responsibility to any person or entity with respect to any loss or damages arising from the information
contained in this book or from the use of the discs or programs that may accompany it.

The opinions expressed in this book belong to the author and are not necessarily those of Cisco Systems, Inc.

Trademark Acknowledgments

All terms mentioned in this book that are known to be trademarks or service marks have been appropriately capitalized. Cisco Press or Cisco Systems, Inc. cannot attest to the accuracy of this information. Use of a term in this book
should not be regarded as affecting the validity of any trademark or service mark.

Feedback Information

At Cisco Press, our goal is to create in-depth technical books of the highest quality and value. Each book is crafted
with care and precision, undergoing rigorous development that involves the unique expertise of members of the professional technical community.

Reader feedback is a natural continuation of this process. If you have any comments regarding how we could
improve the quality of this book, or otherwise alter it to better suit your needs, you can contact us through e-mail at
feedback@ciscopress.com. Please make sure to include the book title and ISBN (1-58705-067-6) in your message.

We greatly appreciate your assistance.

Publisher	John Wait
Editor-In-Chief	John Kane
Cisco Systems Program Manager	Anthony Wolfenden
Managing Editor	Patrick Kanouse
Development Editor	Grant Munroe
Project Editor	Marc Fowler
Copy Editor	Gayle Johnson
Technical Editors	Mark Gallo
	Alex Kamantauskas
	Dave Kurtiak
	Martin Walshaw
Team Coordinator	Tammi Ross
Book Designer	Gina Rexrode
Cover Designer	Louisa Klucznik
Production Team	Octal Publishing, Inc.
Indexer	Tim Wright

CISCO SYSTEMS

llıllı.....ıllın.®

Corporate Headquarters
Cisco Systems, Inc.
170 West Tasman Drive
San Jose, CA 95134-1706
USA
http://www.cisco.com
Tel: 408 526-4000
     800 553-NETS (6387)
Fax: 408 526-4100

European Headquarters
Cisco Systems Europe
11 Rue Camille Desmoulins
92782 Issy-les-Moulineaux
Cedex 9
France
http://www-europe.cisco.com
Tel: 33 1 58 04 60 00
Fax: 33 1 58 04 61 00

Americas Headquarters
Cisco Systems, Inc.
170 West Tasman Drive
San Jose, CA 95134-1706
USA
http://www.cisco.com
Tel: 408 526-7660
Fax: 408 527-0883

Asia Pacific Headquarters
Cisco Systems Australia,
Pty., Ltd
Level 17, 99 Walker Street
North Sydney
NSW 2059 Australia
http://www.cisco.com
Tel: +61 2 8448 7100
Fax: +61 2 9957 4350

Cisco Systems has more than 200 offices in the following countries. Addresses, phone numbers, and fax numbers are listed on the Cisco Web site at www.cisco.com/go/offices

Argentina • Australia • Austria • Belgium • Brazil • Bulgaria • Canada • Chile • China • Colombia • Costa Rica • Croatia • Czech Republic • Denmark • Dubai, UAE • Finland • France • Germany • Greece • Hong Kong Hungary • India • Indonesia • Ireland • Israel • Italy • Japan • Korea • Luxembourg • Malaysia • Mexico The Netherlands • New Zealand • Norway • Peru • Philippines • Poland • Portugal • Puerto Rico • Romania Russia • Saudi Arabia • Scotland • Singapore • Slovakia • Slovenia • South Africa • Spain • Sweden Switzerland • Taiwan • Thailand • Turkey • Ukraine • United Kingdom • United States • Venezuela • Vietnam Zimbabwe

ut the Author

A. Sportack is the Director of Network Engineering for ClearBlue Technologies. By night, he is an essor with Syracuse University's School of Information Studies and Technology, where he teaches a uate courses on data networking. His daytime responsibilities include strategic planning for the net- support the company's Internet data centers, research and evaluation of emerging network technologies, ion of the technology base for the networks thatthe company's Internet-based managed hosting services. ne course of the last 20 years, Sportack has worked in virtually every aspect of information technology, ministering networks and servers to managing technology and technical personnel. He also has written a of books, including *IP Routing Fundamentals,* published by Cisco Press, *Networking Essentials Unleashed,* any others.

out the **Technical Reviewers**

ark Gallo is a technical manager with America Online. His network certifications include Cisco CCNP and isco CCDP. He has led several engineering groups responsible for designing and implementing enterprise LANs nd international IP networks. He has a BS in electrical engineering from the University of Pittsburgh. He resides in northern Virginia with his wife, Betsy, and son, Paul.

Alex Kamantauskas is the hostmaster for ClearBlue Technologies, Inc. He has worked in a wide variety of positions in the Internet sector since 1993, including system and network engineering, network security, and IP allocation services. In his spare time he composes electronic music.

Dave Kurtiak is a principal engineer and Director of Network Computing Services for Loral Skynet, where he leads a team of technical professionals responsible for managing the company's IT and data network infrastructure. He has more than 14 years of experience in the IT and telecommunications industries. Before joining Loral Skynet, he was a senior data communications specialist for AT&T. He specializes in end-to-end network analysis, planning, and troubleshooting. Kurtiak is experienced in many telecommunications technologies, including Ethernet, switches, routers, VPN, point-to-point digital facilities, Frame Relay, and premise wiring topologies. He is also recognized as the resident expert in TCP/IP networking. He has a master's degree in telecommunications from the University of Colorado at Boulder and a bachelor's degree in information systems from the University of North Carolina at Greensboro.

Martin Walshaw, CCIE #5629, CCNP, CCDP, is a systems engineer working for Cisco Systems in the Enterprise Line of Business in South Africa. His areas of specialization include convergence, security, and content delivery networking, which keeps him busy both night and day. During the last 15 years or so, he has dabbled in many aspects of the IT industry, ranging from programming in RPG III and Cobol to PC sales. When Walshaw is not working, he likes to spend all his time with his patient wife, Val, and his sons, Joshua and Callum. Without their patience, understanding, and support, projects such as this would not be possible.

Dedications

I dedicate this book to my precious wife, Karen, for her unflagging love and support throughout the arduous process of developing this book. I'll never know why you tolerate my eccentricities and avocational distractions, but I'm perpetually grateful.

I also dedicate this book to my two children, Adam and Jennifer. You have brought joy and meaning into my life in ways I can't explain.

Acknowledgments

I am indebted to many people for their assistance and support throughout the process of writing this book. Those people include:

David Kurtiak, Alex Kamantauskus, Marc Gallo, and Martin Walshaw for investing their time and expertise as technical editors to make this book the best it can be.

John Kane, Tammi Ross, Grant Munroe, and all the folks at Cisco Press for having enough faith in me (or is that the book?) to agree to its production, and for tolerating the excruciating delays caused by world and business events.

Jeff Harrington for allowing me the use of his technical library and reference materials.

Contents at a Glance

Table of Contents

Introduction

IP Addressing Fundamentals is designed to explain how the IP address space works and how it is used. Many books help you gain a working knowledge of this topic, but none can help you both appreciate the why behind the theory and the how behind the application. My goal is to do both with this book.

The inspiration for this book came as a result of my teaching experiences at Syracuse University. I'm an adjunct professor in SU's School of Information Studies and Technology, where I teach a pair of graduate courses on telecommunications and data networking. Despite the advanced nature of these courses, and the talented students who are attracted to them, I found myself continuously astounded at the limits of their working knowledge of important topics such as IP addressing. After two years of correcting misperceptions, asking students where they picked up their misinformation, and trying to show them a better way to understand the Internet's address space and technologies, I found myself getting frustrated. Just when I started thinking that maybe teaching wasn't such a good idea, I had a pair of experiences that erased my doubts and replaced them with inspiration.

One particularly bright young man explained to me that learning about IP was a lot like trying to piece together a jigsaw puzzle. The only differences were that you didn't know what the puzzle was supposed to look like when it was finished, nor did you have the benefit of a picture fragment on each piece. He appreciated my approach to teaching IP and networking, because I gave them the "big picture," broke it down into subtopics that were easier to grasp, and then correlated those subtopics back to the big picture. A healthy dose of reality, in the form of examining the practical uses and impacts of each subject, was also injected into each class. In the end, he said he not only understood the topic, but also appreciated both its mechanics and relevance.

The other experience occurred in the same semester. One night before class, a student approached me with a new book in his hands. You could tell it was a new book, even from a distance: that shiny, unmarred cover; the smell of fresh ink; the uncracked spine—a thing of beauty! But the look on his face was one of disappointment and anxiety. The book was written by a luminary in the Internet—a founding father who has written countless RFCs and has been instrumental in guiding the Internet's growth and development. Yet my student said the book was disappointing. I suggested that the book should be technically solid given the achievements of its author. He simply replied that it would be a great book if he could understand it! Instead of educating and informing the reader, this book caused anxiety and self-doubt. My student was asking my advice on whether he was smart enough to succeed in this industry. Of course he was, I assured him. It was the book and its author who had failed.

These two events crystallized in my mind the need for this book. I called John Kane, Editor-in-Chief at Cisco Press. We had a long chat about the need for a reader-friendly book that explains the fundamentals of the IP address space from the ground up. A book that unravels the mysteries of subnetting, supernetting, and CIDR. A book that thoroughly explains the binary mathematics of IPv4's addressing space and shows the reader how an IP address becomes an active component in both networks and internetworks. A book that prepares you for success by walking you through some of the issues and traps that lie in wait for anyone daring to either plan or manage the use of an IP address space. Most important of all, a book that doesn't presume that you already know what the puzzle should look like when it is completed. Thankfully, John and the folks at Cisco Press agreed. I hope you enjoy it!

Icons Used in This Book

Throughout this book, you will see a number of icons used to designate Cisco and general networking devices, peripherals, and other items. The following icon legend explains what these icons represent.

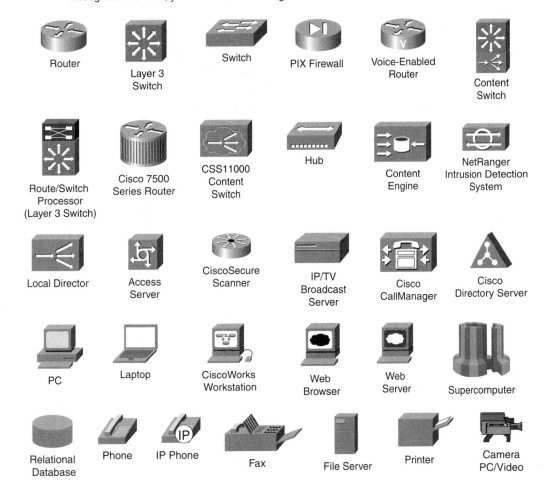

Throughout this book, you will see the following icons used for common network devices

Command Syntax Conventions

The conventions used to present command syntax in this book are the same conventions used in the IOS Command Reference. The Command Reference describes these conventions as follows:

- Vertical bars (I) separate alternative, mutually exclusive elements.

- Square brackets ([ ]) indicate an optional element.

- Braces ({ }) indicate a required choice.

- Braces within brackets ([{ }]) indicate a required choice within an optional element.

- **Boldface** indicates commands and keywords that are entered literally as shown. In actual configuration examples and output (not general command syntax), boldface indicates commands that are manually input by the user (such as a **show** command).

- *Italic* indicates arguments for which you supply actual values.

Introduction to IP Addressing

CHAPTER 1

Developing the Internet's Technologies

To many technical personnel today, the Internet remains a mystery that is taken for granted. Virtually everybody knows what it is and what it can be used for, but few actually know what goes on behind the scenes. The Internet's address space and native protocols have become the de facto standard for many aspects of networking. The Internet Protocol (IP) address space and the various IP-based protocols and mechanisms have been widely deployed around the world. Currently they support more networks than just the Internet. More importantly, these technologies and concepts share a similar origin: Typically, they are developed and ratified in an open and consensus-based forum.

It is this consensus-based approach to developing technologies that creates such confusion among newcomers to the Internet. Worse, the confusion extends beyond the Internet and encompasses all its component technologies, including the IP address space. Understanding any of these technologies requires an appreciation of the context in which it was developed, and a sense of what it was originally intended to do.

This chapter explores how technologies are ratified for use in the Internet. It also looks at the various standards bodies and other organizations that are the Internet's caretakers. This will help you better appreciate what does and does not carry the weight of law on the Internet.

The Internet's Caretakers

Numerous organizations, standards bodies, and even corporations function in different capacities. All of them contribute in some way to the Internet. Some allocate domain names (such as cisco.com) or assign IP addresses to the Internet's end users. Others create the technologies that make the Internet work or that let you use the Internet. All these entities are integral to the Internet's operation. We'll look at each one in this chapter, but only one can truly be considered the Internet's caretaker. That organization is the Internet Engineering Task Force (IETF).

IETF

The manner in which the Internet's technology base is developed and ratified might not be intuitively appreciated. In fact, the arrangement is one of the more unconventional approaches you may ever find. As we start to explore just how it operates, and how standards and other recommendations are developed in this forum, you'll appreciate why I call it unconventional. Nevertheless, it is a model that works using both collaborative and competitive forces.

One of the unique qualities of the IETF is that it consists almost entirely of unpaid volunteers. Don't misunderstand the point; these are highly technical and well-paid engineers who contribute their time to the IETF in addition to the work they do for their employers. Such volunteers don't pay dues to join the IETF. They simply "join" and either lurk in the background or actively contribute to the work being performed.

The IETF, and the way it operates, can be traced back to the nascent days of the Internet when just a few hosts were interconnected directly with serial lines. In those days, the technical personnel responsible for supporting the various interconnected hosts realized that there was great benefit to working together for the sake of deriving consistency in naming conventions, the technology base, communications protocols, and guidelines for using their internetwork. Lacking a central budget, mission, or any of the other trappings of a conventional organization, nothing could be dictated. Only the mutual desire to improve the functionality of their interdependent network bound them together. Everything had to make sense for the entire community to form a consensus. Otherwise, suggestions and recommendations might not be adopted. The technical community supporting this early internetwork (a group of interconnected networks) formed a loose confederation and called themselves an engineering task force. The moniker stuck.

Informal collaboration and communication worked quite well for a number of years, and then the Internet began its exponential growth stage toward the end of the 1980s. The first official meeting of the IETF was held in January of 1986 and was attended by just 21 people. Membership and participation have increased steadily since then and now encompass thousands of people. Although the IETF has grown tremendously, its original essence remains embodied in the way it is organized. Today, technical professionals from competitive companies work side-by-side under the auspices of the IETF to develop and maintain the Internet's technology base. Its membership is an ever-growing group of highly talented individuals who volunteer their time to collaboratively engineer and evolve the Internet's technology base. The IETF's work in spelling out the protocol-level details of new technologies, as well as methods and procedures, is published openly in a series of documents, which include the following:

- Internet drafts
- Requests for Comments (RFCs)
- Internet standards

- Best Current Practices (BCPs)
- FYIs (For Your Information)

Each type of document serves a specific purpose, and we'll look at each one in detail. First we need to examine the hierarchy of the IETF. That will help you better appreciate the inner workings of the IETF as it pertains to the development and ratification of these documents. As we explore the IETF in this chapter, you'll notice how its every nuance, including how the IETF is organized and functions, is recorded in a publicly available document that fits into one or more of the previously mentioned document classes.

NOTE   All of the IETF's documentation is publicly available on its website at www.ietf.org.

Many organizations are affiliated with the IETF, each with loosely defined responsibilities. These groups include the following:

- Internet Society (ISOC)
- Internet Architecture Board (IAB)
- Internet Research Task Force (IRTF)
- Internet Assigned Numbers Authority (IANA)
- Internet Corporation for Assigned Names and Numbers (ICANN)
- Internet Engineering Steering Group (IESG)
- Working groups

Each of these organizations is further explored in the remainder of this section.

ISOC

The ISOC is an international nonprofit organization. It differs from other Internet organizations in that it is not a suborganization of the IETF. Its sole mission is to foster the growth of the global Internet. It does so in fairly abstract and less-than-obvious ways. For example, it theoretically provides oversight to the IETF and its subcomponents, but that oversight is limited to financial, logistic, and legal support. For example, it provides insurance coverage for people involved in the IETF's standards-creation processes, and it functions as a public relations channel whenever an IETF entity needs to communicate via the press.

Perhaps the most visible output of the ISOC is that its trustees ratify the rules and procedures by which standards are developed for the Internet by the IETF. Thus, although the ISOC doesn't directly shape the Internet or its technology base, it sets the rules by which the Internet evolves.

IAB

One of the more critical subentities of the IETF is the IAB. Originally known as the Internet Activities Board, the IAB has evolved and grown over time in response to changes in the Internet. Today, the IAB is known as the Internet Architecture Board. It is responsible for long-range planning and coordinating activities across the various subcomponents of the IETF. As such, it is uniquely positioned to see the big picture of the IETF's cumulative efforts. Part of its role might be to bring issues to the attention of specific area directors if they think a long-term item requires some attention.

IRTF

The IRTF is sponsored and overseen by the IAB. This group conducts research into emerging technologies, and this research becomes an input to the IAB's long-range technology planning activities.

IANA

The IANA is responsible for keeping track of all numbers and numeric values that must be reserved or assigned for the various protocols and technologies maintained by the IETF to work properly. The most obvious example is the IP address space (the sum total of all IP addresses), but IANA's responsibilities also include maintaining the list of TCP and UDP standardized or well-known application port numbers.

IANA is also the Internet's core registrar. This dubious distinction was conferred by the IAB, and it made IANA the "owner" of the root of the Internet's name space. This role has not exactly resulted in a positive perception throughout the Internet community, and unfortunately it has overshadowed some of IANA's other responsibilities. Although IANA once was a relatively autonomous entity within the IETF, and it still is technically charged with maintaining all the unique parameters used on the Internet (addresses, domain names, and port numbers) today, IANA appears to be slowly melding into ICANN.

ICANN

The ICANN is a nonprofit corporation that was established to maintain IP address allocation, assignment of protocol parameters (such as port numbers), and management of the Internet's domain name system (DNS). These functions had previously been performed by IANA, but they have since been delegated to ICANN.

To carry out its duties, ICANN has formed three function-specific supporting organizations (SOs):

- Address Supporting Organization (ASO)
- Domain Name Supporting Organization (DNSO)
- Protocol Supporting Organization (PSO)

ICANN functions as the root of the Internet's domain name space and charters both registries and registrars. The registry function is distributed by regions around the globe. It allows address space to be parsed out and managed regionally. Such registries are known as Regional Internet Registries (RIRs). There are three registries, but some cover more than one region. Table 1-1 lists the regions and their supporting RIRs.

Table 1-1   *RIRs and Their Regions*

Global Region	Supporting RIR
Europe	RIPE NCC
Africa	ARIN and the RIPE NCC
North America	ARIN
Middle East	RIPE NCC
Latin America and the Caribbean	ARIN
Asia-Pacific	APNIC

ARIN stands for American Registry for Internet Numbers. APNIC stands for Asia Pacific Network Information Centre. RIPE NCC is a bit tougher for North Americans to grasp; it stands for Réseaux IP Européens Network Coordination Centre.

Each registry is given a block of IP addresses and is responsible for assigning and managing that space within its region. Two other geographic regions have announced plans to form their own RIRs: Africa and Latin America. ICANN is the only entity that can charter an RIR and assign it an address space.

Within each RIR's region, other entities can apply to become Local Internet Registries (LIRs), much like an Internet Service Provider (ISP) can assign address blocks to its customers' operational networks.

Registrars, on the other hand, are responsible for managing the assignment of Internet domain names. This is a much more contentious issue than merely parsing out numbers. Don't worry just yet about why domain names can be contentious; we'll cover that in detail in Chapter 8, "Internet Names." For now, it is enough that you just appreciate the acronyms, roles, and responsibilities of the various bodies that regulate the Internet's growth, evolution, and operation.

The Internet's Registries and Registrars
by Alex Kamantauskas

The topic of registries on the Internet can cause some confusion. There are multiple "registries" as a direct result of the breakup of the Network Solutions monopoly on domain names. Prior to the advent of ICANN, Network Solutions functioned as both the registry for domain names (the entity responsible for making sure the root servers were updated, the whois servers were maintained, and so on) and the registrar (the point of contact in the trading of domain names as a commodity). When competition was introduced into the domain name market, Network Solutions (and now VeriSign) maintained the registry function, and the registrar function was split among the various competing companies, including Network Solutions. That company was both registry and registrar for a while, but I assure, you they didn't play favorites. In order to become an accredited registrar, you had to agree to—and use—the Network Solutions/VeriSign registry.

However, today the distinction between registry and registrar is growing fuzzier with the advent of sponsored domain names. For instance, NeuLevel is now the registry for the .biz domain name. It provides registry services for the domain name for registrars that are selling names in the .biz space. So, now you have the registry for Internet numbers, multiple registries for Internet names, and competing registrars.

IESG

The Internet Engineering Steering Group (IESG) provides technical management of all IETF activities, as well as its standards-development process. The IESG consists of area directors, each of which are nominated by the IETF's nominations committee and serve a two-year term. The area directors oversee a specific technical area. Current areas include the following:

- Applications
- General
- Internet
- Operations and Management
- Routing
- Security
- Transport
- User Services

These areas correlate almost perfectly with the functional areas of the working groups, which are described in more detail in the next section. The only exception is the General Area, which exists as a catchall mechanism for the IESG. Not many initiatives fall into this category, but those that do can be assigned to whichever area or areas are deemed appropriate.

It's important to note that the oversight of the IESG and its area directors doesn't extend to direct oversight of technical development efforts. Instead, oversight is construed as ratifying the output of the working groups. Thus, the IESG can exert influence on whether any particular proposal advances to the point where it can be implemented. Typically, the IESG accepts the recommendations of working groups, but it can reject a recommendation if it believes the group has either strayed from its charter or has recommended something that will have an adverse effect on the Internet and its technology base.

Working Groups

The detail work of developing specific technical solutions to specific technical problems is performed by transient organizations within the IETF known as *working groups*. The IETF has sought to create a continuity of technical expertise in working groups by organizing them into functional areas. Each functional area is directed by an IESG area director. An area can have multiple working groups operating simultaneously, focused on extremely specific activities. It is important to note that these areas do not necessarily translate cleanly into areas recognized by the IESG. Consider this imperfect correlation between working groups and IESG areas; a feature that enables flexibility, as opposed to a flaw which promotes confusion. The output of any given working group may be reviewed by multiple IESG area directors to obviate potential conflicting technologies or recommendations.

Currently, the IETF has active working groups in the following functional areas:

- **Applications**—Broadly defined as things that use IP networks and security mechanisms, but excluding all security and network mechanisms. Applications that require network connectivity rely on well-defined interfaces to the transport and network layer protocols, and that becomes the bailiwick of the Applications Area working group.

- **Internet**—The Internet Area encompasses developing mechanisms and capabilities for IP itself. For example, developing the ability for IP to be transported over new network technologies such as InfiniBand, Fibre Channel, and cable networks lies in this functional area.

- **Operations and Management**—Anything that defines how things operate is the responsibility of the O&M functional area. Generally speaking, anything involving Simple Network Management Protocol (SNMP), Management Information Base (MIB), or operation of services is done within the O&M area. Specific examples of active working groups in this area include a group investigating the extension of SNMP agents, Domain Name Server (DNS) operations, and the evolution of SNMP.

- **Routing**—The Routing functional area is tightly focused on routing protocols. Some teams active in this area are looking at the Routing Information Protocol (RIP), Open Shortest Path First (OSPF) routing protocol, and the development of a virtual router redundancy protocol (VRRP).

- **Security**—Security is fairly self-evident, in that the teams in this area focus on improving the authentication, privacy, and safety of networked computing assets and data. Security teams are currently working on such things as the creation of an XML-based (extensible markup language) digital signature and an open version of Pretty Good Privacy (PGP) encryption software, among others.

- **Sub-IP**—The Sub-IP Area is one of the hardest areas to describe. At least, I have a difficult time understanding what differentiates it from the Internet functional area. Substantial overlap between the two groups is evident when you consider that two of the currently active Sub-IP groups are developing the specifications for IP over optical facilities and Multiprotocol Label Switching (MPLS).

- **Transport**—The Transport functional area focuses on developing interfaces for higher-level protocols and services. Some of the specific areas of current activity include IP Telephony, IP Storage, Differentiated Services (DiffServ), and audio/video transport.

- **User Services**—Anything that defines how people want things done across a network. This group tends to focus on developing FYIs instead of RFCs. (If these acronyms don't mean anything to you, keep reading. We'll look at all the outputs of the various IETF subentities in the next section, "The Internet Standards Process.") This group also helps users of all levels improve the quality of information available on the Internet. That might sound a bit vague, but you can think of it this way: The User Services group is more of a communications vehicle for the IETF than a technology development group.

If these categorizations sound a bit soft, and it seems there is great potential for overlap, you're right. Many specific technical problems are worked on jointly by two or more working groups. Membership in a working group is voluntary.

If the notion of joining a working group and helping develop new standards for the Internet appeals to you, do yourself and everyone in the IETF a favor, and read RFC 3160. Entitled "The Tao of the IETF," this document helps you better understand the organization, its culture, and everything about the work it produces. The URL is www.ietf.org/rfc/rfc3160.txt.

The Internet Standards Process

The way that technical standards are developed for the Internet might seem arcane from the outside looking in, but this process is eminently logical, and it has served the Internet well for years. This process is documented in the IETF's RFC 2026, which is also currently the Internet's BCP #9. This document can be accessed at www.ietf.org/rfc/rfc2026.txt.

If the terms RFC and BCP are alien to you, read on. The remainder of this chapter is devoted to helping you understand the inner workings of this vital function. The roles of Internet drafts, RFCs, STDs (standards), and BCPs are all explored and explained.

Internet Draft

Virtually every standard published by the IETF starts out as an Internet draft or *I-D* or just plain *draft* in IETF parlance. A draft can be submitted by an individual or can be the product of a working group.

The draft itself conforms to the template used for all RFCs, which only adds to the terminology confusion. Because the RFCs are public documents, virtually anyone in the world can review them and make comments to the author(s) for consideration. If appropriate, the document might be superseded by a modified version, or it might die a quiet death if it fails to resonate within the Internet community. If it does find some support, the document can either become embraced as a de facto standard or undergo the more rigorous standardization process. The remainder of this chapter examines all the document types that the IETF recognizes. Then we'll look at the inner workings of that organization's consensus-based standards adoption mechanisms.

RFCs

The most commonly encountered IETF-produced document is the RFCs. These documents aren't necessarily just requests for comments. In fact, many of them contain the specifications for protocols and technologies that are embraced as standards or built as products. In other words, many RFCs have progressed well beyond the development stage where comments are being solicited. Thus, the full name is actually a misnomer. For this reason, RFCs of all types are almost always referred to as simply RFCs.

NOTE Although the arcane nature and nomenclature of RFCs might be discouraging, rest assured that some of these documents are quite useful. E-mail, as ubiquitous an application as you could hope to find, was first described in RFC 821. Similarly, DNS originated in a pair of RFCs numbered 1034 and 1035. So, you see, they can be quite useful.

There are six different types of RFCs. Each goes through a slightly different process during its journey toward ratification:

- Proposed standards
- Draft standards
- Internet standards
- Experimental protocols
- Informational documents
- Historic standards

Of these six, only the first three qualify as standards within the IETF. Thus, it is imperative to understand that RFCs are not created equal. Some are solid enough to have products designed around them, and others are not intended for use other than to solicit comments or test for interest in an emerging technology. For a much more complete summary of the differences between the various types of RFCs, refer to RFC 1796, "Not all RFCs are Standards." You can find it at www.ietf.org/rfc/rfc1796.txt

Just to prove that things can get even more complicated, there are also three subseries of documents within the RFC architecture—standards (STDs), Best Current Practices (BCPs), and For Your Information (FYI) documents. Each is described in the following sections.

Internet Standards

There are three types standards—the Proposed Standard, the Draft Standard, and the Internet Standard. RFCs that are placed on the standards track first become Proposed Standards. After six months in this status, such RFCs might undergo additional scrutiny and be sanctioned as Draft Standards. Even more scrutiny is required for a Draft Standard to be ratified as an Internet Standard. Internet Standards are often known as Full Standards, but there aren't very many of them. In fact, most standards-track documents never move beyond Proposed Standard. That doesn't mean they aren't useful. In fact, many protocols and products are built around Proposed Standards. The explanation for a standard's inability to move to Draft and then Full Standard might simply be a resource issue: Only so many people can make meaningful contributions. Engineers who develop a Proposed Standard might simply find themselves drawn into other initiatives before they can advance a Proposed Standard any further. Please don't misconstrue that as laziness or anything of the sort. Advancing Proposed Standards is complex, time-consuming work. In fact, it can take several years of work before a Draft Standard can become a Full Standard. The amount of effort required to make this happen limits the number of RFCs that become Full Standards to just those few protocols that are absolutely essential for the Internet to function.

We will examine the IETF's approval process for moving an RFC on the standards track through the various standard stages in a moment.

BCPs

A subset of the RFC series is known as the Internet's Best Current Practices (BCPs). This subset differs from the technical specifications often found in RFCs. BCPs specify operating procedures that are consensually agreed to be the best for the Internet. Alternatively, a BCP can be used to describe how to apply the various technologies described in other IETF documents. Some of the examples of BCPs presented in this chapter should give you a good idea of the type of content that can be found in a BCP.

FYIs

The FYI subseries of documents was created to present information such as big-picture overviews of highly technical topics. Such overviews provide a context within which much more specific RFCs add detail. Other uses of the FYI documents are to introduce a topic or otherwise present information that is perceived to have broad appeal. Working groups within the IETF's User Services Area usually produce this type of document.

Approval Process

The process by which a proposal progresses through the IETF on its way to ratification can be time-consuming and arduous, but it follows a fairly distinct pattern. A proposal is first floated as an Internet draft. Comments are received, and the draft is edited accordingly. This can be an iterative process, as opposed to achieving completion in a single pass. If an individual created the draft, that person might request that an area director take the document to the IESG for review and consideration. If a working group created the document, the chairperson of that group takes it (after achieving consensus in the group, of course) to the area director for forwarding to the IESG. Either way, the IESG must review it in the larger context of existing standards and future desired technology directions. If any changes are deemed necessary by the IESG, the draft goes back to its creator(s) for further work. When there is consensus among the document's creators, area director, and IESG, the draft can be published as an RFC.

It is important to note that additional layers of checks and balances exist in the approval process. For example, if two or more area directors object to an Internet draft, it is blocked from becoming an RFC, and it can't become a standard. This veto power ensures that a technology doesn't get ratified that will have unacceptable impacts on other technologies. This is critical to ensure the ongoing stability of the Internet's open protocols and technologies.

Another check-and-balance mechanism is the "last call." After a draft is submitted to the IESG, an IETF-wide announcement is made to ensure that nothing can escape anyone's notice. In this manner, comments may be solicited from people and/or groups who weren't following a particular draft's development. Such groups include the ISOC, IRTF, IAB, and even other area directors or working groups. Any and all of these parties have the opportunity to submit comments, concerns, and questions to the working group responsible for the document.

After all parties have had a chance to examine the draft (and its implications), the IESG might decide to sanction the draft as an Internet Standard. If that is the case, the draft still has some hurdles to overcome. The IESG requests that the editor of the RFCs (a formal position within the IETF) publish the draft as a Proposed Standard. It has status as a numbered RFC, but it is also explicitly identified as a Proposed Standard. After six months, the author(s) of that RFC can ask their area director to approve it as a draft standard. This is a high hurdle to overcome. The technology must be proven by at least two independent implementations that demonstrate not only interoperability but also validation of the concept's benefits.

As mentioned earlier, it is highly likely that a proposed standard will never make it to full Internet Standard status and yet will still achieve broad acceptance in the market. This can be one of the more confusing aspects of the IETF's standards-setting process. But if an RFC makes it all the way to Full Standard, you can rest assured it has been thoroughly examined and tested. Of course, this is not a guarantee that all products will work perfectly. It just means that the various companies that implement the RFC start with a stable base but are free to interpret it according to their needs. The next section explains this phenomenon and some of its unintended consequences.

NOTE	There is a persistent and pervasive misperception among Internet users that RFCs are the laws of the Internet. In some cases, such as RFCs that are BCPs or STDs, that might be a good analogy. But in the vast majority of cases, RFCs are little more than ideas floated publicly to solicit comments. No one is obligated to comply with an RFC, nor is there any penalty for noncompliance.

The Benefits of Openness

Making publicly available standards documents that stipulate every nuance of a technology is known as *open standards*. Open standards offer tremendous benefits that have been proven time and again since the introduction of this concept. In the days before the Internet, the previous paradigm was tightly integrated proprietary platforms. In other words, every aspect of a networked computing architecture (including endpoint devices, cable interfaces, computing platforms, operating systems, applications, and printers) was tightly linked by the manufacturers. You couldn't mix and match components from different manufacturers; you had to select one vendor for all your needs.

The benefits have proven very compelling. Competition has leveled the playing field, prices have dropped, and manufacturers have continued to innovate in order to develop meaningful (albeit temporary) advantages over their competitors. The Internet standards-setting process is one of the ways in which technologies can be either developed out in the open or, if developed privately, granted openness.

Competitive Advantages of Openness

Although the Internet's standards-setting process might seem very altruistic, especially because virtually all the IETF's members are volunteers, you need to remember that things are not always as they first appear. Joining the IETF, or any of its functional components, as a volunteer can represent a substantial commitment of time and effort. Because the IETF doesn't pay network engineers for these efforts, and most network engineers aren't independently wealthy, it stands to reason that someone must fund or subsidize their involvement. Usually, that is the engineer's employer.

So the obvious question to ask is "What's in it for the employer?". Why would any company fund or subsidize anyone's involvement in the IETF? The answer is remarkably simple: They have a vested interest in the outcome of the proceedings. It is quite common for a company to develop a proprietary technology and then seek to legitimize its standing in the Internet community by presenting the technology to the IETF in the form of an RFC. A working group might or might not then be required to examine the proposal or RFC in more detail and determine what, if any, changes are required to make the proposal more acceptable. Other companies also benefit from participating in that they get the "inside track" on emerging technologies that might or might not become approved for use on the Internet.

At this point, you might be wondering why any company that has developed a great new technology would want to give it away to potential competitors by publishing its technical specifications as an open standard. Wouldn't the company be better off just keeping the technology for itself instead of creating competition? The answer is a resounding no. Consumers of information technologies all but demand open technologies. Thus, a technology manufacturer would find a much larger potential customer base awaiting an open-standards product than it would for a proprietary product. Another benefit is that the company has a distinct advantage over other companies. Simply stated, it has already developed its product, and it can start selling it long before other companies, which have to start from scratch.

Creating Propriety Through Openness

The final nail in the coffin of altruism is found in how some companies manipulate the process of open-standards development. RFC 2119, also known as BCP #14, spells out acceptable language to use in an RFC or similar document used to define new open standard technologies. Acceptable wording describing a function's criticality includes the following:

- MUST
- MUST NOT
- REQUIRED
- SHALL
- SHALL NOT
- SHOULD
- SHOULD NOT

- RECOMMENDED
- MAY
- OPTIONAL

These words are intentionally capitalized, as they are in the various IETF publications, to indicate compliance with their definitions in RFC 2119/BCP #14. This isn't a very long or difficult-to-read document. It should be one of the first things you read as you start to familiarize yourself with the works of the IETF, including the IP address space. It can be found at www.ietf.org/rfc/rfc2119.txt

Despite this careful attempt at creating consistency in products based on open standards, inconsistency continues to abound. Each technology manufacturer is given latitude in defining how closely its product conforms to the recommended specification. The words SHOULD, SHOULD NOT, MAY, RECOMMENDED, and OPTIONAL are almost an invitation for variation. Thus, depending on how well two or more manufacturers adhere to the recommendation of an open-standards document, their products might interoperate with varying degrees of success. The only way to achieve perfect operability is to maintain a single-vendor infrastructure, thereby defeating the very purpose of openness.

Another interesting way that actual products might vary from the open standard is to include additional functions or features that are absent from the standards document. Such technologies or products might still legitimately claim to be "open-standard" and are founded on the belief that they embrace the open standard and then extend it. This belief also leads to the creation of a proprietary architecture within an otherwise open-standards technology.

Summary

The Internet and IP have both enjoyed unprecedented levels of acceptance in the past decade. Despite the attention lavished on the Internet, IP has become more widely used. Many organizations require IP to support their application base—applications that have nothing to do with the Internet. Many other organizations directly contribute to the Internet's evolution and technological advance by letting their technical personnel participate in the IETF in its standards-setting work.

Ben Franklin once said that you should enjoy laws and sausages, but don't even try to understand how either one gets made. His reasoning was that you would lose your appetite for both. I must confess that, to the newcomer, the IETF's standards-setting process also fits this policy. It is a world in which a standard is not necessarily a standard, but an RFC might be. Hopefully, the overview provided in this chapter helps makes things a bit easier to understand.

This book focuses on one particular output of the IETF: the Internet's addressing scheme. Even private networks must conform to the rules and protocols established and enforced through the various mechanisms outlined in this chapter, so an understanding of how those entities operate is essential. The next chapter examines the IP address space (and its underlying mathematics) much more closely.

CHAPTER 2

Classical IP: The Way It Was

The Internet has become so successful and ubiquitous that it is difficult to imagine finding a working professional who isn't an ardent user. The Internet was founded on a suite of communication protocols called the *Internet Protocol (IP)*. IP has undergone some tremendous changes in the last two decades, as has its underlying addressing system. This chapter examines the original form of IP addressing: Classical IP.

Classical IP was a fairly simple approach to carving a large address space into smaller, more usable spaces. This subdivision was achieved by breaking the original space into distinct and hierarchical classes. In theory, different-sized classes would let small, medium, and large entities obtain appropriate-sized address blocks. This chapter explains these humble origins, identifies some of the basic assumptions that underlie the original addressing scheme, and then explores the mathematics of the address space. This forms a solid foundation to give you a better understanding of how the addressing architecture worked and was used.

Evolution of the Address Space

IP and its addressing scheme evolved slowly, sometimes even erratically, over time. They were not, contrary to any current appearances, carefully designed prior to implementation! For example, RFC 1, published in April 1969, tells us that the original IP address space was specified at just 5 bits! As you will see in this chapter, that's enough for just 32 addresses! Strange as that might sound, in 1969 that was more than enough for the embedded base of computers that were being internetworked. Over time, the number of bits allocated to host addressing was increased to 6, and then 8, and finally up to the familiar 32-bit format that is in use today.

The actual format of the "IP address" evolved slowly over time in response to the evolution of the DARPAnet. DARPAnet was the predecessor of the Internet. In essence, it was a network that interconnected various research facilities in support of the U.S. Department of Defense. The notion of classes of addresses, with each class offering a differing combination of bits allocated between network and host identification, was first described in RFC 791, published in September 1981. This RFC is the foundation of what has become Classical IP addressing. Although it is technically obsolete, Classical IP still offers a marvelous opportunity to understand the current state of IP addressing.

The Mathematics of the IPv4 Address Space

The current version of the Internet Protocol is version 4, or IPv4. Discussing the mathematics of the current address space in a chapter titled "The Way It Was" might seem a bit odd. Yet the title isn't misleading nor the topic out of place. How the IPv4 address space is implemented has changed radically since its inception. We'll make more sense of that throughout this chapter. For now, just recognize that IPv4 is still the current version. It is just the old way of carving up the IPv4 address space that has passed into obsolescence.

IP addresses are defined within a mathematical space that is 32 bits in length. *Bit* is an abbreviation of *binary digit*. It is the smallest unit of data, and it can have a value of either 0 or 1. Typically, a pattern of 8 bits is called a *byte,* although purists within the data communications and networking fields insist that 8 bits is an *octet*. In truth, this is only a semantic distinction, so use whatever term you are most familiar with.

It's time for a quick mathematical sanity check. Each bit can represent one of two different values: 0 or 1. Thus, the absolute maximum number of unique addresses you can create with a 32-bit address is 2 to the 32nd power, or 4,294,967,295 addresses. That sounds like a *lot* of addresses. It truly was an inexhaustible supply back in the days when only a few hundred computers were sprinkled around the globe. That was the intent of the architects of IP and its address space: Devise a schema that would be scalable beyond the foreseeable future. However, in today's age of a microprocessor in every household appliance, 4 billion doesn't seem quite so large! There are more than 6 billion people on the earth, so the current address system doesn't even allow one address per person.

The Internet Engineering Task Force (IETF—the caretakers of the Internet's technology base) sought to make the address space more usable in numerous ways. They recognized that even a Base10 number would not be conducive to human use of the address space, because it was too large. Base10 is the decimal number system; it uses ten different symbols to represent numbers that progress in multiples of 10. This is the number system that most humans consider native. Unfortunately, keeping track of numbers from 1 to over 4 billion just isn't practical for humans! Thus, additional steps were taken to develop a logical hierarchy:

- Developing a means by which people could continue using the intuitive Base10 number system for endpoint addressing. Remember, computers and networks are inherently digital. Digital implies binary—the Base2 number system! So, some means of making an inherently binary addressing system intuitive to human users was critically needed.

- Breaking up the numeric address into four equal components. This had the beneficial effect of converting a potentially long address into just four relatively small numbers. In relative terms, that was a huge improvement in usability.

- Subdividing the address space into logical classes of address spaces. Ostensibly, classes would let you predefine addresses for small, medium, and large networks.

These three tactics abetted the usability of the IP address space in different ways. The first two directly facilitated human usage. The last tactic was designed to make the address space more scalable in its application than usable to individual users. These tactics and their impacts on the IP address space are described further in the following sections.

Making the Address Space Human-Friendly

Making the IP address space human-friendly required the use of both a familiar number system and the smallest numbers possible. Addressing the first of these criteria, people think in terms of the Base10 number system, whereas computers are inherently binary. That is, computers process information using one of two possible states: either on/off or 1/0. Either way, information is encoded and processed by computers using very long strings that are made up of just two symbols. It would be well beyond the capability of any person to reliably recall the 32-bit address strings of binary numbers relied upon by computers and computer networks to communicate.

The Internet's original address space was created to be inexhaustible so that the Internet's future growth would not be artificially constrained. Although that design criterion ensured a future for the Internet, it also created a more vexing problem. From a more pragmatic perspective, the raw address space was so large as to be unusable by humans. Again, most humans cannot reliably recall specific 32-bit strings of binary numbers.

Converting any given 32-bit string of binary numbers into decimal numbers would, at least in theory, make the number more human-friendly. After all, the Base10 number system is so familiar to human beings as to be second nature. Unfortunately, a 32-bit binary number can potentially translate into a decimal number so large that it is almost meaningless to human beings. For example, imagine trying to remember whether your computer's address is 4,217,824,125 or 4,217,924,125.

However, those numbers are easier to remember than their binary equivalents (which are 11111011011001101110001101111101 and 11111011011010000110101000011101, respectively, in the Base2 number system). Thus, you could successfully argue that using decimal numbers instead of binary numbers directly reduced the size of the "numbers" that people would have to remember. But they are still far too cumbersome to be useful. You would have great difficulty remembering your own IP address, much less trying to remember the IP addresses of useful destination machines.

NOTE   This discussion about the relative difficulty of remembering numeric IP addresses predates the use of mnemonics as a substitute for numeric addresses. Today's Internet users seldom directly use IP addresses for accessing information stored throughout the Net. The introduction of structured mnemonics for hosts and their domains has all but obviated the practice of using raw IP addresses. These technologies are explored in more detail in Chapter 8, "Internet Names." However, it is important to remember that the logistics of remembering and using large numbers factored into the design of the address space.

Thus, the first priority in making the IP address space human-friendly was to provide a mathematical translation so that people could continue to use the Base10 number system that they are so familiar with! But that still left unsolved the tandem problems of remembering and using large numbers.

The Purpose of the Dots

Although it might seem counterintuitive, especially when we are accustomed to thinking in terms of only decimal numbers, the logical solution to the unmanageably large address space was to break it into a series of smaller numbers. To continue with the example used in the preceding section, a decimal value of 4,217,824,125 presents an interesting case study. Given that this number has four components (groups of billions, millions, thousands, and hundreds/tens/ones), it might seem logical to just split the number along those lines. But several potential problems emerge from such an arbitrary subdivision.

The first potential problem is that such subdivision results in an asymmetric range of valid numbers for each group. The billions group would have a valid range of just 0 to 4, whereas the other three groups' valid ranges would be from 0 to 999. Such asymmetry isn't of great consequence, but it heralds a compromise in the original goal of absolutely minimizing valid numeric ranges. Remember—the smaller the numbers, the easier they are to remember and use!

The next concern is that this scheme is based on decimal numbers but the address space is inherently binary. The same is true of the computers that use the address space directly. Thus, it makes more sense to use binary numbers when evaluating potential techniques for using an address space. Given that the address space is 32 binary digits (bits) in length, segmenting this space is a logical means of creating more manageable numbers. The architects of the Internet's address space saw the wisdom in this approach. They disaggregated the 32-bit numeric address into four equal components of 8 bits. These components are called *octets*.

Such disaggregation had the pleasant effect of reducing the human challenge of remembering a ten-digit number to merely remembering four numbers—each of which is one octet in length. The valid numeric range for these octets is from 00000000 to 11111111. The decimal equivalents are 0 to 255. If you aren't sure why addresses were limited to this range, don't worry. This topic is covered in much more detail in the next section. A dot or period (.) was somewhat arbitrarily selected as the delimiter that would separate the fields. Thus, the convention was set: IP addresses would take this format:

00000000.00000000.00000000.00000000

This is the native form of IP addresses. Yet such a form might be confusing in that IP addresses are most commonly encountered in their decimal form. That is, they use Base10 numbers, which are separated by the dot or period. The term used to describe that form of an IP address is *dotted-decimal notation*. Here is an example of an IP address expressed in dotted-decimal notation:

> 192.168.99.1

All IPv4 addresses adhere to this format. Given the dotted-decimal format, two reasonable questions to ask are "Why bother saying that an IP address is a 32-bit number? Why not simply say that an IP address is four decimal numbers separated by dots?" The answer is that numbers are infinite, but the IP address space is not. It has a hard upper limit established by the 32 bits. It is necessary to explore binary mathematics to understand this statement.

Binary Mathematics

Understanding the IP address space absolutely requires comprehending the binary mathematics on which it is founded. Although this might sound somewhat daunting, it really is quite simple. As with anything, the more you use it, the easier it becomes.

As mentioned earlier in this chapter, the address space is inherently binary; it uses the Base2 number system. Much like the Base10 number system, a digit's significance depends on its location. For example, the value of digits in the Base10 number system changes by a factor of 10 as you change columns. Thus, in the number 111, the numeral 1 has three different values: one group of 1s in the rightmost column, one group of 10 in the middle column, and one group of 100 in the leftmost column. Adding them results in the value 111.

In the Base2 number system, the digits' significance also depends on their location. However, their value changes by a factor of 2 (not 10). The number 111, in binary, translates into one group of 1s, one group of 2s, and one group of 4s, for a total of 7 in Base10. Table 2-1 demonstrates how the binary number 10000000 translates into the Base10 number 128.

Table 2-1   *128 Expressed in Base2*

Decimal Value of Column	128	64	32	16	8	4	2	1
Binary Number	1	0	0	0	0	0	0	0

The eight binary digits and their decimal equivalents shown in Table 2-1 let you count from 0 to 255 in Base10 numbers. The building blocks of this capability are shown in Table 2-2. If the Base10 equivalent does not appear intuitive, refer to Table 2-1 to determine the decimal value of the Base2 columns.

Table 2-2 *The Value of Base2 Number Columns*

Base2	Base10 Equivalent
00000001	1
00000010	2
00000100	4
00001000	8
00010000	16
00100000	32
01000000	64
10000000	128

The entries in Table 2-2 demonstrate the foundation on which the IP address space is built. Each of the four parts of an address contains just 8 bits with which to encode a value. However, only 1 of those 8 bits is actually set to a value other than 0. Notice how the decimal equivalent value doubles as the 1 moves left through the eight possible columns of the binary string of numbers. This demonstrates just the basic decimal values of the binary positions. However, the binary string can be used to encode decimal values that range from 0 to 255. Such values are calculated by adding the decimal values of each column populated with a 1.

Counting in Base2 is fairly simple, because you have only two digits to work with! You increment from 0 to 1. Incrementing above that requires carrying values over into higher columns. This is the same logic that applies to Base10 and every other number system. For example, everyone knows that 9 + 1 = 10, but we seldom think about this equation in terms of columns and their respective values. What we are really saying is that 9 + 1 = one group of 10. The key difference between the Base2 and Base10 number systems is that the amount by which each column's value varies. In Base10, each column (progressing from right to left) is 10 times the value of the preceding column. In other words, the progression is ones, tens, hundreds, thousands. In Base2, the progression is a doubling of the value of the preceding column: 1, 2, 4, 8, 16, 32, 64, 128, and so on. Those values are represented in the Base2 number system by placing a 1 in their respective columns. This is illustrated in Table 2-2.

The next logical step in mastering binary mathematics is learning how to count numbers that aren't factors of 2. See Table 2-3.

Table 2-3   *Counting in Base2*

Base2	Base10
00000000	0
00000001	1
00000010	2
00000011	3
00000100	4
00000101	5
00000110	6
00000111	7
00001000	8
00001001	9
00001010	10
00001011	11
00001100	12
00001101	13
00001110	14
00001111	15
00010000	16
↓	↓
11111111	255

Without subjecting you to the tedium of counting all the way up to 255 in Base2, Table 2-3 attempts to demonstrate how to count in that number system. At first, the progression of the pattern of 1s and 0s might seem counterintuitive, but it follows the same logic as any other number system. There are only two symbols with which to encode values, so the highest "number" you can place in any column is a 1.

To illustrate this point, suppose that the binary number is 00000001. Incrementing it by one unit requires resetting the rightmost column to 0 and carrying a 1 over into the column to its left. This yields 00000010. This is the same logic that is applied in decimal numbers when we increment 9 by 1 to get 10. In that equation, a group of nine 1s is increased by 1 to yield one group of 10 with no 1s. The difference lies in the number of valid numbers and the value of the columns. Quite literally, our binary number translates into decimal as follows: no groups of 128, no groups of 64, no groups of 32, no groups of 16, no groups of 8, no groups of 4, one group of 2, and no units. Summing up the groups yields a decimal value of 2.

Another, slightly more complex example is the binary number 10101010. This binary number translates into decimal as follows: one group of 128, no groups of 64, one group of 32, no groups of 16, one group of 8, no groups of 4, one group of 2, and no units. Summing up the groups yields a decimal value of 170 (128 + 32 + 8 + 2).

Therefore, to convert binary to decimal, you must sum up the decimal equivalents of all columns in the binary string that have a 1 instead of a zero. This summation must be done separately for each octet in the IP address.

No Zero Suppression, Please!

One of the oddities that you might have noticed in Tables 2-2 and 2-3 is that leading 0s are not suppressed. In other words, you wouldn't express the numeric value of 1 as 00000001 in Base10—you would suppress the leading zeroes. They're meaningless and therefore are deleted. However, it is important to remember that IP addresses consist of a single 32-bit number; you artificially segment them into groups of 8 bits. Thus, suppressing leading 0s might actually truncate numbers in the middle of a larger string. Such an action would change the value of the IP address and would result in an invalid value.

Although it is customary in mathematics to suppress leading 0s, this does not hold true in the IP address space. That's because a 32-bit number is arbitrarily segmented into four smaller groups of bits. Suppressing leading 0s in any of those groups truncates the whole number, thereby changing the total values. It is imperative to remember that, even though you are accustomed to thinking of IP addresses in terms of four numbers that range from 0 to 255, an IP address is really a single 32-bit string of binary numbers.

The Address Space Hierarchy

Having examined the mathematics upon which the IP address space is founded, it is time to explore its hierarchical organization. The hierarchy is best described as being compound, because there are two aspects:

- Two levels of addressing within each IP address.
- Classes of addresses based on differing bit allocations to the two levels of addresses. Having segmented the address's bit string into four 8-bit components makes it very easy to create address classes because you have logical groupings to work with.

Each of these hierarchical aspects is explored in the following sections.

Two-Level Addresses

Each IP address consists of two parts: a network address and a host address. Together, they enable the specific and unique identification of endpoints. More importantly, they enable a level of operational efficiency within an internetwork. Such an efficiency improvement is made possible by reducing the workload of the routers and switches that interconnect networks. Simply stated, they don't have to "remember" the path to each individual endpoint. All endpoints must have a unique IP address, but they can share a common network address. Thus, it is sufficient to "remember" the path to each network and to entrust the networking components of each destination network to deliver transmitted packets of data after they are routed through the internetwork and arrive at their destination network.

NOTE   An *internetwork* is two or more networks that are interconnected.

To better illustrate this point, consider the internetwork shown in Figure 2-1.

Figure 2-1   *Network Addresses Serve as Destinations*

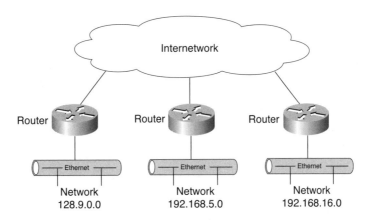

In Figure 2-1, routers provide interconnectivity between the various networks by remembering routes to each network. In each of these examples, the nonzero octets of each IP address identify the network address.

There is no reason for a router to calculate or store a route to each host. Instead, the router merely calculates and stores routes to each network. The local-area networks (LANs) are responsible for extending interconnectivity down to the individual endpoints. It is only at this level that host addresses become significant. For this reason, routes to destinations are described in terms of the destination's network address. All host addresses within that network address are said to belong to the same *address block*.

Classes of Addresses

The second aspect of the IP address space hierarchy is a bit more complex: the entire address space is segmented into numeric ranges. Each numeric range is tailored to a specific purpose based on differing allocations of bits between the host and network portions of the address. Simply stated, the IETF sectioned the four-octet address space into distinct classes that were reserved for small, medium, and large companies or organizations. Each class offered a different number of definable host addresses. The expectation was that most of the companies or organizations that would use the Internet Protocol would fit into one of these categories.

Logically, there would be more smaller companies than larger companies, so there would have to be many address blocks that offered a relatively small number of usable host addresses. Extending this logic, small companies wouldn't need very many host addresses, but large companies would require a significant number of host addresses. This logic became the foundation for the classes of IP addresses.

The classes of IP addresses were identified with a single alphabetic character: Classes A, B, C, D, and E. Each of these represents a different compromise between the number of supportable networks and hosts.

Class A

The Class A address space was conceived to satisfy the scenario of a precious few extremely large entities requiring a large number of host addresses. In general terms, only the first octet is used for the network address. The remaining three octets identify potential host addresses within that network. At first glance, this might lead you to conclude that there are 255 possible Class A addresses (excluding 0). Such a conclusion would assume that the entire first octet could be used to identify Class A network addresses. Unfortunately, that's not quite the case. The first octet does, indeed, range from 0 to 255, but that must satisfy the entire IP address range, not just the Class A networks. All-0s addresses are reserved and unusable. Consequently, the Class A address space starts at 1.0.0.0 instead of 0.0.0.0.

Clearly, an upper mathematical boundary needed to be established that separated the upper limits of the Class A space from the lower limits of the Class B space. A remarkably uncomplicated answer was embraced: The first bit (which should automatically get you thinking in binary terms rather than decimal numbers) of a Class A address is always a 0. Table 2-4 lists the rules governing the Class A address space. Bits in each octet that may have either a 0 or 1 value are designated with a -.

Table 2-4   *Bit Allocation for the Class A Address Space*

	First Octet	Second Octet	Third Octet	Fourth Octet
Usage	Network	Hosts	Host	Host
Required Binary Values	0-------	--------	--------	--------

The highest value of the first octet, in binary, is 01111111. In theory, and expressed in decimal form, the highest Class A address is 127 (64 + 32 + 16 + 8 + 4 + 2 + 1). This mathematically limited the Class A address space to networks numbered 1.0.0.0 up to 127.0.0.0. However, the Class A space was further impinged! The address space 127.0.0.0 was reserved for use with loopback testing. Thus, even though it appears to satisfy the criteria for being a Class A space, it is not usable as such. Thus, the range of possible Class A addresses is from 1.0.0.0 to 126.0.0.0. Within each Class A address space, the valid range for hosts ranges from x.0.0.0 to x.255.255.255, where x denotes any valid number in the Class A range. To illustrate this point, 10.1.99.240 and 10.235.5.111 are hosts that reside on the same network: 10.0.0.0.

NOTE   Throughout this chapter, I'll use an x as a wildcard character to represent a valid mathematical value in lieu of an actual value for an octet in an IP address structure.

The last three octets (the last three dotted-decimal numbers) of a Class A address represent possible host addresses within each specific network number. It is important to note that the entire address must be unique. Therefore, individual host addresses (99.100.101, for example) can be duplicated within each Class A network. This can be a potential source of confusion, which is why it is always a good idea to reference entire IP addresses rather than just partial addresses. No one will be confused as to the uniqueness of 10.99.100.101 compared to 76.99.100.101.

Given that each Class A address offers three full octets for unique host addresses, the number of mathematically possible addresses ranges from x.00000000.00000000.00000000 to x.11111111.11111111.11111111, where x identifies an unspecified network address number. This range equates to 16,774,215 unique host addresses per network number, with a maximum of 126 possible network addresses. As you can see, the architects of the Internet's address space achieved their objective: a fairly small number of incredibly large address spaces.

Class B

The Class B address space was conceived as a middle ground between two polar extremes: Class A (very few networks with a very large number of endpoints) and Class C (lots of networks, each with a very small number of endpoints). The architects of the address space followed their convention of using octet boundaries. Whereas a Class A network address was defined with just a single octet, a Class B network address was treated to half of the four octets in an IP address.

Having 16 bits for host addresses means that each Class B network has 65,535 mathematically possible addresses. You might assume that, because 16 bits are also used for defining unique network addresses, there are 65,535 mathematically possible network addresses as well. Unfortunately, that's not quite the case. Remember, some of the overall address space has already been allocated for Class A addresses, and more will be needed for other addresses. The Class B space must be constructed so as to occupy a separate mathematical range—ideally, contiguous to the Class A space—and yet leave enough address space for other classes of networks. Again, the solution was remarkably simple: the first 2 bits of the first octet must be 10.

Starting the bit pattern of the first octet with a 10 separates this space from the upper limits of the Class A space. Table 2-5 lists the rules governing the Class B address space. Again, bits in each octet that may have either a 0 or 1 value are designated with a -.

Table 2-5   *Bit Allocation for the Class B Address Space*

	First Octet	**Second Octet**	**Third Octet**	**Fourth Octet**
Usage	Network	Network	Host	Host
Required Binary Values	10------	--------	--------	--------

The highest value of the first octet is 10111111. Thus, expressed in decimal form, the highest Class B address is 191 (128 + 32 + 16 + 8 + 4 + 2 + 1), which mathematically limits the Class B address space to networks numbered from 128.0.0.0 to 191.255.0.0.

The last two octets of a Class B address represent possible host addresses within each specific network number. As with the Class A address space, the entire address must be globally unique. Individual host addresses can be duplicated within each network address. Valid Class B host addresses range from $x.x$.00000000.00000000 ($x.x$.0.0 in dotted-decimal notation) to $x.x$.11111111.11111111 ($x.x$.255.255 in dotted-decimal notation), where x identifies an unspecified network address number. This range yields a maximum of 65,535 unique host addresses per Class B network. The range of possible Class B network addresses is from 128.0.0.0 to 191.255.0.0, for a total of 16,385 possible network addresses. Valid host addresses for Class B networks range from $x.x$.0.0 to $x.x$.255.255. Thus, 160.10.1.32 and 160.10.242.17 would be on the same network (160.10.0.0).

Within this range of valid numbers, each numeric combination of the first two octets represents a different IP network address. Thus, 191.2 is as separate and distinct from 191.3 as 128.1 is from 191.254. To better illustrate this point, consider Table 2-6, which demonstrates how incrementing network addresses works with both decimal and binary numbers. Given that we're exploring the incrementation of network addresses, the host portion of the address is represented solely with the character x.

Table 2-6   *Incrementing Class B Network Addresses*

Decimal Network Address	Binary Network Address
128.0.*x*.*x*	10000000.00000000.*x*.*x*
128.1.*x*.*x*	10000000.00000001.*x*.*x*
128.2.*x*.*x*	10000000.00000010.*x*.*x*
128.3.*x*.*x*	10000000.00000011.*x*.*x*
128.4.*x*.*x*	10000000.00000100.*x*.*x*
↓	↓
128.254.*x*.*x*	10000000.11111110.*x*.*x*
128.255.*x*.*x*	10000000.11111111.*x*.*x*
129.0.*x*.*x*	10000001.00000000.*x*.*x*
129.1.*x*.*x*	10000001.00000001.*x*.*x*
129.2.*x*.*x*	10000001.00000010.*x*.*x*
129.3.*x*.*x*	10000001.00000011.*x*.*x*
129.4.*x*.*x*	10000001.00000100.*x*.*x*
↓	↓
129.254.*x*.*x*	10000001.11111110.*x*.*x*
129.255.*x*.*x*	10000001.11111111.*x*.*x*
130.0.*x*.*x*	10000010.00000000.*x*.*x*
130.1.*x*.*x*	10000010.00000001.*x*.*x*
130.2.*x*.*x*	10000010.00000010.*x*.*x*
↓	↓
191.255.*x*.*x*	10111111.11111111.*x*.*x*

When an IP network address is viewed as a binary string, the incrementing appears much more logical; the rightmost bit of the network address determines how incrementing occurs. If that bit is a 0, it is incremented by converting it to a 1. If that bit is a 1, it is incremented by converting it to a 0 and then carrying a value over to the column immediately to its left. This process is repeated until a 0 is encountered and nothing further needs to be "carried over." Although this should be a repetition of what you saw in Table 2-2, the idea of carrying over a value from one octet to another is the key difference reinforced in this table.

Class C

The Class C address space offers a large number of network addresses, although each one can support only a very limited quantity of host addresses. The architects of the address space again followed their convention of using octet boundaries. The Class C network address is three octets in length, leaving just one octet for use in identifying unique hosts within each network.

Having just 8 bits for host addresses means that each Class C network has only 256 mathematically possible addresses. However, using 24 bits for network addresses means that there can be a lot of them. Although these 24 bits must be defined so that they don't overlap with other address classes, 2,097,151 Class C network addresses are still mathematically possible.

Delineating the Class C space from the Class B space requires starting the bit pattern of the first octet with a 110. This separates the Class C space from the upper limits of the Class B space while simultaneously leaving some higher network numbers available for use in defining other classes. Table 2-7 demonstrates how this is achieved. As with Tables 2-4 and 2-5, bits in each octet that may have either a 0 or 1 value are designated with a -.

Table 2-7   *Bit Allocation for the Class C Address Space*

	First Octet	**Second Octet**	**Third Octet**	**Fourth Octet**
Usage	Network	Network	Network	Host
Required Binary Values	110-----	--------	--------	--------

The highest value of the first octet is 11011111. Thus, expressed in decimal form, the highest Class C address is 223 (128 + 64 + 16 + 8 + 4 + 2 + 1), which represents the highest network number that can be defined in this class. Given that the address space starts at 192 (128 + 64, or 11000000 as a binary string), the Class C network address space ranges from 192.0.0.0 to 223.255.255.0. Valid host numbers range from $x.x.x.0$ to $x.x.x.255$. Thus, 192.168.127.144 and 192.168.127.254 are hosts on the same Class C network: 192.168.127.0.

Incrementing a Class C network address is relatively simple. You have three octets for this purpose, so the first network address is 192.0.0. Next are 192.0.1, 192.0.2, and 192.0.3, until you get to 192.0.255. This is where an appreciation of binary mathematics helps: The next available network address above 192.0.255 is 192.1.0. In decimal, this might not be very intuitive, but it becomes perfectly clear in binary. Consider Table 2-8.

Table 2-8   *Incrementing Class C Network Addresses*

Decimal Network Address	Binary Network Address
192.0.0.x	11000000.00000000.00000000.x
192.0.1.x	11000000.00000000.00000001.x
192.0.2.x	11000000.00000000.00000010.x
↓	↓
192.0.254.x	11000000.00000000.11111110.x
192.0.255.x	11000000.00000000.11111111.x
192.1.0.x	11000000.00000001.00000000.x
192.1.1.x	11000000.00000001.00000001.x
192.1.2.x	11000000.00000001.00000010.x
↓	↓
192.1.254.x	11000000.00000001.11111110.x
192.1.255.x	11000000.00000001.11111111.x
192.2.0.x	11000000.00000010.00000000.x
192.2.1.x	11000000.00000010.00000001.x
192.2.2.x	11000000.00000010.00000010.x
↓	↓
192.255.254.x	11000000.11111111.11111110.x
192.255.255.x	11000000.11111111.11111111.x
193.0.0.x	11000001.00000000.00000000.x
193.0.1.x	11000001.00000000.00000001.x
193.0.2.x	11000001.00000000.00000010.x
↓	↓
223.255.255.x	11011111.11111111.11111111.x

This table provides the correlation between decimal and binary numbers. Although it would be impractical to list every mathematically possible Class C network address, this subset should amply demonstrate the key aspects of incrementing these network addresses. After you become comfortable with incrementing binary numbers, understanding the IP address space becomes easy!

Valid Class C host addresses range from 00000000 to 11111111, or 0 to 255 if you prefer dotted-decimal notation. Remember, only one octet is available for host identification, so the range is limited to just these 256 addresses (0 through 255). Initially, not all of these addresses were usable, even though they were mathematically possible; the highest and lowest addresses were reserved. Address 0 was conventionally reserved for identifying the network itself, whereas address 255 was used as a broadcast address within that network. Such reservations held true throughout the entire Classical IP architecture and were not unique to Class C addresses. It is still possible to find information sources that declare that the number of possible addresses in a Class C-sized address block is either 254 or 255.

Class D

The Class D address space is a radical departure from the first three classes. Unlike the previous three classes we've examined, this class does not adhere to the convention of dividing the bit string into network and host address subcomponents. As you might expect, this makes it rather difficult to use in uniquely identifying networked hosts in an internetwork. Quite simply, you cannot define a network address. This is by design; this uniquely flat address space is not used for endpoint addressing. Instead, it serves as a code that lets a host send a single stream of IP packets to numerous destination machines simultaneously.

Multicasting is a complex topic that uses a unique binary string in the Class D space to correlate to a predefined list of IP endpoints. A multicast address is a unique IP address that directs packets with that destination address to predefined groups of IP addresses. Thus, there is no need for the hierarchical division of bits between network and host addresses in this class.

Despite this break from architecture, the Class D address space must adhere to other constraints. For example, it too must have its own range of addresses. To achieve this, the first 4 bits of a Class D address must be 1110. Binary mathematics dictates that, given the location of this 0, the lowest address in this class can be 11100000, or $128 + 64 + 32 = 224$. The highest mathematically possible address, given this constraint in the first octet, is 11101111, or $128 + 64 + 32 + 8 + 4 + 2 + 1 = 239$. Thus, Class D multicast group addresses are from 224.0.0.0 to 239.255.255.255. Table 2-9 follows the format of the preceding tables and demonstrates how the octets are used in this class.

Table 2-9 *Bit Allocation for the Class D Address Space*

	First Octet	**Second Octet**	**Third Octet**	**Fourth Octet**
Usage	Multicast Group	Multicast Group	Multicast Group	Multicast Group
Required Binary Values	1110----	--------	--------	--------

Class E

A Class E address has been defined but is reserved by the IETF for its own research and other nonroutable purposes. Thus, Class E addresses exist, but they have not been released for use in the Internet. This address class begins at 240.0.0.0 and ends at the top of the address space, 255.255.255.*x*. This topmost range might appear familiar; it is the basis of the subnetting mask. Subnetting is covered in Chapter 3, "Fixed-Length Subnet Masks," and Chapter 4, "Variable-Length Subnet Masks," so you'll become much more familiar with this aspect of the IP address space.

Drawbacks of Class-Based Addressing

There is a simple elegance to this original IPv4 addressing architecture. The entire address space is neatly cleft along octet boundaries, and upper limits are established via the first octet's initial bit sequence. It's so clean and simple that it is brilliant. Unfortunately, this scheme was developed absent any knowledge of future Internet-user demographics. This class-based architecture satisfied the needs of the Internet community for more than a decade. The relatively slow growth rate masked the architectural inefficiencies of the IP address space. Quite simply, the architecture was founded on an absolute lack of data. Thus, the architecture is inherently more logical than practical.

Evidence of this is found in the great gaps between the classes. The Class C-sized network offers 255 hosts, but the next step up in size is Class B, which offers 65,535 host addresses. That's a huge gap! The difference between the Class B-sized network and Class A is even worse: Class A supports 16,774,215 unique host addresses. Ostensibly, organizations that required a number of addresses that fell in between these coarse classes could obtain multiple address spaces. If they mixed and matched them from the three classes, they could fairly closely match the number of addresses provided to their requirements. Or, they could simply rationalize the need for "growth" and obtain a lot more address space than they actually needed.

The point is that the tremendous disparities between the three primary address classes (A, B, and C) created the potential for inefficiency and waste. This has proven to be the Achilles' heel of IPv4. In subsequent chapters, you will learn more about the various methods that were developed to enhance the efficiency with which IP addresses could be deployed and used.

Summary

The binary mathematics and binary to decimal conversions presented in this chapter are essential to understanding the IP address space. Although the various classes of addresses have passed into obsolescence, their memory lingers on. Quite a few network-savvy people still think in terms of classes and often describe their network as being a Class A, B, or C. More importantly, the topics presented in this chapter formed the foundation on which other innovations advanced the usefulness and longevity of the IPv4 address space. The next two chapters focus on splitting a network address block into subnetworks. Subnetting, as that process is called, is extremely useful in building efficient address allocation schemes.

CHAPTER 3

Fixed-Length Subnet Masks

The first significant feature retrofitted to the IPv4 address space was the introduction of support for a third tier in its architecture. As discussed in Chapter 2, "Classical IP: The Way It Was," the IP address space features a two-tier hierarchy in which each address consists of a network address and a host address within its 32-bit structure. Such flatness distinctly limits scalability in a number of ways. Perhaps the most confining limitation is that the address space assumes that all networks fit into one of just three different sizes of networks small, medium, and extremely large.

Creating a third tier for identifying subnetwork addresses is a relatively straightforward concept that involves "borrowing" bits from the host portion of the address. These bits are used to create subnetwork addresses as an extension of the network address. In other words, smaller networks can be created—and uniquely addressed—from larger networks and network address spaces. Implicit in the word "subnetwork" is the fact that the third tier of address information is of only local significance and use. The presence or absence of subnetworks does not affect routing to that network address from a global perspective. Within a subnetted network, the subnetwork address is used for routing.

This chapter explains what benefit is derived from the creation of a third tier of addressing and explores the mathematics that support the use of fixed-length subnetwork masks (FLSMs). Keep in mind that this chapter explains how subnetting used to be done (emphasis on the past tense). Although fixed-length subnetting is functionally obsolete, you might still encounter it in legacy networks. Despite this functional obsolescence, FLSM serves as a simplified introduction to a still-relevant concept. Even more important, FLSM is still a highly relevant topic for many proprietary technical certification exams.

Introduction to Subnetting

Subnetting, as this process is more commonly called, is a remarkably logical and mathematical process. Understanding the mathematics of subnetting helps you develop and implement efficient subnetting schemes that make better use of available address spaces. That is the explicit goal of subnetting: to use an address space more efficiently. Unfortunately, subnetting is the most confusing and least-understood aspect of IPv4 . This is largely due to the fact that it makes sense only when viewed in binary numbers, yet most people think in terms of decimal numbers. For that reason alone I rely extensively on the use of binary-to-decimal translations to demonstrate the concept and applications of subnetting throughout this chapter.

Some of the specific topics we'll examine include

- The rationale for developing a third tier of addressing
- The logic and mathematics that form the basis of a subnet
- The subnet mask that is used to specifically identify which bits of the IP address are used for network and subnetwork identification
- The concept of an extended network prefix

Examining these topics prepares you for a more thorough investigation of fixed-length subnetting. In the last half of this chapter you will see how subnetting works in different-sized networks and with different-sized subnets.

The Need for a Third Tier of Addressing

In essence, subnetting offers a third tier within the IP addressing hierarchy. The need for a third tier of addressing became apparent fairly early on in the Internet's development. The Internet's two-level hierarchy assumed that each site connected to the Internet would contain only a single network. Therefore, each site would contain only a single local-area network (LAN) that could be satisfied by a single block of IP addresses (characterized by multiple contiguous host addresses within a single network address). Consequently, only a single connection to the Internet would suffice for interconnectivity needs.

By 1985, this was no longer a safe assumption. Although most organizations connected to the Internet could continue to operate with just one connection to the Internet, few organizations had just one LAN. The dawn of the client/server era was at hand, and a two-level address hierarchy was suddenly obsolete. Organizations suddenly began experiencing the effects of reaching either the technological or scalability limits of their technology platforms.

In other words, some networks needed to be broken into subcomponents to improve performance. This was particularly true of early, shared Ethernet LANs. Other organizations found themselves with different LAN technologies within the same location. That's not uncommon when budgets are distributed and each group in the organization makes its own purchasing decisions. Other organizations might have found themselves simply trying to span too great a distance with their LAN.

Thus, several motivating forces pointed in the same direction: An enhancement to the IP address architecture was needed—specifically, a third, local, hierarchical tier of addressing.

To better appreciate why this is the case, consider Figure 3-1.

Figure 3-1   *The Emergence of Multiple Networks Per Site Created Problems for the IP Address Space's Two-Level Hierarchy*

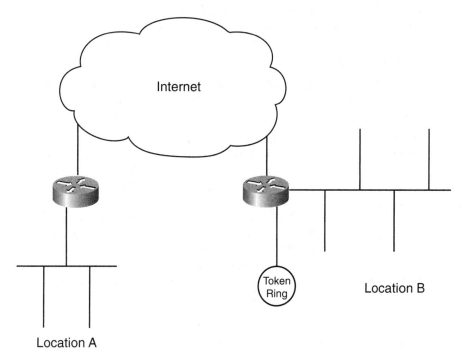

In Figure 3-1, you can see that the router in Location B hosts two different LANs. Each network must have its own network address; otherwise, other networks won't be able to communicate with devices connected to it. This holds true for the two networks at the same location. They are connected to different interfaces on the same router, and the router is responsible for governing and/or facilitating communications between them. Depending on how that router is configured, it has several main responsibilities. Without getting into a dissertation on the mechanics and functions of routing protocols, suffice it to say that the router is responsible for the following:

- Advertising the presence of the two networks directly connected to it

- Forwarding outbound traffic

- Enabling communications between its two directly-connected networks

- Forwarding inbound traffic to the appropriate network

Implicit in these responsibilities is the assumption that the router has a means of discriminating between the two local networks. In other words, they must each have their own network address. In the Classical IP environment, each of these networks would have required its own address space. So, if you assume that each LAN consisted of just 40 total devices, two Class C networks would have been required. That translates into the assignment of 512 IP addresses when just 100 would have sufficed, with a bit of room to spare. That's a remarkable waste of addresses. It doesn't take a tremendous amount of imagination to envision how such waste could rapidly deplete a finite supply of addresses. Clearly, a better approach was required.

In theory, both networks could easily share a single Class C network address and still have a lot of room for growth, if only there were a way to split up a network address locally. This is where subnetting comes in.

Each network at a location requires its own network address in order to internetwork, but that network address (which is really just a subnetwork address) needs to be unique only *locally*. So, if you assigned a single Class C network, such as network 192.168.9.0, to this location, the entire Internet would use the address 192.168.9 to communicate with machines at this location, regardless of which LAN they were on. That address—192.168.9—is the network address. It remains the basis of reaching all the subnetworks within this network. Addresses from 192.168.9.1 through 192.168.9.128 could be assigned to the Ethernet LAN shown in Figure 3-1, and 192.168.9.129 through 192.168.9.255 could be assigned to the Token Ring LAN. However, that puts the onus on the router at that location to determine which interface to use in forwarding inbound packets. How the router does this requires a closer look at the mathematics of subnetting.

The Concept of Subnetting

The problem described in the preceding section demonstrates why a third tier of addressing is necessary. What the example didn't provide is an explanation of how to develop that tier. Subnetting was first explored and defined in a series of loosely-related RFCs numbered 917, 940, and 950. These RFCs called for the creation of a third, logical, but local tier of addressing to be created from the existing address architecture. Recall from Chapter 2 that IP addresses are 32 bits in length and consist of two components—a network address and a host address. The network address cannot be touched, because it is used globally for routing to and from the network it identifies. That leaves the host address as the only viable means of developing a third tier of addressing.

Per RFC 950, the host address may be carved up to create a subnetwork address. Thus, the three tiers of addressing are

• Network address

• Subnet address

• Host address

Your ability to subnet depends directly on the number of bits allocated between a network and host address. That's because the subnet address is carved from the host address. The more host bits an IP address has, the more subnets that can be created. However, there is an inverse correlation between the number of subnets that are created and the number of hosts that can be supported in each subnet. In effect, you borrow bits from the host address to create the subnet address. Logically, the more bits you borrow from the host field to create subnets, the fewer bits that remain for the identification of hosts. Of course, not all IP address spaces were created equal. The Class A address space offers more than 16 million host addresses. Borrowing bits from a field of that size wouldn't appreciably reduce the available pool of addresses. In fact, subnetting a Class A address space would have the tremendous benefit of making more efficient use of the available pool of addresses. Subnetting a Class C network address space—with just 256 total available host addresses—makes you quickly aware of the finite nature of those addresses. We'll delve into more examples of subnetting later in this chapter. The next significant concept to acknowledge is that it is crucial to have a means of tracking how many bits are borrowed. IP addresses that are subnetted look exactly like IP addresses that aren't subnetted, so another mechanism is required to keep track of subnet sizes. This mechanism is called the *subnet mask*. Subnet masks are statically defined on each endpoint device (such as a printer or desktop computer) connected to the network. The concept of a mask can be difficult to grasp. Many people gain a working appreciation of how to make networked devices function without really understanding masks. We'll look at subnet masks in much more detail in the following section.

The Subnet Mask

A subnet mask is a 32-bit binary number that can be expressed in either dotted-decimal or dotted-binary form. In this regard, a subnet mask is structurally similar to an IP address. However, there are some important distinctions. For example, a mask is not routable, nor does it have to be unique. However, a subnet mask does serve an important function: It is used to tell end systems (including routers and hosts in the LAN) how many bits of the IP address's host field have been borrowed to identify the subnet. The bits in the mask that identify the network address, as well as the subnet address, are set to 1s. The remaining bits, which are used for host addresses within each subnet, are set to 0s.

One potentially confusing point about masks is that they can be used to identify a network, a subnetwork, or both. A network mask identifies just the bits used to identify a network address. A subnet mask identifies *all* the bits used for network and subnetwork identification. This leads us to the concept of the extended network prefix, which we'll examine in the next section.

Extended Network Prefix

It is important to note that the borrowed bits are always the leftmost bits in the host field. Thus, the subnet address is numerically contiguous with the network address. Together, they form the *extended network prefix*. The remaining bits are used for host identification.

To better demonstrate this concept of an extended network prefix, consider the contents of Table 3-1, which shows the dotted-binary and dotted-decimal equivalents of network (not subnet) masks for the various classes of IP addresses. Note that the masks in this table are just *network* masks.

Table 3-1   *Network Masks*

Address Class	Dotted-Decimal Form	Dotted-Binary Form
Class A	255.0.0.0	11111111.00000000.00000000.00000000
Class B	255.255.0.0	11111111.11111111.00000000.00000000
Class C	255.255.255.0	11111111.11111111.11111111.00000000

Because the masks in Table 3-1 are network masks, not subnetwork masks, only those bits that are used to identify the network address are set to 1s. Thus, a network mask lets you see that, in the old Class A network address space, exactly 8 bits are used to identify the network and 24 are used for host identification. Similarly, the Class C network space features 24 bits for network identification, but only 8 for host identification.

Designing a Subnet

The next step is to take a basic network mask and add a subnet field to create the extended network prefix. Table 3-2 shows the dotted-decimal and dotted-binary forms of subnet masks that are permissible when you subnet a Class C address. The borrowed bits are indicated in bold.

Table 3-2   *Subnet Masks*

Borrowed Bits	Dotted-Decimal Form	Dotted-Binary Form
2	255.255.255.192	11111111.11111111.11111111.**11**000000
3	255.255.255.224	11111111.11111111.11111111.**111**00000
4	255.255.255.240	11111111.11111111.11111111.**1111**0000
5	255.255.255.248	11111111.11111111.11111111.**11111**000
6	255.255.255.252	11111111.11111111.11111111.**111111**00

You can better appreciate the concept of an extended network prefix by comparing the dotted-decimal notations in Table 3-2 to the entry for a Class C network in Table 3-1. The next thing to notice is the dotted-decimal notation for each dotted-binary string. Recalling the principles of converting binary to decimal from Chapter 2, it should be much easier to understand those strange strings of numbers called subnet masks. A mask of 255.255.255.192 means that only 2 bits have been borrowed from the host field to create the subnet field. These 2 bits (in this specific context) carry the decimal equivalents of 128 and 64, which add up to 192. A mask of 255.255.255.192, when applied to a Class C network address, yields exactly four subnets of equal size. Each subnet has exactly 64 mathematically possible host addresses. If you multiply 4×64, you get 256, which is the total number of IP addresses contained in Class C.

This leads to the inevitably confusing notion that the larger the decimal number in the mask, the smaller the number of hosts available in the defined subnet. This is caused by that inverse relationship I mentioned earlier: The more bits you allocate for subnet identification, the fewer bits that are left for host identification. Thus, the number of bits used for subnetting determines both how many subnets are mathematically possible and how many hosts can be defined within each of those subnets. Later in this chapter, we will explore this trade-off in much more detail. Before we do that, you need to understand some other minor details. These include the rules for forming subnets.

Subnetting Rules

Having seen how useful subnetting can be, it is important to understand that FLSMs are severely limited in that they all must be the same size. RFC 950 stipulates that a network address space *could be* (an important caveat that we'll explore later) split up locally into subnets. However, the Internet Engineering Task Force (IETF) knew that any mechanism developed had to be readily backward-compatible, should not impose a punishing load on routers, and yet should still offer enough benefit to warrant broad acceptance.

One Size Must Fit All

In the world of fixed-length subnets, one size truly must fit all. Under the rules of FLSM, a network can be subdivided into only equal-sized subnetworks. I don't think many people would believe, even for a second, that LANs are so homogenous that they are all the exact same size. Instead, they come in all different shapes, sizes, and technologies. The practical implication of this criterion is that the mask selected must accommodate the largest of the LANs being addressed out of an FLSM address block. Thus, those subnets all had to be the same size—hence the term fixed-length subnet masks.

Ostensibly, this was originally a simplifying assumption. Routers were still fairly immature by today's standards, and every effort was made to reduce their workload. Sticking to just one size of subnet helped reduce the CPU and memory intensity of supporting subnets, which meant that those resources remained as unencumbered as possible so that they could be applied to routing and packet forwarding.

The more immediate impact of this policy was that much space was wasted. Seldom, if ever, can all subnetting needs be solved with the same size mask. So, designing a subnetting scheme became either a matter of picking a mask arbitrarily or surveying the subnetworks and selecting a mask that accommodated the largest of them. With the benefit of hindsight, it becomes evident that FLSM was inefficient and wasted a significant number of addresses. However, you must temper that realization with the fact that FLSM was a tremendous improvement over the previous method of operation.

All 0s and All 1s

Conventional thinking today holds that Classical IP rules reserved "all 0s" and "all 1s" in an IP address for establishing the network's identity and broadcasting within a network, respectively. However, if you read RFC 950, you'll see that its authors went out of their way to ensure backward compatibility for subnetting, and this extended to support for the technical shorthand in use at the time.

That shorthand called for using 0 to mean "this" and all 1s to mean "all." That might not seem very useful, but consider how it would have helped in specific situations. For example, the term 0.0.0.37 translates into "just host 37 on *this* network." Translating the first three octets depended completely on your location. This is a very useful tool. It is still used to develop rule sets for routers and firewalls.

The "all-1s" address was equally useful. Rather than specifically enumerating all hosts on a network, you could use this convention as follows: The address 128.9.255.255 means "all hosts on network 128.9." Again, this is a remarkably useful shorthand that is still in use today.

Unfortunately, preserving this shorthand also had a direct and costly impact on subnetting. In the immortal words of J. Mogul and Jon Postel in RFC 950:

> It is useful to preserve and extend the interpretation of these special addresses in subnetted networks. This means the values of all zeros and all ones in the subnet field should not be assigned to actual (physical) subnets.

This statement has significant implications for fixed-length subnetting. In Table 3-2, you might have noticed that even though 8 bits are available in the host field, a maximum of 6 bits and a minimum of 2 bits can be borrowed. The reason for these limitations is mathematical. If you limit yourself to just two digits, counting in binary is as follows: 00, 01, 10, 11. That's it. That's the entire universe of numerically possible combinations and, consequently, numerically possible addresses. If you adhere to Mogul and Postel's admonition, only two of the four numerically possible subnets with a 2-bit mask are usable. In the simplest of terms, you've wasted half your available number of subnets just for the sake of maintaining tradition and not muddling nomenclature.

NOTE   Times have changed, and subnets previously reserved from use can now be used. In fact, given how close some portions of the IPv4 address space came to depletion, it was inevitable that some changes be made. One of these was support for Subnet 0. Subnet 0 is aptly named: It is the first subnet created from a network, and it bears a subnet address of all 0s. Although introducing support for Subnet 0 affords some relief from the inefficiencies of fixed-length subnet masking, it is far from a panacea. This is still very much a gray area, and it can still generate disagreement even among networking professionals. A large part of the reason for this disagreement is caused by the consensus-driven nature of the IETF's RFC process.

The RFCs contain suggestive guidelines that are embraced because they make sense. They are not edicts carved in stone and handed down from on high. Thus, they can be—and are—interpreted differently by different parties. Consequently, the way subnetting logic is implemented on network hardware varies from vendor to vendor. In some cases, such disparities are introduced intentionally as a means of differentiating one's products from the competition. Subnet 0 is certainly not an exception. Before attempting to use Subnet 0 in your network environment, research the issue thoroughly with your hardware vendor (such as Cisco Systems) and make certain you understand all the implications.

A slightly more subtle implication of this example is that a 2-bit mask is the absolute minimum size. If you drop to a 1-bit mask, your range of mathematically feasible addresses becomes just 0 and 1. Both are reserved values, so a mask of 255.255.255.254 yields no usable subnets.

This logic also works when applied to the maximum number of bits that can be allocated to a subnet address. Allocating 6 bits to the subnet address results in just four host addresses within that subnet. The 00 address would be used to identify that subnet, and the 11 address is reserved for broadcasts within that subnet. Thus, a subnet of 6 bits in a Class C-sized network would yield only two usable host addresses. In other words, with a mask of that size (255.255.255.252), you would get lots (2^6) of tiny subnets. Increasing the size of the mask would result in unusable subnets. Thus, the largest permissible mask is 255.255.255.252.

The mathematically inverse correlation between the number of fixed-length subnets and hosts per subnet is the key to understanding the concept of subnetting. Why this mathematical correlation is so critical is explored throughout the remainder of this chapter.

Forming Subnets from 24-Bit Network Addresses

Having explored the basics of subnetting, you are ready for a more in-depth examination of how they are formed and the mathematics on which they are founded. Starting with a 24-bit network address (equivalent to a Class C network), the formation of subnets is limited to between 2- and 6-bit masks. The limited size of masks in a 24-bit network makes for an ideal case study to demonstrate the potential for confusion as to where a subnet begins and ends and why some addresses look valid but aren't.

Let's start by examining the basic trade-off proposition that exists between the number of subnets that can be formed with any given mask size and the subsequent number of usable hosts per subnet. This information is presented Table 3-3.

Table 3-3   *Hosts Versus Subnets in a 24-Bit Network*

Number of Bits in the Network Prefix	Subnet Mask	Number of Usable Subnet Addresses	Number of Usable Hosts Per Subnet
2	255.255.255.192	2	62
3	255.255.255.224	6	30
4	255.255.255.240	14	14
5	255.255.255.248	30	6
6	255.255.255.252	62	2

NOTE   You might find other reference sources that report the data presented in Table 3-3 slightly differently. Many information sources apparently prefer to use "mathematically feasible" quantities as opposed to usable quantities. I define "usable" in the historical context of Classical IP and FLSM to exclude the mathematically feasible values of all 0s and all 1s. Thus, all my numbers are 2 less than other sources describing the mathematical potential of each subnet.

At first glance, the inverse correlation between subnets and hosts should be obvious. You can get either two subnets of 62 addresses each or 62 subnets of two addresses each. Another combination is six subnets of 30 hosts or 30 subnets with six hosts in each. Finally, a 4-bit subnet mask gives you exactly 14 subnets with 14 hosts. As I said, the inverse correlation between subnets and hosts in a 24-bit network should be obvious. What might not be so obvious are the inefficiencies inherent in each of the subnetting schemes or the areas of possible confusion. The potential inefficiencies of subnetting are explored later in this chapter.

Subnetting is confusing because you create artificial subdivisions within a network. This means that instead of host addresses within a "network" address starting predictably at 0 and ending at 255, initial host addresses can be almost any value in between. For the sake of understanding (and using) subnetwork addressing, you need to be able to identify three significant host addresses within each subnet:

- **Base address**—Each subnet begins with a host address of all 0s. This address is usually reserved for use in identifying the subnet itself and is not assigned to a specific host.

- **First assignable address**—The host address that is one up from the base is regarded as the first address that can be used for host identification.

- **Broadcast address**—Each subnet ends with the broadcast address. All hosts within the subnet accept incoming packets addressed to either themselves or the subnet's broadcast address. Thus, the broadcast address is a way of sending a single stream of IP packets to *all* the connected devices within a given subnet. In a properly designed addressing scheme, the broadcast address of any given subnet has a value of all 1s.

It is essential that you be able to map out these key addresses within a subnetted network, but the irony is that doing so won't really help you understand how subnets are formed. The logic behind subnetting is obvious only when you view those addresses in their binary form. Using just decimal numbers can become intuitive if you work with IP addresses long enough, but it is not intuitive at first, and it's certainly not the easy way to learn about subnetting.

In this section, you can see how flexible a tool subnetting can be, as well as how confusing. The role of certain addresses varies with the size of the mask. For example, it would be extremely useful to know the base address, first assignable address, and last address in a subnet. Unfortunately, these arbitrary designations absolutely require understanding how the subnets are formed. For the sake of example, we will take the address block of 192.169.125.0 and show you all the different ways it can be subnetted with fixed-length masks.

Subnetting with a 2-Bit Mask

A 2-bit mask identified via the subnet mask 255.255.255.192 yields a total of two usable subnet addresses, each containing 62 usable host addresses. There are 64 addresses in each subnet, but only 62 are usable due to the need to reserve the all-0s and all-1s addresses.

In the example presented in Table 3-4, the Class C address 192.169.125 is subnetted with a 2-bit mask. Notice how the base or starting address of each subnet is exactly 64 addresses higher than the preceding subnet. In other words, we are counting in multiples of 64. This is perfectly logical when you consider that the decimal equivalent value of the rightmost bit of the subnet field is 64. A hyphen is used to further highlight where the subnet address ends, and where the host field begins. You will not find "real" IP addresses formatted this way!

Table 3-4   *Subnetting with a 2-Bit Mask in a 24-Bit Network*

	Binary Network Plus Subnet Address	Decimal Translation
Base	**11000000.10101000.01111101**.00000000	192.168.125.0
Subnet 0	**11000000.10101000.01111101.***00*-000000	192.168.125.0
Subnet 1	**11000000.10101000.01111101.***01*-000000	192.168.125.64
Subnet 2	**11000000.10101000.01111101.***10*-000000	192.168.125.128
Subnet 3	**11000000.10101000.01111101.***11*-000000	192.168.125.192

Mapping Significant Addresses

Subnetting, by virtue of logically segmenting a host address into two different fields, still must adhere to the precept of uniqueness. Host addresses, although they are duplicated across each newly created subnet, remain unique in the context of the extended network prefix. To better illustrate this point, consider the following example. You can have a value of 000001 in the 6-bit host address field in each of the subnets created. Host 000001 in subnet 2 (10 in binary) translates into 192.169.125.129. This is because the last octet, which is used for both host and subnet identification, is 10000001 in binary. Translated into decimal, the string is 129. Thus, the host addresses are not unique when viewed across subnets, but because each subnet has a unique 2-bit prefix, the entire octet remains unique. More importantly, this example demonstrates how unintuitive subnetting can be. Who would expect that host address 0.0.0.129 would be the first assignable number in a subnet?

As I mentioned earlier, subnetting really makes sense only when you look at the binary numbers. To better illustrate the logic behind this potentially confusing situation, Table 3-5 walks you through the process of mapping out the base address, first usable address, and broadcast address in 2-bit subnets.

Table 3-5   *Mapping Important Addresses with a 2-Bit Mask*

	Binary Network Plus Subnet Address	**Decimal Translation**
Base	11000000.10101001.01111101.00000000	192.169.125.0
Subnet 0	11000000.10101001.01111101.*00*-000000	192.169.125.0
Subnet 0	11000000.10101001.01111101.*00*-000001	192.169.125.1
Subnet 0	↓	↓
Subnet 0	11000000.10101001.01111101.*00*-111111	192.169.125.63
Subnet 1	11000000.10101001.01111101.*01*-000000	192.169.125.64
Subnet 1	11000000.10101001.01111101.*01*-000001	192.169.125.65
Subnet 1	↓	↓
Subnet 1	11000000.10101001.01111101.*01*-111111	192.169.125.127
Subnet 2	11000000.10101001.01111101.*10*-000000	192.169.125.128
Subnet 2	11000000.10101001.01111101.*10*-000001	192.169.125.129
Subnet 2	↓	↓
Subnet 2	11000000.10101001.01111101.*10*-111111	192.169.125.191
Subnet 3	11000000.10101001.01111101.*11*-000000	192.169.125.192
Subnet 3	11000000.10101001.01111101.*11*-000001	192.169.125.193
Subnet 3	↓	↓
Subnet 3	11000000.10101001.01111101.*11*-111111	192.169.125.255

In Table 3-5, you can see the skeleton of the mappings within a 24-bit network address (192.169.125) that is subnetted using a mask of 255.255.255.192. A complete table would have 256 entries and would consume several pages. Rather than subject you to so exhaustive a review of this topic, I've opted for this approach. Each subnet is identified in the left column. The middle column presents the binary string for a specific address within the specified subnet, and the last column gives a decimal translation.

Walking through this table, you can see each subnet's base address. A base address is the starting point—the first address within a subnet. The base address for the entire block is easy to find, because all 8 bits in the host address octet are set to 0. Each subnet also has a base address and features a host address of 0s. However, subnet host addresses in Table 3-5 contain only 6 bits. Logically, then, each subnet (00, 01, 10, and 11 in this case) begins with the base host address of 000000. Each subnet also ends with the same highest possible address value: 111111. Incrementing beyond this number results in an increment in the subnet field, so that's an unmistakable sign of the boundaries between subnets.

Viewing the subnet and host addresses as a single, concatenated field lets you appreciate the mathematical beginning and ending points of each subnet. The ↓ symbols indicate a sequential incrementing of the host field by one binary digit at a time from 000001 through 111110.

Using a 3-Bit Mask

Continuing with our examination of subnetting Class C type networks (24 network address bits), a 3-bit subnetwork mask offers a different combination of subnets and hosts. The mask is 255.255.255.224 because you have the 3 highest-order bits of the last octet to use in defining subnets, so 128 + 64 + 32 = 224. Under strict classical rules, this mask enables the definition of six usable subnets, each with 30 usable host addresses. These are identified in Table 3-6.

Table 3-6   *Subnetting with a 3-Bit Mask in a 24-Bit Network*

	Binary Network Plus Subnet Address	Decimal Translation
Base	11000000.10101001.01111101.00000000	192.169.125.0
Subnet 0	11000000.10101001.01111101.*000*-00000	192.169.125.0
Subnet 1	11000000.10101001.01111101.*001*-00000	192.169.125.32
Subnet 2	11000000.10101001.01111101.*010*-00000	192.169.125.64
Subnet 3	11000000.10101001.01111101.*011*-00000	192.169.125.96
Subnet 4	11000000.10101001.01111101.*100*-00000	192.169.125.128
Subnet 5	11000000.10101001.01111101.*101*-00000	192.169.125.160
Subnet 6	11000000.10101001.01111101.*110*-00000	192.169.125.192
Subnet 7	11000000.10101001.01111101.*111*-00000	192.169.125.224

As is evident in Table 3-6, the base address in each subnet represents an increase of 32 addresses from the previous subnet's starting point. This is because 32 is the decimal equivalent of the lowest-value bit allocated to the subnet mask. Table 3-7 builds on this example by mapping out the following significant addresses within a subnet:

- The first, or base, address
- The first assignable address
- ˙ The last, or broadcast, address

The base address has a host address field of all 0s, the broadcast address has a host address field of all 1s, and the assignable addresses have a host address field populated by a combination of 1s and 0s.

Table 3-7 *Mapping Significant Addresses with a 3-Bit Mask*

	Binary Network Plus Subnet Address	**Decimal Translation**
Base	11000000.10101001.01111101.00000000	192.169.125.0
Subnet 0	11000000.10101001.01111101.*000*-00000	192.169.125.0
Subnet 0	11000000.10101001.01111101.*000*-00001	192.169.125.1
Subnet 0	↓	↓
Subnet 0	11000000.10101001.01111101.*000*-11111	192.169.125.31
Subnet 1	11000000.10101001.01111101.*001*-00000	192.169.125.32
Subnet 1	11000000.10101001.01111101.*001*-00001	192.169.125.33
Subnet 1	↓	↓
Subnet 1	11000000.10101001.01111101.*001*-11111	192.169.125.63
Subnet 2	11000000.10101001.01111101.*010*-00000	192.169.125.64
Subnet 2	11000000.10101001.01111101.*010*-00001	192.169.125.65
Subnet 2	↓	↓
Subnet 2	11000000.10101001.01111101.*010*-11111	192.169.125.95
Subnet 3	11000000.10101001.01111101.*011*-00000	192.169.125.96
Subnet 3	11000000.10101001.01111101.*011*-00001	192.169.125.97
Subnet 3	↓	↓
Subnet 3	11000000.10101001.01111101.*011*-11111	192.169.125.127
Subnet 4	11000000.10101001.01111101.*100*-00000	192.169.125.128
Subnet 4	11000000.10101001.01111101.*100*-00001	192.169.125.129
Subnet 4	↓	↓
Subnet 4	11000000.10101001.01111101.*100*-11111	192.169.125.159

Table 3-7   *Mapping Significant Addresses with a 3-Bit Mask (Continued)*

	Binary Network Plus Subnet Address	Decimal Translation
Subnet 5	11000000.10101001.01111101.*101*-00000	192.169.125.160
Subnet 5	11000000.10101001.01111101.*101*-00001	192.169.125.161
Subnet 5	↓	↓
Subnet 5	11000000.10101001.01111101.*101*-11111	192.169.125.191
Subnet 6	11000000.10101001.01111101.*110*-00000	192.169.125.192
Subnet 6	11000000.10101001.01111101.*110*-00001	192.169.125.193
Subnet 6	↓	↓
Subnet 6	11000000.10101001.01111101.*110*-11111	192.169.125.223
Subnet 7	11000000.10101001.01111101.*111*-00000	192.169.125.224
Subnet 7	11000000.10101001.01111101.*111*-00001	192.169.125.225
Subnet 7	↓	↓
Subnet 7	11000000.10101001.01111101.*111*-11111	192.169.125.255

As you saw in Table 3-5, you cross over from one subnet into the other whenever you hit an all-1s address. The next address becomes an all-0s address in the next-higher subnet number. The decimal values offer scant clues to those who are not intimately familiar with subnetting as to the identity of a subnet's base, initial, or broadcast address.

Using a 4-Bit Mask

The next way you can slice up a 24-bit network address is with a 4-bit subnet mask. Subnets of this size are identified with the mask 255.255.255.240 because the first 4 bits of the last octet are used for subnet identification. Mathematically, 240 = 128 + 64 + 32 + 16. Table 3-8 identifies the mathematically possible subnets that such a mask lets you create.

Table 3-8   *Subnetting with a 4-Bit Mask in a 24-Bit Network*

	Binary Network Plus Subnet Address	Decimal Translation
Base	**11000000.10101001.01111101**.00000000	192.169.125.0
Subnet 0	**11000000.10101001.01111101**.*0000*-0000	192.169.125.0
Subnet 1	**11000000.10101001.01111101**.*0001*-0000	192.169.125.16
Subnet 2	**11000000.10101001.01111101**.*0010*-0000	192.169.125.32
Subnet 3	**11000000.10101001.01111101**.*0011*-0000	192.169.125.48
Subnet 4	**11000000.10101001.01111101**.*0100*-0000	192.169.125.64

continues

Table 3-8   *Subnetting with a 4-Bit Mask in a 24-Bit Network (Continued)*

	Binary Network Plus Subnet Address	Decimal Translation
Subnet 5	11000000.10101001.01111101.*0101*-0000	192.169.125.80
Subnet 6	11000000.10101001.01111101.*0110*-0000	192.169.125.96
Subnet 7	11000000.10101001.01111101.*0111*-0000	192.169.125.112
Subnet 8	11000000.10101001.01111101.*1000*-0000	192.169.125.128
Subnet 9	11000000.10101001.01111101.*1001*-0000	192.169.125.144
Subnet 10	11000000.10101001.01111101.*1010*-0000	192.169.125.160
Subnet 11	11000000.10101001.01111101.*1011*-0000	192.169.125.176
Subnet 12	11000000.10101001.01111101.*1100*-0000	192.169.125.192
Subnet 13	11000000.10101001.01111101.*1101*-0000	192.169.125.208
Subnet 14	11000000.10101001.01111101.*1110*-0000	192.169.125.224
Subnet 15	11000000.10101001.01111101.*1111*-0000	192.169.125.240

This size of mask enables the creation of 14 usable subnets (16 total that are mathematically definable) with 14 usable host addresses each. By now, it should be relatively obvious that you find subnet base addresses by counting in multiples of the decimal value set by the lowest-order bit in the subnet. In a 4-bit subnet, that value is 16. This is reinforced by the Decimal Translation column in Table 3-8.

Given that the tables are getting quite lengthy, and because I'm confident that you get the idea, it isn't necessary to continue mapping the base, initial, and broadcast addresses of each subnet. That would run up the page count, and other topics need to be covered. Therefore, the remainder of this section continues mapping out the base addresses of different-sized subnets in both binary and decimal numbers but foregoes the additional step of mapping out the progression of addresses across the sequential subnets.

Using a 5-Bit Mask

A 5-bit subnet mask is the inverse of a 3-bit mask. In other words, instead of enabling the creation of six subnets of 30 hosts each, a 5-bit mask offers you 30 subnets of six hosts each. The mask for this size of subnet is 255.255.255.248, because 128 + 64 + 32 + 16 + 8 = 248. Table 3-9 gives the breakdown of this mask, as well as the decimal translation of its subnet base addresses.

Table 3-9   *Subnetting with a 5-Bit Mask in a 24-Bit Network*

	Binary Network Plus Subnet Address	**Decimal Translation**
Base	**11000000.10101001.01111101**.00000000	192.169.125.0
Subnet 0	**11000000.10101001.01111101.**_00000_-000	192.169.125.0
Subnet 1	**11000000.10101001.01111101.**_00001_-000	192.169.125.8
Subnet 2	**11000000.10101001.01111101.**_00010_-000	192.169.125.16
Subnet 3	**11000000.10101001.01111101.**_00011_-000	192.169.125.24
Subnet 4	**11000000.10101001.01111101.**_00100_-000	192.169.125.32
Subnet 5	**11000000.10101001.01111101.**_00101_-000	192.169.125.40
Subnet 6	**11000000.10101001.01111101.**_00110_-000	192.169.125.48
Subnet 7	**11000000.10101001.01111101.**_00111_-000	192.169.125.56
Subnet 8	**11000000.10101001.01111101.**_01000_-000	192.169.125.64
Subnet 9	**11000000.10101001.01111101.**_01001_-000	192.169.125.72
Subnet 10	**11000000.10101001.01111101.**_01010_-000	192.169.125.80
Subnet 11	**11000000.10101001.01111101.**_01011_-000	192.169.125.88
Subnet 12	**11000000.10101001.01111101.**_01100_-000	192.169.125.96
Subnet 13	**11000000.10101001.01111101.**_01101_-000	192.169.125.104
Subnet 14	**11000000.10101001.01111101.**_01110_-000	192.169.125.112
Subnet 15	**11000000.10101001.01111101.**_01111_-000	192.169.125.120
Subnet 16	**11000000.10101001.01111101.**_10000_-000	192.169.125.128
Subnet 17	**11000000.10101001.01111101.**_10001_-000	192.169.125.136
Subnet 18	**11000000.10101001.01111101.**_10010_-000	192.169.125.144
Subnet 19	**11000000.10101001.01111101.**_10011_-000	192.169.125.152
Subnet 20	**11000000.10101001.01111101.**_10100_-000	192.169.125.160
Subnet 21	**11000000.10101001.01111101.**_10101_-000	192.169.125.168
Subnet 22	**11000000.10101001.01111101.**_10110_-000	192.169.125.176
Subnet 23	**11000000.10101001.01111101.**_10111_-000	192.169.125.184
Subnet 24	**11000000.10101001.01111101.**_11000_-000	192.169.125.192
Subnet 25	**11000000.10101001.01111101.**_11001_-000	192.169.125.200
Subnet 26	**11000000.10101001.01111101.**_11010_-000	192.169.125.208
Subnet 27	**11000000.10101001.01111101.**_11011_-000	192.169.125.216
Subnet 28	**11000000.10101001.01111101.**_11100_-000	192.169.125.224

continues

Table 3-9   *Subnetting with a 5-Bit Mask in a 24-Bit Network (Continued)*

	Binary Network Plus Subnet Address	Decimal Translation
Subnet 29	11000000.10101001.01111101.*11101*-000	192.169.125.232
Subnet 30	11000000.10101001.01111101.*11110*-000	192.169.125.240
Subnet 31	11000000.10101001.01111101.*11111*-000	192.169.125.249

A mask of 255.255.255.248 in a fixed-length subnet environment is probably pushing the point at which the subdivision of address space is becoming ridiculous—at least as far as subnets for end users are concerned. With just six usable host addresses, the value of a subnet becomes questionable for such a purpose. This is particularly true because, in a fixed-length subnetting scheme, the subnet size selected must be able to accommodate the largest of the subnets.

Using a 6-Bit Mask

If a 5-bit mask bordered on ridiculous, surely a 6-bit fixed-length subnet mask is lunacy. Yet FLSM rules let you implement such a scheme. The subnet mask for this scheme in a 24-bit network is 255.255.255.252. Mathematically, you arrive at that value because $128 + 64 + 32 + 16 + 8 + 4 = 252$. In binary terms, that mask is 11111111.11111111.11111111.11111100. In other words, not many bits are left for host addresses. In terms of Classical IP rules, with this scheme you could create 62 usable subnets, each bearing just two usable host addresses.

Don't worry. I have no intention of dragging you through a multipage table, exhaustively perusing the incremental binary math of this scheme. Instead, I'll treat you to a very abridged version that still adequately demonstrates the limited utility of such a scheme. Table 3-10 presents the abridged data, again using the 24-bit network address 192.169.125.0.

Table 3-10   *Subnetting with a 6-Bit Mask in a 24-Bit Network*

	Binary Network Plus Subnet Address	Decimal Translation
Base	11000000.10101001.01111101.00000000	192.169.125.0
Subnet 0	11000000.10101001.01111101.*000000*-00	192.169.125.0
Subnet 1	11000000.10101001.01111101.*000001*-00	192.169.125.4
Subnet 2	11000000.10101001.01111101.*000010*-00	192.169.125.8
Subnet 3	11000000.10101001.01111101.*000011*-00	192.169.125.12
Subnet 4	11000000.10101001.01111101. *000100*-00	192.169.125.16
Subnet 5	11000000.10101001.01111101. *000101*-00	192.169.125.20
Subnet 6	11000000.10101001.01111101. *000110*-00	192.169.125.24
↓	↓	↓
Subnet 63	11000000.10101001.01111101.*111111*-00	192.169.125.252

NOTE   The /30 subnet might seem thoroughly useless, given how few addresses it contains. However, it might well be one of the most commonly used subnet masks. It is ideally suited for addressing serial links (such as T1 or other point-to-point leased lines) on routers. However, the usefulness of so small a subnet is apparent only when you escape the confines of fixed-length subnetting schemes.

Notice in Table 3-10 how the base address of each subnet increments by four addresses. As demonstrated earlier in this chapter, half of these mathematically possible addresses remain reserved under the classical rules of subnetting. The four addresses are 00, 01, 10, and 11. The 00 and 11 addresses function as the subnet identity and the broadcast address for each subnet, respectively. Thus, a 6-bit mask gives you a plethora of subnets, but with a dearth of host addresses per subnet.

Hopefully, this review of the trade-offs between subnet and host addresses has helped reinforce the basic concepts of subnetting and has given you a lot to think about. I wouldn't want to leave you with the misimpression that only Class C (24-bit) networks can be subnetted. Far from it! Any network address can be subnetted. To help demonstrate this, the next section briefly examines how subnetting works with a Class B network (16-bit) address.

Subnetting a 16-Bit Network Address

A Class B network contains many more addresses than a Class C. As explained in Chapter 2, the Class B network uses 16 bits of its address space for host identification and the other 16 bits for network identification. That means that each Class B network can uniquely identify 65,536 possible endpoints—quite a difference from the paltry 256 available within a Class C network!

Having so much address space to work with means that there is a lot more flexibility in forming subnets. However, the limitations of FLSM still apply. The limitations of FLSM were noticeable in a Class C network, and those same limits are experienced on an even greater scale within a Class B network.

Apart from the sheer size difference, subnetting a Class B network with FLSM is much like subnetting a Class C. Some of the basic rules that must be adhered to are that a minimum of 2 bits and a maximum of 14 may be used to identify subnets. These 16 bits are the third and fourth octets in the 32-bit IPv4 address. Implicit in these statements is that a subnet address can spill over between two of an IP address's octets. That can make things a bit trickier to understand, but it's an extension rather than a violation of the subnetting rules you are now so familiar with. These bits also must start out with the highest-order bits of the host address in order to ensure that the extended network prefix remains a contiguous block of bits. Table 3-11 presents the basic set of trade-offs between the number of subnets and the number of hosts per subnet that you can create with FLSM.

Table 3-11   *Subnetting a 16-Bit Network*

Number of Bits in the Network Prefix	Subnet Mask	Number of Usable Subnet Addresses	Number of Usable Hosts Per Subnet
2	255.255.192.0	2	16,382
3	255.255.224.0	6	8,190
4	255.255.240.0	14	4,094
5	255.255.248.0	30	2,046
6	255.255.252.0	62	1,022
7	255.255.254.0	126	510
8	255.255.255.0	254	254
9	255.255.255.128	510	126
10	255.255.255.192	1,022	62
11	255.255.255.224	2,046	30
12	255.255.255.240	4,094	14
13	255.255.255.248	8,190	6
14	255.255.255.252	16,382	2

The sheer size of a Class B network should be evident from Table 3-11. A mask of 255.255.192.0, for example, yields only two usable subnets, but each one offers 16,382 host addresses.

Using 172.16.0.0 as our sample network block, let's look at how it can be subnetted and which addresses become base subnet addresses. Without subjecting you to the tedium of an exhaustive exploration of how a 16-bit network can be subnetted, refer to Table 3-12 for a much-condensed version. This table simply demonstrates the key difference between subnetting a Class B versus a Class C. That difference lies in how the address bits are allocated between network, subnet, and host fields. I have again followed the convention of using bold for the network address, bold italic for the subnet address, and plain text for the host address to help you more readily appreciate the boundaries between these fields.

Table 3-12 *Subnetting a 16-Bit Network*

Subnet Mask	Binary Equivalent
255.255.192.0	**11111111.11111111.***11*-000000.00000000
255.255.224.0	**11111111.11111111.***111*-00000.00000000
255.255.240.0	**11111111.11111111.***1111*-0000.00000000
255.255.248.0	**11111111.11111111.***11111*-000.00000000
255.255.252.0	**11111111.11111111.***111111*-00.00000000
255.255.254.0	**11111111.11111111.***1111111*-0.00000000
255.255.255.0	**11111111.11111111.***11111111*.00000000
255.255.255.128	**11111111.11111111.***11111111.1*-0000000
255.255.255.192	**11111111.11111111.***11111111.11*-000000
255.255.255.224	**11111111.11111111.***11111111.111*-00000
255.255.255.240	**11111111.11111111.***11111111.1111*-0000
255.255.255.248	**11111111.11111111.***11111111.11111*-000
255.255.255.252	**11111111.11111111.***11111111.111111*-00

Table 3-12 has some interesting points to consider. First, did you notice that there is a mask of 255.255.255.128? That mask would be illegal in a Class C network, because it would use only 1 bit for subnet identification. However, in the much larger Class B space, that mask indicates that 9 bits (not 1) are being used for subnet identification. Thus, you should recognize that the legality of any particular mask depends directly on the size of the network address block.

Other interesting subnets are last five, which range from 255.255.255.192 through 255.255.255.252. These masks are identical to those found in Class C networks. However, recognize that in this particular case, each one has 8 additional bits being used for subnet identification. Thus, the number of hosts per subnet may remain equal to the Class C counterpart, but the number of possible subnets that can be created is much greater. Again, the size of the network address block being subnetted has tremendous implications for the subnetting scheme. Context is everything.

At this point in the chapter, you are probably very tired of staring at tables of numbers. Fear not: You're almost through with this topic. The remainder of this chapter points out some of the specific weaknesses and inefficiencies inherent in FLSM. These are the reasons why FLSM has become functionally obsolete. You can still use it, but as you will learn in the next chapter, you have better options.

Sources of Inefficiencies with FLSM

Fixed-length subnet masking was a tremendous step in the evolution of the IP address architecture. It offered the capability to develop locally significant subnetworks without affecting global routability and gave network administrators the flexibility to create whichever sized subnet suited their needs best. Despite this radical leap forward, the potential for waste remained high. Thus was born the great irony of subnetting. Subnetting, in general, was designed to enable more efficient use of address space by permitting class-based network address blocks to be subdivided into smaller address blocks. Yet the way subnetting was originally implemented was far from efficient.

Sources of waste and inefficiency included the following:

- Subnet 0 and subnet "all 1s" were reserved.
- All-0s and all-1s host addresses were reserved.
- There was one size of mask for all subnets.

The manner in which each of these contributed to inefficiency and waste is further described in the following sections.

Subnet Addresses

I've probably beaten this one to death throughout this chapter, but it remains an important point. The original rules for subnetting in RFC 950 stressed the significance of reserving the subnets whose addresses were constructed of all 0s and all 1s. Depending on the size of the mask being used, this could translate directly into a substantial number of addresses being wasted. Consider a mask of 255.255.255.192 in a Class C network. That size of network has only a mathematically possible 256 host addresses. The subnet mask we've selected would yield four possible subnets, each with 64 mathematically possible host addresses. Reserving subnets 0 and 3 (as per Table 3-4) immediately translates into the loss of 128 of the host addresses. Pragmatically, wasting 128 addresses is better than wasting 384, as you would do if you acquired just two Class C networks and didn't bother subnetting. However, the fact remains that the classical rules are not perfectly efficient.

Host Addresses

A much more subtle form of loss is found in the host addresses themselves. Again, the all-0s and all-1s addresses are reserved, but this time there's a pair within each subnet. Thus, for each subnet formed, two host addresses can't be used. To continue expanding on the example from the preceding section, the all-0s and all-1s addresses in subnets 1 and 2 are as shown in Table 3-13.

Table 3-13   *Subnetting with a 6-Bit Mask in a 16-Bit Network*

Subnet Number	Binary Value of the Last Octet	All 0s
Subnet 1	*01*-000000	192.169.125.64
Subnet 1	*01*-111111	192.169.125.127
Subnet 2	*10*-000000	192.169.125.128
Subnet 2	*10*-111111	192.169.125.191

Table 3-13 demonstrates that, in addition to losing all of Subnets 0 and 3 (the all-0s and all-1s subnet addresses), you lose four more addresses. That brings the total of unusable addresses to 132 out of the original 255—a more than 50% loss rate.

Sizing the Mask

As you learned earlier in this chapter, there can be only a single mask for each network being subnetted with FLSM. Thus, an additional source of inefficiency lies in the fact that the appropriate size of mask for the largest of the local networks is probably too big for the others. The numbers of addresses wasted in this manner are incalculable, because they vary widely from implementation to implementation. Suffice it to say that the waste is in direct proportion to the size difference between the smallest and largest LANs being serviced with a subnetted network address block.

Given this potential for waste, network administrators are motivated to size their subnets as carefully as possible. A contravening point to consider is that it is often difficult to accurately project growth over time. Thus, a network administrator might be tempted to build in a substantial amount of fluff to accommodate this unspecified future growth requirement. Despite not having good data to work with, a network administrator is the one who would suffer the consequences of an overly conservative subnetting scheme. Users, after all, tend to care more about their own convenience than they do about the global availability of IP addresses. Thus, sizing a network mask often is influenced more by fear than by actual requirements.

Although this might seem trivial, reflect on how radically the base (or first), initial, and broadcast addresses per subnet change with mask size. These were presented in a series of tables in this chapter. Now consider how difficult it would be to change the mask size in an established FLSM network. The vast majority of your endpoints would have to be renumbered. Although tools such as Dynamic Host Configuration Protocol (DHCP) might reduce the burden of renumbering, it still would be a logistical nightmare to plan, and implementing it would cause some downtime. Besides, even the most sophisticated network likely wouldn't be completely supported by DHCP or some other automated tool. Quite simply, many hosts can't afford to have a dynamic address. Servers and network nodes, for example, all but require a static address to function reliably from the perspective of the user community.

Summary

Subnetting was an invaluable extension of the original IP address space's hierarchy. As useful as it was, its original form quickly demonstrated its limitations. These limitations, as you've seen in this chapter, are directly related to the inflexibility of carving a network address into fixed-length subnetwork blocks. Simply put, one size seldom fits all. Out of this inflexibility were borne waste and inefficiency. In retrospect, fixed-length subnet masks seemed revolutionary at their inception but have proven themselves more valuable for leading the way to the future. Thus, even though the original concept was vindicated, the execution left much to be desired.

Over time, a more sophisticated approach to subnetting was developed that enabled much greater flexibility. This approach, known as variable-length subnet masking (VLSM), is explained in the next chapter.

CHAPTER 4

Variable-Length Subnet Masks

The preceding chapter examined the powerful innovation known as subnetting in its original form: Fixed-Length Subnet Masking (FLSM). At its introduction, FLSM was called simply subnetting. By any name, it was a revolutionary and necessary evolution of the IP address architecture that enabled a tremendous reduction in the waste of IP addresses. With the benefit of hindsight, we can see that FLSM was but a half step in the right direction. Its single greatest benefit was that it validated the concept of borrowing bits from the host field of an IP address to create locally significant subnetwork identification addresses. But the simplifying assumption of permitting just one subnet mask for all subnets created from a network address proved to be both unnecessary and inefficient.

In reality, subnets are hardly ever of the same approximate size. Consequently, FLSM's one-size-fits-all design philosophy created a substantial number of wasted addresses. Solving this conundrum was easy: Permit the creation of variable-length subnets. In theory, this would enable subnets to be created more efficiently by making each subnet mask specifically tailored to each subnet.

To help make this esoteric concept a bit more real, I'll use a sample network to show you how subnetting works mathematically. Throughout this chapter, we'll build on this sample network and look at some interesting things, including practical implications. We'll also look at the challenges of managing an address space subnetted into flexibly sized subnets using a technique known as Variable-Length Subnet Masking.

Variable-Length Subnetting in the RFCs

Ordinarily, I would point out an IETF source document that is the basis for an Internet technology and then expound on that technology. In the case of Variable-Length Subnet Masking (VLSM), there is no clear-cut genesis document. Searching the Internet or the RFC Editor's database turns up a variety of references, mostly in documents dedicated to other topics. The more salient of these tangential reference documents are RFC 1009 and RFC 1878. They provide you with the context for the development of variable-length subnets and supporting mathematics and helps you appreciate a more thorough examination of VLSM. The following sections discuss each of these RFCs.

RFC 1009

The first "official" acknowledgment that you could use multiple subnet masks came in June 1987 with RFC 1009. Although this RFC focused on requirements for Internet gateways, the perceived benefits of a flexible approach to subnetting were identified. The rationale for supporting flexible or variable subnet masks was an acknowledgment of the inefficiency of trying to use a single mask for multiple subnets. Additionally, the RFC's authors acknowledged that subnetting was strictly a local phenomenon that had no impact on global routing. Consequently, enabling subnets to be created with different sized masks within the same network address offered tremendous benefits with no disadvantages. The flexibility was deemed critical to a continued ability to cope with the Internet's future expected growth.

Here are some of the rules stipulated in this RFC:

- Not assigning subnet addresses with values of either all 1s or all 0s.

- It was recommended, but not required, that the host address's highest-order bits be used to create the subnet addresses. This ensured that both network and subnetwork addresses remained contiguous. For example, let's see what happens if the Class C-sized network address 192.168.125.0 is subnetted with a subnet mask of 255.255.255.224. Translating that address to binary results in **11000000.10101000.01111101.000**00000. The last 8 bits are the only ones used for host addresses, so you are exhorted by the RFC to use this field's highest-order bits to create your subnet address. I have indicated those bits in bold italic to make it very clear what is meant by highest-order bits.

- The Internet would route to the subnetted location using only the network portion of the IP address. Local gateways (known more commonly today as routers) would be required to route to specific destinations using the entire extended network prefix. The *extended network prefix,* to refresh your memory, is the network address plus the subnet address. This prefix can be seen only when you view the address in binary form. Let's look at this a little closer using the same example as before. The extended network prefix for address 192.168.125.0 with a subnet mask of 255.255.255.224 is indicated in bold italic in the following bit string: ***11000000.10101000.01111101.000***00000. The local router makes its forwarding decisions based on both the network and subnetwork portions of an IP address.

Remember that because a subnet mask is of local significance only, nothing you do at the subnet level has any impact whatsoever on routing *to* your network. At the time RFC 1009 was published, many network administrators had figured out the mathematics of VLSM on their own and were not only creating variable-length subnets, but also nesting multiple levels of subnets within other subnets! Thus, the Spartan description of guidelines on how to support variable-length subnets in RFC 1009 amounted to little more than an acknowledgment of what was already becoming common practice.

The term *VLSM* is not used in RFC 1009. Instead, the RFC's authors seem to prefer describing this phenomenon as *flexible subnet masks*.

Standardization Without Ratification

It is generally understood and accepted that VLSM was an evolutionary step forward that was made possible by the successes of FLSM. However, few understand that VLSM wasn't explicitly and separately defined until long after it was in common use.

You might be wondering how on earth someone could use something like VLSM if it hasn't been formally developed or sanctioned by the IETF. That's a fair question. It certainly isn't the normal way a technology becomes accepted and deployed throughout the Internet user community. The answer is remarkably simple: VLSM didn't have to be sanctioned, because the capability already existed. We just lacked the sophistication to appreciate it. That probably sounds a little cryptic, so let me try explaining it in more-tangible terms. In a local-area network (LAN), subnet masks are configured in three general locations:

- A router's interface to a LAN
- Management ports on all LAN devices such as hubs or switches
- All the hosts connected to that LAN

In order for everything to work properly in an FLSM environment, all interfaces within a network must use the same mask. This includes all the hosts, the router interface, and the management ports on the LAN hubs or switches. But each of these interfaces is configured separately. No requirement in the FLSM specifications mandated a sanity check across all of a router's interfaces to ensure that the same-sized mask was being used. Some early routing platforms gave the administrator a caution but accepted the flawed configuration. Thus, nothing stopped you from assigning different-sized subnet masks to different router interfaces, even though each of those interfaces might have been configured with IP addresses from the same network address.

In lieu of IETF standardization, grassroots creativity allowed FLSM to deliver greater capability than its creators ever imagined possible. The IETF first acknowledged the informal practice of "flexible" subnetting in RFC 1009, released way back in June 1987. However, they didn't grant legitimacy to that practice until they started developing another technology, *Classless Interdomain Routing* (CIDR). A rather inauspicious start for an invaluable capability!

RFC 1878

RFC 1878 is an Informational RFC released in December 1995. It defined no new technology or protocol, but it offered greater clarification on the mathematical trade-offs between the number of hosts and the number of subnets that could be created with various-sized network blocks. In fact, RFC 1878 was titled "Variable Length Subnet Table for IPv4."

One of the more useful tables in this RFC is excerpted in Table 4-1. This table demonstrates the correlation between the number of subnets and hosts you can define with any given-size mask. The mask size is indicated in both the familiar decimal terms and a new notation that was introduced in CIDR. This notation explicitly identifies the extended network prefix by using a slash (/) followed by a number. The slash can be thought of as a flag that indicates that the following numbers specify how many bits in the IPv4 address are used for network and subnetwork addresses. Thus, the number after the slash, when subtracted from 32, yields the number of bits allocated to host addressing.

Please note that all values in Table 4-1 are gross and are not adjusted for usability.

Table 4-1 *Mathematical Correlation Between Subnets and Hosts*

Decimal Mask	CIDR Notation	Number of Possible Host Addresses	Size in Terms of Class-eBased Networks
128.0.0.0	/1	2,147,483,648	128 Class A
192.0.0.0	/2	1,073,741,824	64 Class A
224.0.0.0	/3	536,870,912	32 Class A
240.0.0.0	/4	268,435,456	16 Class A
248.0.0.0	/5	134,217,728	8 Class A
252.0.0.0	/6	67,108,864	4 Class A
254.0.0.0	/7	33,554,432	2 Class A
255.0.0.0	/8	16,777,216	1 Class A
255.128.0.0	/9	8,388,608	128 Class B
255.192.0.0	/10	4,194,304	64 Class B
255.224.0.0	/11	2,097,152	32 Class B
255.240.0.0	/12	1,048,576	16 Class B
255.248.0.0	/13	524,288	8 Class B
255.252.0.0	/14	262,144	4 Class B
255.254.0.0	/15	131,072	2 Class B
255.255.0.0	/16	65,536	1 Class B
255.255.128.0	/17	32,768	128 Class C
255.255.192.0	/18	16,384	64 Class C
255.255.224.0	/19	8,192	32 Class C
255.255.240.0	/20	4,096	16 Class C
255.255.248.0	/21	2,048	8 Class C
255.255.252.0	/22	1,024	4 Class C
255.255.254.0	/23	512	2 Class C
255.255.255.0	/24	256	1 Class C

Table 4-1   *Mathematical Correlation Between Subnets and Hosts (Continued)*

Decimal Mask	CIDR Notation	Number of Possible Host Addresses	Size in Terms of Class-eBased Networks
255.255.255.128	/25	128	1/2 Class C
255.255.255.192	/26	64	1/4 Class C
255.255.255.224	/27	32	1/8 Class C
255.255.255.240	/28	16	1/16 Class C
255.255.255.248	/29	8	1/32 Class C
255.255.255.252	/30	4	1/64 Class C
255.255.255.254	/31	2	1/128 Class C
255.255.255.255	/32	1	Single-host route

Table 4-1 should exhibit some interesting mathematical patterns. If these patterns aren't yet self-evident, fear not: It gets easier with practice! Basically, you will see a repetition of a numeric sequence in the Decimal Mask column. A single bit set equal to 1 in the leftmost column of a binary octet carries a decimal value of 128. The initial 2 bits, when set to 11, yield a decimal equivalent of 192. Thus, the increments of decimal numbers must follow the pattern you first saw in Chapter 2: 128, 192, 224, 240, 248, 252, 254, and 255.

The next interesting pattern you should recognize is that, starting with the /32 mask (which references just one host address), you are doubling the number of possible host addresses with each bit you add to the host field. This doubling is complemented with a halving of the number of subnets available. Start at the bottom of the Number of Possible Host Addresses column. For every bit you add to the host address field, you double the quantity of addresses available. With each bit you remove from the host field, you are halving the number of available hosts in that sized network. Thus, a /25 network offers exactly half the number of host addresses that are available in a /24 network. Understanding this relationship is necessary for understanding both VLSM and CIDR. We'll look at CIDR in much more detail in Chapter 6, "Classless Interdomain Routing (CIDR)."

If you'd like to read more about the guidelines for VLSM contained in RFC 1878, here's the URL:

www.ietf.org/rfc/rfc1878.txt

The Inefficiencies of FLSM

Chapter 3, "Fixed-Length Subnet Masks," showed you how FLSM lets you conserve the IP address space by creating locally significant subnetwork addresses. The benefit of this is that you can use a single network address to service multiple local networks. But in the real world, those local networks are seldom the same size. Thus, implementing FLSM actually wastes IP addresses. To better illustrate this point, consider the network shown in Figure 4-1. We will use this basic network diagram as the basis for exploring VLSM throughout this chapter.

Figure 4-1   *Sample Network*

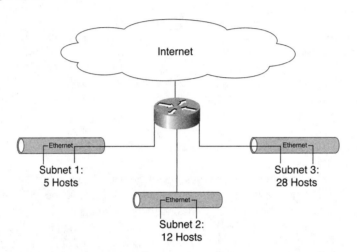

This example is simplified throughout this chapter for the sake of demonstrating the relative efficiencies of VLSM versus FLSM. It is not intended as a realistic example, nor is it indicative of how you would actually subnet a block of network addresses. Consequently, you might notice that there are no IP addresses in the subnets assigned to LAN switch or hub management ports. Similarly, some of the subnet address ranges do not end neatly on the bit boundaries indicated by their mask. Although this scheme would work, it is not ideal. Again, it is intended solely to demonstrate relative efficiencies. It's not a guide for how to subnet on the job. We'll look at how to do that in subsequent chapters. For now, we'll just concentrate on the basics, and that requires some simplifying assumptions.

In Figure 4-1, you can see that the local subnets are of very different sizes. Subnet 1 contains just five hosts. Subnet 2 contains 12 hosts, and Subnet 3 contains 28 hosts.

Without any form of subnetting, you might have to resort to using three different Class C networks for each of these subnetworks. That would be a tremendous waste of addresses: 765 total addresses for just 45 hosts! Subnetting a traditional Class C network using fixed-length subnet masking requires you to use a mask large enough to satisfy the largest of the three subnets. That would be Subnet 3 with its 28 hosts. As you saw in Chapter 3, this would require subnetting the entire 24-bit network address with a mask of 255.255.255.224. That mask borrows 3 bits from the host field to create a 27-bit extended network prefix. The result is a 5-bit host field that lets you define six usable subnets, each with 30 assignable IP addresses. When I say "assignable," I'm referring to the reservation of both the all-0s and all-1s addresses. There are 32 mathematically possible addresses per subnet, but you need to reserve one host address (the all-0s address) for subnet identification and the all-1s address for IP-based broadcasting within that subnet.

NOTE   The notion of reserving all 0s and all 1s is found throughout the history of the Internet and the Internet's address space. Confusion results because this convention has been applied to both subnet addresses and host addresses.

As *host* addresses, these values are necessary within a subnet for subnet identification and broadcasting. Broadcasting is a transmission technique that sends the same packets of information to every connected host within a specific scope. In this particular case, the all-1s host address within any given subnet would be used to communicate with all hosts within that subnet.

This practice differs starkly from the obsolete practice of reserving all-0s and all-1s *subnet* addresses. Reserving those subnet addresses was arbitrary and was recommended solely for the sake of maintaining consistency of language within the network engineering community.

In this example, a total of 45 addresses are wasted through inflexibility. Using a mask of 255.255.255.224 to accommodate the needs of your largest subnet (Subnet 3) results in varying surpluses of addresses available in each subnet. Table 4-2 demonstrates how FLSM wastes addresses through the inflexibility of its subnetting mask.

Table 4-2   *Inefficiencies in FLSM*

Subnet Number	Number of Hosts	Excess IPs
Subnet 1	5	25
Subnet 2	12	18
Subnet 3	28	2

Using FLSM saves IP addresses in this example when compared to just giving each subnetwork its own Class C network address. Of course, you could make a very convincing argument that you would never want to precisely size a subnet, even if doing so were technically feasible. Such an effort might well result in a very painful renumbering exercise in the future when growth inevitably occurs. We'll look at how you can manage growth within a subnet later in this chapter. For now, let's look at how VLSM can improve on the efficiency with which you can use an address space.

Comparing VLSM to FLSM

VLSM greatly improves the efficiency with which the sample network can be subnetted. Instead of just using a 3-bit subnetwork field (mask of 255.255.255.224) for all fields, you can use whichever size mask makes sense for each subnet. In Chapter 3, we looked at a table that correlated the trade-offs between the number of hosts and the number of subnets that could be created from a 24-bit network address. That table, and that entire chapter, were focused on Classical IP—in other words, the way things used to be! Reserving the all-0s and all-1s subnets is no longer necessary or desirable. Consequently, the tables in this chapter reflect the availability of all mathematically possible subnet addresses.

With that caveat in mind, take a look at Table 4-3. Notice the gaps between subnet sizes? This should be a very familiar pattern by now, because it is a function of binary mathematics. Intuitively, you should recognize that VLSM won't be perfectly efficient, simply because subnet sizes (created from a 24-bit network address) increment from two usable host addresses to 6, to 14, to 30, and then to 62. We'll talk about this phenomenon later in this chapter, including why such gaps might be useful.

Table 4-3   *Hosts Versus Subnets in a Traditional Class C Network*

Number of Bits in the Network Prefix	Subnet Mask	Number of Usable Subnet Addresses	Number of Usable Hosts Per Subnet
2	255.255.255.192	4	62
3	255.255.255.224	8	30
4	255.255.255.240	16	14
5	255.255.255.248	32	6
6	255.255.255.252	64	2

Armed with this information, you can return your attention to the sample network. Looking at Table 4-2, Subnet 3 (which contains 28 hosts) would still require 5 bits for host addressing, so the best-size mask would still be 255.255.255.224. Subnet 1, however, would be better off with a mask of 255.255.255.248. That mask allocates 5 bits to the subnet identification field and 3 bits to host identification. A 3-bit host field yields six usable host addresses, which is perfect for the five-host subnet, and it still leaves an extra address for future growth. Subnet 2, with its 12 hosts, would be best-served with a mask of 255.255.255.240, because that mask evenly splits the host address into 4 bits for the subnet and 4 bits for host identification. This lets you assign 14 unique host addresses within a subnet.

Table 4-4 demonstrates the binary and decimal mathematics of the right-sized mask for each of the three subnets. Given that the first three octets are all high values of 255 or 11111111 in binary, I conserve space and save your eyesight by showing only the contents of the mask's last octet. The first three octets are indicated with the constant *n*. The binary values in this table adhere to my convention of showing the bits representing the subnet ID in a bold italic font.

Table 4-4   *Finding the Right Mask Size Per Subnet*

Subnet Number	Number of Hosts	Mask	Binary Value of Mask's Last Octet
Subnet 1	5	255.255.255.248	*n.n.n.**11111**000*
Subnet 2	12	255.255.255.240	*n.n.n.**1111**0000*
Subnet 3	28	255.255.255.224	*n.n.n.**111**00000*

As you can see, the most efficient subnet mask for each of the three subnets differs for each network. The downside of carefully tailoring a subnet mask to a subnet is the limitation of capacity for future growth. Ideally, you want some room for future growth, but predicting how much growth will be experienced is more of an art than an exact science. For the sake of the example, you need only 3 bits for host addressing in Subnet 1, 4 bits for host addressing in Subnet 2, and 5 bits for host addressing in Subnet 3. Using VLSM lets you use those three different masks within the same network address to achieve a dramatic reduction in wasted or unusable IP addresses.

Table 4-5 compares the relative efficiency of FLSM versus VLSM in the sample network.

Table 4-5   *Comparing the Relative Efficiency of FLSM Versus VLSM*

Subnet Number	FLSM with a Mask of 255.255.255.224		VLSM	
	Number of Hosts Supported	Number of IPs Wasted	Number of Hosts Supported	Number of IPs Wasted
Subnet 1	5	25	5	1
Subnet 2	12	18	12	2
Subnet 3	28	2	28	2

Quickly summing the number of IP addresses wasted using FLSM for the sample network vis-à-vis VLSM reveals that there can be a dramatic improvement. In the sample network, FLSM requires you to use a 3-bit mask, resulting in a waste of 45 IP addresses in just three subnets. That wasted amount drops to just five with a VLSM scheme.

A Practical Application

To better demonstrate how VLSM works in practical terms, Table 4-6 shows the progression from the sample network's base address (192.168.125.0) through the defined subnets. Pay particular attention to the binary and decimal translations for each subnet's base and terminal addresses. In decimal terms, you are progressing sequentially through the address space. In binary terms, you can see that each network uses a different combination of high-order bits in the last octet to identify the subnet. This might seem strange, but it is eminently logical. I distinguish between host and subnet bits in the binary address by indicating the subnet bits in bold italic and then delineating the two subfields with a dash (-). Ordinarily, you wouldn't find a dash in the middle of a bit string.

Table 4-6 *Subnetting with VLSM in a 24-Bit Network*

	Binary Network + Subnet Address	**Decimal Translation**
Base	**11000000.10101000.01111101.**00000000	192.168.125.0
Unassigned (Subnet 0)	**11000000.10101000.01111101.***00*000000	192.168.125.0
Unassigned (Subnet 0)	↓	↓
Unassigned (Subnet 0)	**11000000.10101000.01111101.***000*11111	192.168.125.31
Subnet 1	**11000000.10101000.01111101.***00100*000	192.168.125.32
Subnet 1	↓	↓
Subnet 1	**11000000.10101000.01111101.***00100*111	192.168.125.39
Subnet 2	**11000000.10101000.01111101.***00101*000	192.168.125.40
Subnet 2	↓	↓
Subnet 2	**11000000.10101000.01111101.***00101*111	192.168.125.47
Subnet 3	**11000000.10101000.01111101.***001*10000	192.168.125.48
Subnet 3	↓	↓
Subnet 3	**11000000.10101000.01111101.***001*11111	192.168.125.63
Unassigned	**11000000.10101000.01111101.**01000000	192.168.125.64
Unassigned	↓	↓
Unassigned	**11000000.10101000.01111101.**11111111	192.168.125.255

The unassigned space illustrated in Table 4-6 can be used in a number of different ways. Here are two of the more feasible scenarios for using this space:

- Any existing subnet can suddenly expand beyond the surplus afforded by its current mask.

- A new group of users might have to be supported, which necessitates the creation of a new subnet.

Both of these scenarios and their implications on subnetting schemes are explored in the remainder of this section.

Adding a Subnet

In the example used throughout this chapter, Subnets 1 through 3 have been used, with Subnet 0 idle. It is equal in size to a subnet defined with a mask of 255.255.255.224, but the 32 addresses it would contain are not used. I did this on purpose to show you that in many cases, old subnetting rules can be very persistent. Consequently, it is not uncommon to find Subnet 0 unused in networks today. Under today's rules for subnetting, this space doesn't have to lie fallow. To continue with the sample network, if a requirement emerges for a new subnet with 30 or fewer devices, Subnet 0 could be pressed into service.

Additional unallocated addresses remain in the high end of the network address block. Addresses 64 through 255 are unused, so it is possible for additional subnets to be created in the future. Thus, you have some options for satisfying new requests for subnets. Depending on the number of hosts in a new subnet, you could assign Subnet 0 or carve Subnet 4 out of the currently unassigned address space (addresses 64 through 255). A more nettlesome question is how you accommodate growth within the existing subnets.

Outgrowing a Subnet

As you were looking at Tables 4-4 and 4-5, did you notice that even VLSM isn't perfectly efficient? There are still wasted addresses. That's a direct function of the binary math that is the foundation of the address space itself, rather than a flaw in any particular approach to carving the space into subnets. You can create a subnet on any bit boundary, but each bit increments by a factor of 2. Remember: The rightmost bit in an octet has a decimal value of 1, the bit to the immediate left carries a value of 2, then 4, then 8, then 16, then 32, then 64, and ultimately 128 for the leftmost bit in the octet. Consequently, you must form your subnets in this sequence from powers of 2.

You could look at this architectural feature as a negative in that it results in wasted space. Alternatively, you could take a more pragmatic perspective and appreciate the positive implications of this feature. For example, even if it were possible to create subnets of the precise size you require for any given subnet, would you really want to tailor it so concisely? Many things can happen that would require you to add endpoints to a subnet. For example, the user community on any of your subnets might hire someone new. The same thing would hold true for technological innovation. It wasn't that many years ago that printers didn't have a built-in network interface card (NIC), and you had to use a server to spool print requests to them. A more commonly encountered scenario is that the group you are supporting can simply outgrow its subnet.

The point is that there are many reasons why the number of host addresses in any given subnet could change over time. Trying to add a few addresses to a tightly constructed subnetted scheme can be painful. Depending on the extent of the growth, you might find it necessary to completely renumber one or more subnets! That might not sound so bad, but it is not fun, and your users might not appreciate having to experience it either. Plus, you might discover a relatively common practice: application developers who hard-code IP addresses into their software. Renumbering a network will cause every such application to fail!

To illustrate this point, let's assume that Subnet 2 of the sample network needs to grow by five endpoints. Unfortunately, that subnet has only two available IP addresses within its assigned range (192.168.125.40 through 192.168.125.47), and Subnet 3 picks up right where Subnet 2 ends, so there is no opportunity to just change the mask's size to encompass sequential but unassigned addresses. Because Subnets 2 and 3 are numerically contiguous, your only choices both involve renumbering the endpoints within Subnet 2. You have to move them to a section of the address space that offers more addresses. Your two options are as follows:

- Move the endpoints from Subnet 2 to Subnet 0.

- Move the endpoints from Subnet 2 to the newly created Subnet 4 using previously unassigned addresses from the high end of the address block.

Table 4-7 shows you what the subnetting scheme would look like if you were to renumber the endpoints in Subnet 2 to use the range of addresses in Subnet 0. Doing so results in the allocation of 30 usable host addresses to a group of users that requires only 17, but you don't have any better options! The coarseness of the architecture works against you. A mask of 255.255.255.240 would yield only 14 usable hosts, which is inadequate. However, a mask of 255.255.255.224 (1 less bit in the subnet prefix) yields 30 usable hosts and is the only feasible solution. This should seem familiar to you, but if it doesn't, just refer back to Table 4-4.

Table 4-7   *Moving Subnet 2 Hosts to Subnet 0*

	Binary Network + Subnet Address	**Decimal Translation**
Base	11000000.10101000.01111101.00000000	192.168.125.0
Subnet 0	11000000.10101000.01111101.*000*00000	192.168.125.0
Subnet 0	↓	↓
Subnet 0	11000000.10101000.01111101.*000*11111	192.168.125.31
Subnet 1	11000000.10101000.01111101.*00100*000	192.168.125.32
Subnet 1	↓	↓
Subnet 1	11000000.10101000.01111101.*00100*111	192.168.125.39
Unassigned (formerly Subnet 2)	11000000.10101000.01111101.00101000	192.168.125.40
Unassigned (formerly Subnet 2)	↓	↓
Unassigned (formerly Subnet 2)	11000000.10101000.01111101.00101111	192.168.125.47
Subnet 3	11000000.10101000.01111101.*001*10000	192.168.125.48

Table 4-7   *Moving Subnet 2 Hosts to Subnet 0 (Continued)*

	Binary Network + Subnet Address	Decimal Translation
Subnet 3	↓	↓
Subnet 3	**11000000.10101000.01111101.***001*11111	192.168.125.63
Unassigned	**11000000.10101000.01111101.**01000000	192.168.125.64
Unassigned	↓	↓
Unassigned	**11000000.10101000.01111101.**11111111	192.168.125.255

Your second option for satisfying the outgrowth of Subnet 2 is to create a new subnet from the unassigned addresses. Table 4-8 demonstrates how this would be done. Pay particular attention to the binary and decimal translations for Subnet 4 to see how that would be accomplished.

Table 4-8   *Moving Subnet 2 to the Newly Created Subnet 4*

	Binary Network + Subnet Address	Decimal Translation
Base	**11000000.10101000.01111101.**00000000	192.168.125.0
Unassigned (Subnet 0)	**11000000.10101000.01111101.**00000000	192.168.125.0
Unassigned (Subnet 0)	↓	↓
Unassigned (Subnet 0)	**11000000.10101000.01111101.**00011111	192.168.125.31
Subnet 1	**11000000.10101000.01111101.***00100*000	192.168.125.32
Subnet 1	↓	↓
Subnet 1	**11000000.10101000.01111101.***00100*111	192.168.125.39
Unassigned (formerly Subnet 2)	**11000000.10101000.01111101.**00101000	192.168.125.40
Unassigned (formerly Subnet 2)	↓	↓
Unassigned (formerly Subnet 2)	**11000000.10101000.01111101.**00101111	192.168.125.47
Subnet 3	**11000000.10101000.01111101.***001*10000	192.168.125.48

continues

Table 4-8   *Moving Subnet 2 to the Newly Created Subnet 4 (Continued)*

	Binary Network + Subnet Address	**Decimal Translation**
Subnet 3	↓	↓
Subnet 3	**11000000.10101000.01111101.***001*11111	192.168.125.63
Subnet 4	**11000000.10101000.01111101.***01*000000	192.168.125.64
Subnet 4	↓	↓
Subnet 4	**11000000.10101000.01111101.***010*11111	192.168.125.95
Unassigned	**11000000.10101000.01111101.**01100000	192.168.125.96
Unassigned	↓	↓
Unassigned	**11000000.10101000.01111101.**11111111	192.168.125.255

If you look carefully at the progression of numbers—particularly the binary numbers—you will see a very familiar pattern. Both Subnets 3 and 4 use a 3-bit subnet mask. This makes it easy to see why one subnet ends with *00111111* and another begins with *01000000*. In the other cases, mismatched subnet prefixes make it a bit tougher to follow the logic. In those cases, ignore my visual cues about subnet formation and just look at the 8-bit string as a whole. Then, things make more sense.

Keep Careful Records!

Looking back over the previous three tables, you must draw one simple, inescapable conclusion: It is critical to maintain an accurate and up-to-date record of address assignments! Subnetting, in its original incarnation, was deemed practical only if you used a fixed-length mask to subdivide an entire network address. Although this wasn't the most efficient way to subdivide a network, it was still far more efficient than the previous method of operation, which was to secure separate network addresses for each of your subnets.

The grassroots innovation of flexible subnetting happened outside the auspices of the IETF. Thus, there was no solid base of research to draw on, no well-worn trail to follow, and no set of tools to rely on. If you chose to ignore the recommendation of using a single-sized subnet mask for your subnetting, you were on your own! This was a simplifying assumption embedded in the original subnetting RFCs. It gave ordinary network administrators a chance to improve the efficiency with which they consumed IP address space without creating a mathematics exercise that could have qualified as a Herculean task.

Despite the risks of stepping outside the safe confines of an RFC, flexible subnetting became the dominant paradigm. Technical personnel realized that the price they had to pay for this was the creation and maintenance of an accurate database of address assignments. This has never been more true!

Summary

Despite its beginning as an illegitimate child of an IETF ratified technology, "flexible subnetting" proved itself vastly superior to the original form of subnetting with fixed-length masks. In and of itself, VLSM (as it later became known) represented a tremendous advance in the sophistication of the IP address space. Yet it would have an even greater contribution in the future—a contribution that no one could have foreseen. You see, in the mid-1990s, the Internet was experiencing unprecedented, phenomenal growth. This growth rate sorely tested the scalability of the Internet's mechanisms, including its address space.

Sadly, the IP address space demonstrated that its original architecture was not up to the task. The IETF sprang into action, launching numerous working groups to evaluate how best to shore up the failing address space. Numerous efforts were focused on developing stopgap fixes to shore up the sagging address space. These fixes are outlined and described in the next chapter. One notable development was Classless Interdomain Routing (CIDR). CIDR was made possible by having VLSM break the psychological barrier of variable-length network prefixes. CIDR is an important-enough aspect of the IP address space to warrant its own chapter. We will explore it in detail in Chapter 6.

The Evolution of IPv4

CHAPTER 5

The Date of Doom

The Internet, as well as its parent, DARPAnet, grew very slowly at first. This slow growth led to complacency with respect to the finite supply of addresses, and it masked the limits inherent in the Internet's addressing system. The general belief was that there were so many addresses relative to demand that the supply would never be exhausted. The combination of latent architectural inefficiencies and wasteful assignment practices would rear its ugly head soon after the Internet's commercialization.

It wasn't long before the IETF could extrapolate the date by which a portion of the IPv4 address space would become depleted. That projected date became known as the *Date of Doom*. The IETF responded via a flurry of activities geared toward buying enough time to prevent the Date of Doom from becoming reality. These activities ranged from the very simple to the remarkably complex. This chapter focuses on just the short-term initiatives. Chapter 6, "Classless Interdomain Routing (CIDR)," and Chapter 7, "Private Addresses and NAT," round out the arsenal of technologies developed to combat the crisis by looking at the more-complex initiatives: Classless Interdomain Routing (CIDR), private addresses, and Network Address Translation (NAT).

Each of the time-buying activities outlined in this chapter achieved varying levels of success, but they have had an indelible impact on how the Internet's address space is managed today.

Responding to the Crisis

By 1992, the Internet was growing at rates that were straining it, its address space, and its physical and logical support infrastructures. Concern was running high among the techies behind the scenes at the IETF, but nobody else really seemed to grasp the problem. In November 1992, RFC 1380 was released. This RFC was strictly informational in nature, but it caused a sensation the likes of which the network engineering community has seldom experienced!

Certain parties within the IETF had already calculated the projected date by which the remaining supply of Class B address spaces would be exhausted. After that point, the other address classes would also come under increased pressure, and the failure would increase exponentially. The bottom line was that everything would start crashing sometime around

March 1994. This Date of Doom became the rallying cry for mobilizing engineering resources to resolve all sorts of problems, big and small, short-term and long-term, for the sake of maintaining the Internet's viability.

The Problems

The problems dated back to the beginning but remained latent. During the Internet's early days, it grew very slowly. That slow rate of growth was caused by two primary factors:

- These were the halcyon days before client/server computing architectures.

- The Internet was still not a commercial vehicle; the only entities connected to it were academic, research, and military organizations. They all used it to facilitate their mutual research.

These two factors led to the mistaken belief that the 32-bit address space, the class-based address architecture, and all the Internet's physical and logical support infrastructure would service the Internet far into the future. Not much time passed before that was proven untrue. The symptoms of commercialization, and their projected impacts, appeared likely to cause numerous problems. The most immediate problem areas foreseen by the IETF included the following:

- **Impending exhaustion of the Class B address space** — Subsequent exhaustion of the other areas of the IPv4 address space.

- **Routing performance problems caused by an explosion in the size of the Internet's routing tables** — Human impacts of having to support an increasingly larger set of routes in an ever-growing internetwork.

Let's take a look at these two points, because they are highly correlated.

Address Space Exhaustion

The class-based IPv4 address architecture was flawed from the start. Only the very slow initial growth of the Internet masked its deficiencies. The slow growth vis-à-vis the sheer size of the address space (remember, an 8-bit address space with just 256 addresses was upgraded to a 32-bit address space with more than 4 billion addresses) created a false sense of security. This resulted in wasteful address assignment practices. Not the least of these included the following:

- **Hoarding of address blocks** — Early adopters of the Internet tended to register far more blocks of addresses than they needed. Many large, early Internet users grabbed Class A address spaces just because they could. In retrospect, it seems the only criterion in handing out IP address blocks was the size of the organization, not the size of its needs. This was justified as "planning" for unknown and unspecified future requirements.

- **Inefficient assignments**—Because IP addresses were so plentiful, many organizations assigned their numbers in a wasteful manner. This too could be attributed to planning.

- **Inefficient architecture**—As you saw in Chapter 2, "Classical IP: The Way It Was," the class-based architecture contained inordinately large gaps between the classes. These gaps wasted a considerable number of addresses. Under strict classical rules, a medium-sized company that requires 300 IP addresses would have been justified in requesting a Class B address. In effect, more than 65,000 addresses would be wasted due to the architectural inefficiency.

The inadequacy of the original address space and architecture was being felt most acutely in the Class B range. It was believed, based on an examination of address-space assignments, that this range would be exhausted first, and that continued explosive growth would rapidly exhaust the remaining address classes in a chain reaction.

Routing Table Explosion

A slightly more subtle implication of the rapid consumption of IP address blocks was the commensurate increase in the size of the Internet's routing table. A routing table, in simple terms, is a router's list of all known destinations, correlated with which interface should be used to forward datagrams to those destinations. Logically, then, the greater the number of network addresses, the larger a routing table becomes. When a router receives a packet to be forwarded to a destination, it must first examine that packet's destination IP address and then do a table lookup to find out which port it should use to forward that packet. The larger the table, the greater the amount of time and effort required to find any given piece of data. This means that the time it takes to figure out where to send each datagram increases with the size of the routing table. Even worse, the demands on physical resources also increase.

That's a bit of an oversimplification, but it serves to illustrate my point: The Internet was growing rapidly, and this was directly increasing the size of the routing tables needed by the Internet's routers. This, in turn, caused everything to slow down. It was also straining the physical capabilities of the Internet's routers, sometimes right to the outer edges of the router's capabilities. In other words, simply plugging in more memory or upgrading to the next-larger router or CPU wouldn't help.

The bloating of the Internet's routing tables had the potential to become a vicious, self-sustaining cycle: The larger the tables became, the more time was required to process any given packet. The more time was required to process a packet, the more memory and CPU time were consumed. As you consumed more CPU cycles to process a packet, the more packets became backlogged. This was a problem that could, if left unchecked, cause the Internet to collapse—especially since the Internet continued to grow at a phenomenal rate.

Clearly, something had to be done.

The Long-Term Solution

Being able to identify a problem's root cause is always the necessary first step in solving the problem. Thus, you could argue that the IETF was perfectly positioned to rectify the problems inherent in the IPv4 address space: It understood precisely the sources of its impending problems. But the IETF faced a catch-22. This was the type of problem that couldn't be solved quickly, yet time was not a luxury the IETF could afford! They had to act, and act quickly, to ensure the Internet's continued operability.

The IETF realized that the right answer—long-term—was to completely reinvent the Internet Protocol's address space and mechanisms. But that would require a tremendous amount of time and effort. Something had to be done in the short term. They had to find ways to buy the time needed to come up with a new IP addressing system. This new protocol, and preferred long-term solution, became known as *IPv6*. We'll examine IPv6 in Chapter 15, "IPv6: The Future of IP Addressing."

For now, let's focus on the emergency measures deployed to shore up the ailing IPv4. The vast majority of these measures were simple quick fixes. Although none of these, individually, would solve the larger problem, each would help forestall the impending Date of Doom in some small way. We'll call these quick fixes *interim solutions* and look at them in the next section.

Interim Solutions

The old saw still cuts true: Every little bit helps. In that spirit, the IETF attacked in all directions as it tried to stave off the impending, projected Date of Doom. Some of the measures, as you've seen so far in this chapter, were fairly dramatic, big-ticket items. Others were remarkably simple and easy, yet effective. In this section, I'll show you some of the simple items that helped the Internet cope with its addressing crisis. These efforts included some measures to increase the pool of available address space. Others were intended to set the stage for abolishing class-based network architectures in favor of a classless architecture.

Here are some of the quick fixes employed by the IETF:

- Emergency reallocation of classful address spaces
- Emergency rationing of the remaining address spaces
- Urging holders of over-sized class-based addresses to return any unused or underused blocks
- Reserving address blocks for use in private networks but not across the Internet
- Changing the criteria for obtaining address spaces to make it significantly more difficult for enterprises and organizations to get their own address space

Each of these tactics helped, in some small way, to stave off the Date of Doom. Cumulatively, they revolutionized how the Internet is accessed and used. Internet users are still experiencing the impacts of these changes today, sometimes for the first time. Throughout the remainder of this chapter, we'll examine each of these tactics and their impacts on IP network users so that you can better appreciate some of the subtle challenges inherent in obtaining and managing an IP address space in today's environment.

One of the other, more-significant proposals that emanated from the IETF's emergency effort was to more fully embrace the concepts proven in VLSM. Although VLSM was just a grassroots innovation, there was tremendous benefit in being able to flexibly devise subnet masks. Logic fairly dictates that there would be even more benefit if network masks (as opposed to just subnet masks) were equally flexible. Imagine being able to define network addresses at any bit boundary! Unfortunately, that would require an almost complete rewrite of the IPv4 address space and its supporting protocols. That's nearly as big a change as IPv6. This proposal ultimately came to be known as Classless Interdomain Routing (CIDR). CIDR would abandon class-based addresses in favor of bit-boundary network definitions. We'll look at CIDR and its architecture, symmetry, benefits, and uses in Chapter 6. For now, let's continue to focus on the IETF's quick fixes.

Emergency Reallocation

One of the simpler devices in the IETF's bag of tricks to buy time was documented in RFC 1466. This document basically called for the as-yet still-unused Class C network address space to be reallocated into larger, equal-sized blocks. These blocks could then be allocated to regional registries to satisfy the growing and increasingly global demand for Internet access.

Table 5-1 shows the new allocation scheme, including the specific address blocks that were reallocated.

Table 5-1   *RFC 1466 Renumbering*

CIDR Block Size	Base Address	Terminal Address
/7	192.0.0.0	193.255.255.255
/7	194.0.0.0	195.255.255.255
/7	196.0.0.0	197.255.255.255
/7	198.0.0.0	199.255.255.255
/7	200.0.0.0	201.255.255.255
/7	202.0.0.0	203.255.255.255
/7	204.0.0.0	205.255.255.255
/7	206.0.0.0	207.255.255.255

These blocks are huge. In fact, they represent the equivalent of two Class A network blocks. You might question how serious the impending address shortage could have been given that so many addresses were still available. That's a fair question, but you have to remember that this was a *proactive* initiative to shore up the impending depletion of the *Class B* address space. The IETF was using all the resources at its disposal to ensure that a failure did not occur.

The important thing to note about this reallocation was that it set the stage for two things:

- Due to the fact that the large reallocated blocks were to be handed out to global registries, route aggregation could be done much more effectively as the Internet scaled to global proportions.

- Migration away from a class-based address architecture toward a more flexible bit-level definition. (This approach came to be known as Classless Interdomain Routing [CIDR]. It is thoroughly examined in Chapter 7.) Removing so many addresses from the pool of available Class C networks was a powerful statement of the IETF's intention to evolve away from the class-based addressing system.

Each of these aspects warrants closer inspection.

Improving Aggregatability

Reallocation of unassigned Class C network blocks enabled a dramatic improvement in route aggregatability in comparison to the previous size-based classful architecture. Aggregatability is a mouthful of a word that simply means the ability to be aggregated, or lumped together. Stop and think about that: This inventory of Class C blocks was previously handed out directly to end-user organizations solely on the basis of size. This meant there was little, if any, correlation between numeric contiguity (which is an absolute prerequisite to route aggregation) and geographic location. There was, however, a near-perfect correlation between numeric contiguity and the size of end-user networks. Unfortunately, for routing purposes, that's a useless correlation!

RFC 1466 sought to correct this deficiency inherent in the original class-based IPv4 architecture by creating an inventory of "superblocks" that could be distributed to regional Internet registries. In Chapter 1, "Developing the Internet's Technologies," you learned that registries are entities responsible for parsing address blocks within global regions. Examples that might jog your memory include APNIC, RIPE, and ARIN.

Creating very large blocks of addresses for those registries to distribute within their region automatically meant that, over time, route aggregation around the world would improve. This was deigned necessary to bring the Internet's address space into alignment with its evolving needs. Specifically, commercialization meant globalization. Globalization meant scales previously unheard of for a single internetwork. It also meant that distributing addresses in a manner that precluded any meaningful aggregation could no longer be afforded.

Introduction to a Classless Environment

The other aspect of RFC 1466's impact was to set the stage for introducing a classless address system. This aspect is very subtle and requires some thought to appreciate. The reallocation of Class C-sized networks into superblocks meant that *all* demands for address spaces within geographic regions would be satisfied via those superblocks, regardless of the size of those demands. Having examined the mathematics of the class-based IPv4 architecture in Chapter 2, you know how early routers determined how many bits of an IP address were used for the network portion of the address. They examined the 32-bit address (in binary) and looked to see where the first binary 0 appeared in the leftmost octet of that address. RFC 1466 undermined this old approach, because all the superblocks (and, consequently, all the network addresses created from them) were from the old Class C range. Thus, another mechanism would be absolutely essential in determining how many bits of an IP address from this range were used for the network address.

This is where CIDR comes in. It is, unarguably, the most significant of the IPv4 enhancements to come out of the Date of Doom mobilization, and it is complex enough to warrant its own chapter. For now, suffice it to say that RFC 1466 set the stage for deploying CIDR globally. The basis for CIDR predated RFC 1466, but the version that became standard came later, in RFCs 1517 through 1520. Thus, the chronology fits. The IETF knew how it wanted to evolve the address space, so it used RFC 1466 to create a pool of addresses to support this evolution. Doing so allowed it to finalize the details of classless addressing.

The Net 39 Experiment

An initiative closely related to RFC 1466 was a series of experiments designed to demonstrate how the huge Class A address space could be used more efficiently. Dubbed the *Net 39 Experiment* for its use of address space 39.0.0.0, these tests validated the concept of routing to variable-length network masks. This was important because the IPv4 address space itself wasn't in danger of depletion. Indeed, plenty of Class A and C network blocks were left! Only Class B was coming under pressure. But using addresses from different numeric ranges meant completely rewriting IP's address architecture and supporting protocols. You wouldn't want to undertake such an endeavor without first testing your concepts extensively.

The Class A address space was particularly important to test because it represented fully half the total IPv4 addresses. Unfortunately, each Class A block was so huge as to be impractical for end-user organizations. Consequently, many of those blocks sat idle while the Class B space was endangered. The experiments to understand Class A subnetting were documented in RFCs 1797 and 1879. Knowing how much address space was locked away in impractically large blocks, the IETF was very motivated to find a way to use them. There were more than enough addresses there to stave off the impending addressing crisis almost indefinitely.

NOTE	RFC 1897, published in January 1996, presents an interesting juxtaposition that helps you better appreciate the stopgap nature of many of the technologies presented in this chapter. That RFC, published concurrently with many of the other RFCs mentioned in this chapter, allocated addresses for use in testing IPv6.

The output of this trial was used to figure out what would happen if an address block from one class were used in a way that was inconsistent with its original intent. For example, a Class A address (network 39.0.0.0 was used) could be assigned to an ISP. That ISP could then carve it into smaller networks for assignment to end users. Thus, a customer could be given a Class C-sized network created within 39.0.0.0. For the sake of continuing this example, let's say an ISP customer was given 39.1.1.0/24. One of the more obvious problems encountered was that routers would tend to look at 39.1.1.0/24 and treat it as 39.0.0.0/8. That was always true if a classful interior routing protocol were used. In retrospect, that shouldn't be so surprising.

From this research came the conclusion that the Class A address space could be carved up to shore up the rapidly depleting IPv4 address spaces. However, some constraints were necessary to ensure that routing across the Internet was not adversely affected.

One of the constraints deemed necessary for the Internet to continue functioning properly was how convoluted its topology could become. The IETF recommended against end-user organizations connecting to more than one ISP, because this meant that the network block of such organizations would have to be supported by each of their ISPs. That would directly increase the number of routes that the Internet would have to support. Perhaps the most intriguing aspect of the Net 39 Experiment RFCs was that, at this stage of the IPv4 address space's development, the IETF was thinking in terms of both classful and classless (CIDR) addressing and routing. However, they recognized that you couldn't ensure problem-free internetworking if you needed to support both simultaneously. Thus, all classful interior routing protocols (known more commonly as *Interior Gateway Protocols* [IGPs]) were deemed historic. The message was clear: The tests were successful, and that opened the door for a classless address architecture—CIDR.

Emergency Call for Unused Addresses

Not wanting to overlook even the most obvious of opportunities in their quest to prop up the failing IPv4 address space, the IETF issued RFC 1917 in February 1996. Although it doesn't stipulate any technology and, consequently, could be termed an information RFC, this document has achieved the status of an Internet *Best Current Practice*. It remains in effect as BCP #4.

This RFC was unarguably the simplest of the stopgap measures: It called for people to voluntarily surrender any unused or underutilized address spaces. In theory, this would result in a temporary increase in their inventory of available and assignable address spaces and would let that inventory be parsed out in aggregatable blocks to Internet service providers (ISPs). Two primary target audiences were identified in this RFC:

- Holders of IP address blocks that were too large for their requirements
- Holders of IP address blocks that required IP addresses to support IP-based applications but who were isolated from the Internet

For different reasons, each of these communities represented an opportunity to reclaim addresses that were currently being wasted.

Oversized Block Assignments

The more pragmatic side of this request was an acknowledgment that many existing holders of IP address blocks were given blocks larger than they needed due to the inefficiency of the class-based architecture. In a classless environment, network prefixes can be established on any bit boundary. Thus, it is possible to more precisely tailor a network block to an Internet user community's actual needs. For example, if an organization needed 450 IP addresses, in a classful environment they would have been given a Class B address block. However, in a classless environment, they could be given a network with 512 addresses instead of 65,535. You could logically expect that a large number of the holders of Class B space would be able to return at least half of the space they were originally allocated. The point is that *many* very usable and routable blocks could be harvested from organizations that grabbed a Class B network space but needed only hundreds of addresses. These blocks could be freed up for reallocation to other organizations if and only if a mechanism were developed that enabled the definition of network blocks on bit boundaries instead of octet boundaries.

Isolation from the Internet

Many companies required IP and, consequently, IP addresses to support a base of networked applications without really requiring access to the Internet. Others chose to embrace IP for their internal communication requirements but could not connect to the Internet for fear of compromising the security of their networked computing assets. In theory, obtaining legitimate IP addresses was the "right" thing to do. I can remember very specific instances in which two network engineers would be on opposite sides of this issue. One would argue that, because the network in question would never be connected to the Internet, there was no reason to obtain "legal" IP addresses. The other would invariably argue from the purists' perspective. You can't predict the future, and your requirements might change, so do it right the first time! With that supporting logic, they would advocate obtaining real IP addresses.

There was no good way to settle this argument. Neither position was clearly right or wrong. It was more a matter of what you believed. Even the existence of RFC 1597, with its private address spaces, didn't really settle the argument. Those addresses were reserved for private networks but didn't mandate their use. With RFC 1917, the correct answer was that in the best interests of the Internet community, you shouldn't waste "real" IP addresses for an isolated network. Instead, the IETF urged you to save those addresses for use in routing across the Internet. Private IP networks, regardless of size, should use the addresses stipulated in RFC 1918 (which were previously reserved in RFC 1597, but as class-based address blocks).

The great debate had finally been settled: Don't use real IP addresses unless you need to route over the Internet. This gave the caretakers of the Internet's address space (IANA and its myriad delegate organizations) a clear directive as well as a means of enforcement.

Although that was all very well and good, and it would certainly help slow down the rate of address consumption, something still needed to be done about all the past decisions that had already been made. Quite simply, the purists of the world were sitting on a substantial number of address blocks that were being used on isolated networks! This represented a tremendous potential pool of addresses that could greatly mitigate the address crisis being experienced. The IETF and IANA would embark on an aggressive campaign to identify and reclaim unused and underused address spaces. This effort was largely successful, but, as you'll see in Chapter 13, "Planning and Managing an Address Space," it did induce some very unexpected behaviors in terms of evolving address-space management tactics!

Preserving Address Block Integrity

One of the more subtle problems plaguing the Internet during the early to mid-1990s was a side effect of address space depletion. This side effect was the rate at which the Internet's routing tables were growing. As you saw earlier in this chapter, the size of a network's routing tables are crucial to that network's end-to-end performance. Routing tables can expand for numerous reasons. In addition to the exponential rate of growth it was experiencing, the Internet's tables were expanding for three primary reasons:

- Class-based addresses still being assigned to new customers had legacy effects. RFC 1466, as you just saw, was a huge step toward minimizing such legacy effects. By converting so many class-based network addresses into classless address space, the IETF sought to make as clean a break as possible from the old, obviously inefficient, class-based IPv4 addressing.

- Customers leaving their ISPs did not return their address blocks. This forced the new ISP to support routing for those specific blocks of addresses.

- End users of the Internet were applying for their own address blocks instead of using blocks assigned to them by an ISP.

The last two items are interrelated. Rather than trying to explore them separately, it makes more sense to my twisted way of thinking to examine them from the perspective of their practical impacts on the Internet. Essentially, how well or how poorly you manage an address space is evident in how well the routes for that space aggregate or fragment. Aggregation is rolling smaller network addresses into larger network addresses without affecting routes to those networks. For example, instead of listing 10.10.1.0/24, 10.10.2.0/24, 10.10.3.0/24, and so on up to 10.10.255.0/24, you could aggregate all those network blocks into just 10.10.0.0/16. This larger block tells the rest of the world how to access all the smaller network blocks that may be defined from that /16 block.

Fragmentation is the opposite of aggregation: Network addresses are so numerically dissimilar and discontiguous as to defy aggregation. If aggregation isn't possible, the routers in the internetwork must remember a discrete route to each network. This is inefficient and can hurt the internetwork's performance.

Aggregation and fragmentation are best thought of as extremes, with infinite room for compromise in between. The politics of Internet governance have basically pitted Internet end-user organizations against ISPs in an ongoing struggle between these two idealistic extremes.

These impacts include route aggregation (and how it was damaged by rapid growth using Classical IP addressing rules) and the effects of directly registered customer address blocks. Examining these two impacts from a practical perspective will help you better appreciate how the Internet's address-space policies and rules have evolved over time and why things are the way they are.

Aggregation Versus Fragmentation

The addition of lots of new networks to the Internet would not necessarily contribute to the bloat of the Internet's routing tables. In theory, new networks (and their addresses) could be added to the Internet without increasing its routing tables if those network addresses were correlated regionally and/or by service provider. In other words, a clever approach to managing address assignment could accommodate tremendous growth with little to no impact on the Internet's routing tables simply by keeping numerically similar network addresses clumped together in a region. You could route from around the world to that region using only the highest-order bits of those related network addresses.

Although this might sound like a Utopian ideal, it is actually quite practical and realistic. To better demonstrate how such a scheme would work, consider the following example. An ISP is granted a relatively large block (let's say a Class B-sized block). It then carves this block into smaller blocks that it can assign to its customers. As far as the rest of the Internet is concerned, a single routing table entry would be required to that Class B-sized (/16) network address. This concept is known as *route aggregation*.

To see how this works, refer to Figures 5-1 and 5-2. Figure 5-1 demonstrates four ISP customers buying access to the Internet but using their own IP address space. For the sake of this example, I have used the addresses reserved in RFC 1918 instead of real addresses. The last time I used a real host address in a book, I caught an earful from the administrator of that box! Getting back to the point, even though these addresses are fictitious, they are too far apart numerically to be reliably aggregated. Thus, the ISP would have to advertise each one individually to the rest of the Internet.

Figure 5-1 *ISP Supporting Directly-Registered Customer Address Blocks*

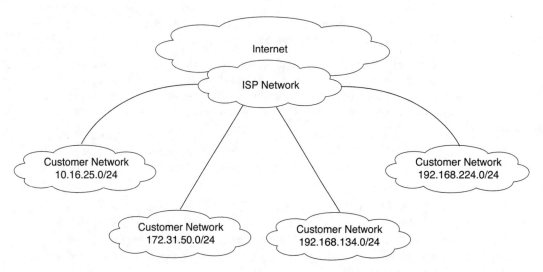

In real life, a service provider would probably have hundreds of customers, but that would make for a very cluttered illustration! Figure 5-2 shows how those customers could each use a smaller block carved from the ISP's 16-bit network address.

Figure 5-2 *Route Aggregation of an ISP Using ISP-Provided Address Blocks*

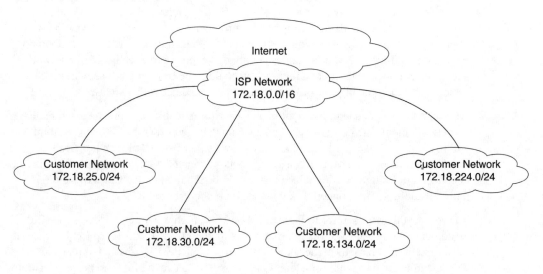

Route aggregation, in the simplistic interpretation shown in Figure 5-2, directly contributes to a reduction in the size of the Internet's routing tables. If each of the ISP's customers had its own unique network addresses, each would have to be announced to the Internet. More to the point, each network address would require its own entry in every routing table of every router in the Internet. Instead, four routing table entries can be satisfied with a single entry in the Internet, because the route through the Internet is the same for each of the four customer networks. The routes start to differ only within the network of their mutual service provider. This is the only part of the Internet that needs to track routes to the four distinct customer network addresses. Thus, the entire world uses just the first two octets of the service provider's network address to reach all its customer networks. Within that service provider's network, the third octet becomes significant for routing packets to their destination.

When viewed from this perspective, it seems perfectly logical that the right way to provide Internet addressing is via a service provider's larger address blocks. But some problems are inherent with this approach. Implementing an IP address scheme represents a potentially huge investment in planning and effort. From an Internet user's perspective, changing IP addresses is undesirable, because it forces you to make the same investment in time and effort without having anything to show for it.

Thus, although using service provider addresses does minimize routing table bloat, and makes sense for the Internet, you have to realize that benefits of this approach are asymmetrically distributed. That's a euphemistic way of saying that it is better for the Internet and ISPs than it is for the owners/operators of networks that connect to the Internet. For those entities, this approach can actually be harmful!

The danger of obtaining and using IP addresses from a service provider is that the service provider "owns" them. In effect, you are leasing the addresses for the duration of your service contract with that provider. If you wanted to change service providers (maybe you found a better deal, or maybe your provider doesn't meet your performance requirements), you would have to relinquish the "leased" addresses and obtain a new range from your new provider. Changing service providers therefore would necessitate renumbering all your IP endpoints! Renumbering becomes a very effective barrier to changing service providers.

Directly-Registered Address Spaces

It's not difficult to see why ISP customers are motivated to avoid changing their IP addresses. Renumbering endpoints is that onerous and risky a proposition! The surest way to avoid having to renumber is to "own" your IP addresses. Of course, you know that nobody really "owns" IP addresses except IANA, but ownership in this sense means that an organization would have IP addresses *registered directly in its name*. As soon as an address block is registered directly to you, it is yours forever—provided, of course, that you don't outgrow it or forget to pay the annual fee.

In the early days of the Internet, it was relatively easy to obtain directly registered address spaces. Such spaces were said to be *portable*, because they were independent of service provider address blocks. Thus, the holder of a directly registered address block enjoyed the unparalleled freedom to change service providers at will without having to worry about changing address blocks at the same time.

The drawback of this approach is, of course, the impact on the Internet's routing tables. Portability, more than any other factor, fragments large, contiguous (and therefore aggregatable) address blocks. Unfortunately for those end users, the Internet's routing tables were outpacing technology in their growth. They were becoming bigger at a faster pace than CPUs were increasing in speed. Consequently, Internet performance was deteriorating quickly, and the trend didn't look good. This was one of the facets of the impending Date of Doom that the IETF sought to obviate. One of the easy scapegoats was the portability of network addresses.

Preventing Further Fragmentation

End-user organizations highly prize portable address spaces. But they are the bane of the Internet. The IETF sought to protect the Internet by more specifically constraining address assignment practices to prevent any further address space fragmentation. This effort was documented in RFC 2050. RFC 2050 is still in effect and is also Internet Best Current Practice #12. Specifically, this document stipulated the rules and regulations regarding subassignments of IP address spaces by ISPs.

The way it works is simple. An ISP's customer—if it didn't already have directly registered address blocks of its own—could obtain addresses from its service provider. However, to preserve the integrity of large service provider address blocks, those addresses had to be surrendered when the contract for service ended. In other words, these addresses were *nonportable* and remained with the service provider with which they were registered. That way, the ISP could advertise just a single, large network address to the Internet that encompassed all its customer networks created from that large block.

But if a customer wanted to move to a different service provider to obtain a lower monthly recurring cost, it found itself in the uncomfortable position of having to quickly renumber its entire network and all its addressed endpoints. Adding insult to injury, the range it had to migrate to was another nonportable address range supplied by the new service provider. Each time the customer wanted to change providers, it had to go through the same expensive, risky, painful process of renumbering endpoints.

RFC 2050/BCP 12 doesn't do anything to mitigate this pain for end users. Rather, it compels service providers to treat all their assignable address space as nonportable, regardless of whether any given subset of it may be globally routable. If an ISP chooses to disregard RFC 2050 and let ex-customers keep their assigned space, it will eventually exhaust its address space. That ISP will find it impossible to convince its regional Registry to entrust it with more address space. An ISP without an inventory of available network addresses cannot service any new customers. RFC 2050 seeks to prevent further fragmentation of the Internet's address space (which directly increases the size of the Internet's routing tables) by giving ISPs the incentive to preserve the integrity of their existing blocks.

Rationing Directly Registered Addresses

RFC 2050, in the absence of any other policy changes, was a tweak to the nose of the Internet's end-user community. It wasn't intended to be painful. Rather, it was designed as an emergency effort to ensure the Internet's continued operability. Such austerity measures are often palatable provided that the pain is shared somewhat equitably. Because the end-user community bore the brunt of the inconvenience caused by that RFC, they had every reason to be upset. The only mitigating factor was that those organizations could shield themselves from any pain just by having their own directly registered address spaces—that is, they could until IANA started rationing new directly registered address blocks.

This is where things started getting ugly. IANA exacerbated the routability versus portability conflict when it tightened its policy on directly registered address spaces. Organizations that wanted their "own" address spaces would have to meet very stringent requirements before that privilege would be granted. The cumbersome and bureaucratic application process alone was enough to deter most would-be applicants. Those persistent enough to successfully complete an application with their Registry quickly discovered that did not guarantee their request would be granted.

Although this policy shift was a necessity caused by the impending address-space crisis, it meant that it was now almost impossible for an end-user organization to obtain its own directly registered address space. When you view this fact in conjunction with the bias against end-user organizations in RFC 2050, it becomes clear that end-user organizations bore the full brunt of the policy changes necessary to prevent the Internet's address space from collapsing.

Ostensibly, this policy shift was designed to immediately curtail the outflow of the finite supply of the remaining IPv4 addresses. This, all by itself, would buy a lot of time and forestall the crisis. However, it also forced Internet users to seriously consider alternative options for their IP addressing, such as the following:

- Using ISP-provided addresses
- Using nonunique addresses
- Using a translation function between your network and the Internet

We've already looked at why using ISP-provided addressing isn't very attractive to end-user organizations. We'll look at the other two options much more closely in the next chapter. For now, just realize that none of these were very palatable, nor as convenient as directly registered address space. The fact that these unattractive options were forced on end-user organizations created the potential for a tremendous backlash that is still being experienced today.

End-User Backlash

In some cases, the backlash has been extremely aggressive and creative. The goal is simple, and it can be summed up in just one word: portability. The extent to which end-user organizations pursue this grail is remarkable. It is characterized by aggressive — if not desperate — attempts. The stakes are that high!

Part of the problem, or maybe I should say part of the game, is that there is tremendous confusion about what constitutes portability. Internet Registries, for example, interpret portability to mean global routability.

Determining global routability from a Registry's perspective is simple: Is the address block large enough to be worth routing on the Internet? That criterion has absolutely nothing to do with block ownership. As you have seen, service providers are bound by a different criterion: compliance with RFC 2050/BCP 12. Consequently, they have a different interpretation of portability. Service providers have an obligation to interpret portability to mean *both* global routability and directly registered to the end-user organization. They might provide a range of addresses to a customer that is large enough for routing over the Internet, but they cannot consider it portable, because it is theirs.

End-user organizations try desperately to exploit this chained ambiguity of definitions by insisting their service-provider blocks meet the criteria of global routability. Therefore, their argument continues, those addresses should be handed over when they change providers! Sometimes this argument works, and sometimes it doesn't. If it doesn't, the game doesn't end there for some end-user organizations. I've seen quite a few ex-customers simply refuse to return their address blocks! Although I won't pretend to understand the rule of law well enough to pass judgment on the legality of such hijacking of address space, I can tell you it certainly violates Internet BCP 12 and does nothing to help the Internet's performance.

Sadly, these unintended consequences caused by RFC 2050 and the emergency rationing of directly registered address spaces continue to haunt the Internet. We've spent quite a bit of time looking at them for the simple reason that they form an unavoidable constraint in today's IP network environment. The more you know about these and the other constraints, the better you'll be able to deal with them on the job.

Hijacked Address Spaces

Since its inception, RFC 2050 has done wonders for minimizing the expansion of Internet routing tables. However, it has created potentially serious tension between ISPs and their customers — or should I say their ex-customers? One of the less-heralded side effects of RFC 2050, in combination with IANA's crackdown on granting privately registered address spaces, has been the hijacking of ISP address blocks.

When a customer leaves an ISP, it is required to return its IP address space to that ISP. That ISP can, in theory, put those addresses back in its inventory of unused addresses with which it satisfies new customer requests for addresses. However, it is not uncommon for a customer to terminate service with one ISP, start service with a new ISP, and then insist that new ISP support its existing blocks. By refusing to stop using an address space, an end-user organization can effectively convert a nonportable address space to a de facto portable space! Even though this is a violation of an Internet Best Current Practice, some ISPs are reluctant to do anything to upset a paying customer. Money talks!

An ISP whose addresses have been hijacked in this manner faces few good options. ARIN and IANA don't offer any active help, but they still insist that you reclaim your blocks. I've found that contacting the ex-customer's new service provider and demanding that it immediately cease supporting the hijack of addresses meets with only mixed success. Some ISPs are much more reputable than others and will jump at the opportunity to help you reclaim your lost property. Others require a bit of coercion. Letting them know that you will be advertising the hijacked addresses as null routes and that they should expect a trouble call from an unhappy and out-of-service customer usually does the trick.

Summary

When the IPv4 address space started to suffer under the strain of the Internet's explosive growth, the IETF responded quickly with a broad series of parallel efforts. Some of these efforts, as we've seen in this chapter, were the simplest of mechanisms. Others were remarkably complex and required years to develop. The hope was that the combination of the various short-term initiatives would buy enough time for the real solution (IPv6) to be developed. It is imperative that you appreciate the significance of many of these mechanisms. They have become so successful at recovering addresses and reducing the need for unique addresses that they have, together, become quite viable long-term solutions to the original problem of a vanishing address space. Consequently, they are still very much in effect today, and you need to understand their implications and constraints on IP addressing.

Initiatives notably absent from this chapter are private addresses, Network Address Translation (NAT), and Classless Interdomain Routing (CIDR). Together, these initiatives represent nothing less than a complete rewrite of the rules and architecture that governed the IPv4 address space. As such, they merit more than just a passing mention in a chapter. At the very least, they require their own chapters. The next chapter focuses on private addresses and NAT. We'll conclude our examination of the IETF's emergency evolution of IPv4 in Chapter 7 when we look at CIDR.

CHAPTER 6

Classless Interdomain Routing (CIDR)

By June 1992, it had become apparent that the rapid growth of the Internet, caused by its commercialization, was straining its address architecture and space to their breaking points. A portion of the address space was in danger of depletion and the Internet's routing tables were growing so large as to be almost unmanageable. The *Internet Engineering Steering Group (IESG)* deliberated various approaches as to how best to go about fixing what was ailing the Internet. We looked at many of the subsequent stopgap fixes in Chapter 5, "The Date of Doom."

As a result of these deliberations, consensus within the IESG was that the old class-based IPv4 architecture had to be replaced with a new classless architecture. A classless architecture would enable the formation of network prefixes on any bit boundary within the IP address. This would have the immediate and direct effect of eliminating the ridiculous gaps between Class A-, Class B-, and Class C-sized networks. The new technology was directly based on the concepts and mathematics proven via *Variable-Length Subnet Masking (VLSM)*. It came to be known as *Classless Interdomain Routing (CIDR)*. This chapter explores CIDR's structure, nature, and operational mechanics.

CIDR: An Historic Review

CIDR was defined in RFCs 1517 through 1520, published in September 1993. As you peruse these documents, you can't help but notice the sense of urgency with which the IETF was grasping for a solution to its impending address crisis. The Internet's commercialization wrought a dramatic and rapid evolution in its size, scope, and user base. Once just populated with a few academic and research bodies collaborating on DARPA, the Internet quickly grew to global proportions. Its user community also spanned the gamut, including an ever-increasing number of users who tried desperately to figure out how to make money off the Net. The effect was rapidly increasing pressure on all the Internet's internal support mechanisms, including its address space, that threatened to collapse the Internet itself.

Specific areas of concern for the IESG included the following:

- **Impending depletion of the Class B address range**—The tremendous gap between the number of hosts available on a Class C network versus a Class B network meant that many Class B networks were being assigned to small companies that needed more addresses than the Class C network could provide.

- **Bloating of the Internet routing tables**—Determining which route any given packet should take requires a table lookup. The larger the Internet's routing table, the more time on average any given routing decision takes. The Internet's rapid expansion can best be explained by pointing out that the size of the Internet's routing tables was doubling approximately every 12 months during the early 1990s. According to Moore's Law, processing power doubles approximately every 18 months. Consequently, the routing tables were growing faster than technology could keep up! That slowed down routing across the Internet and threatened to disrupt its functionality unless checked.

- **IP address space exhaustion**—Ostensibly, the Class B space would deplete first, and that would trigger a chain reaction that would place increasing pressure on the remaining classes.

With these concerns for their motivation, the IESG studied the problems plaguing the IP address space extensively. They documented their recommendations in RFC 1380, which was published in November 1992. This document posited CIDR as the solution to the first two problems. CIDR remained to be developed, but enough of its desired functionality was spelled out in RFC 1380 that the Internet community could appreciate the impending changes.

At this point in time, nobody within the IETF was certain exactly how to solve the looming address crisis. Consequently, they attacked in all feasible directions. Specifying a classless IP architecture was but one of the myriad tactics deployed to buy enough time for IPv6 to be developed. Implicit in this statement is the fact that, like the various stopgap technologies we examined in Chapter 5, nobody really expected CIDR to be more than just another stepping-stone to IPv6.

CIDR: An Architectural Overview

The IETF witnessed the successful grassroots innovation of VLSM and appreciated the significance of moving beyond octet boundaries in the IP addressing architecture. With subnets, this was a trivial endeavor: A subnet mask, regardless of whether it is of fixed or variable length, is of local significance only. In other words, routers do not use subnet addresses to decide on optimal paths through a network. However, embracing a bit-level definition of network addresses would have a tremendous impact on routers and how they calculate routes.

The previous method of operation was the class-based addressing architecture that we examined in Chapter 2, "Classical IP: The Way It Was." Classical IP used the leftmost bits of leftmost octet to determine an address's class. It was possible to identify the class of any IP address simply by examining its first octet in binary form. By identifying in which bit position a 0 first appeared, you could determine whether it was a Class A, B, C, or D. After establishing an address's class, a router would know precisely how many bits of the 32-bit address it should use to make routing decisions.

Abandoning the class-based approach enables a more efficient use of an address space via more finely tunable address allocation. An even more important change was that the mathematical boundaries of the old address classes were done away with. Thus, the once-threatening problem of the depletion of Class B addresses was solved. The solution came in two forms:

- Reducing demand for Class B address space
- Increasing the potential supply of Class B-sized network addresses

The demand for Class B network addresses was seriously reduced simply by letting network addresses be created by bit boundaries, as opposed to octet boundaries. Thus, if a Class C (24-bit) network were too small, you could get a 23-bit, 22-bit, 21-bit, and so on network instead of just jumping right to a 16-bit network block.

The potential supply of 16-bit-sized networks was greatly increased by eliminating the mathematical boundaries of the old address classes. Under the CIDR rules, any sized network block could be created from anywhere in the 32-bit addressing system. An additional benefit of CIDR was that smaller networks could still be carved from larger network blocks. In the class-based architecture, this was known as subnetting. Subnets, as you have seen in previous chapters, violated the class-based architecture. Thus, they couldn't be routed but were invaluable for creating local subnetworks.

In a CIDRized environment, abandoning the rigid hierarchy of class-based addresses in favor of bit-level boundaries created a huge problem for routers: How do you figure out how many bits are significant for routing? The answer was to expand the use of subnet masks and to make them routable instead of just of local significance. In this fashion, the boundary or distinction between subnet masks and network blocks became perfectly blurred. Today, the distinction is almost semantic. It depends on how aggregatable your address distribution scheme is and how your routers are configured. If the word aggregatable leaves you scratching your head, fear not! It's not as complex as it sounds. We will look at aggregatability later in this chapter. For now, let's take a closer look at CIDR notation.

CIDR Notation

It is imperative that you understand CIDR notation, including what it is and what it isn't. CIDR notation has become the predominant paradigm for conveying the size of a network's prefix. But it is just a human-friendly form of shorthand. When you configure routers, you must still use the dotted-quad style of IP mask. For example, 255.255.255.248 is the equivalent of a /29. It should be obvious which one is easier to use.

Table 6-1 shows the valid range of CIDR block sizes, the corresponding bitmask, and how many mathematically possible addresses each block contains. If this table looks familiar, it's because of the similarities between CIDR and VLSM. You've seen some of this data before, in Table 4-1. CIDR notation was included with that table simply to make it easier for you to go back and compare VLSM with CIDR.

Table 6-1 *CIDR Notation*

CIDR Notation	Decimal Mask	Number of Possible Host Addresses
/5	248.0.0.0	134,217,728
/6	252.0.0.0	67,108,864
/7	254.0.0.0	33,554,432
/8	255.0.0.0	16,777,216 (Class A network)
/9	255.128.0.0	8,388,608
/10	255.192.0.0	4,194,304
/11	255.224.0.0	2,097,152
/12	255.240.0.0	1,048,576
/13	255.248.0.0	524,288
/14	255.252.0.0	262,144
/15	255.254.0.0	131,072
/16	255.255.0.0	65,536 (Class B network)
/17	255.255.128.0	32,768
/18	255.255.192.0	16,384
/19	255.255.224.0	8,192
/20	255.255.240.0	4,096
/21	255.255.248.0	2,048
/22	255.255.252.0	1,024
/23	255.255.254.0	512
/24	255.255.255.0	256 (Class C network)
/25	255.255.255.128	128
/26	255.255.255.192	64
/27	255.255.255.224	32
/28	255.255.255.240	16
/29	255.255.255.248	8
/30	255.255.255.252	4
/31	255.255.255.254	2
/32	255.255.255.255	1

This table omits network masks /1 through /4 because they are invalid. The largest network permitted under current CIDR rules is a /5. A /5 is sometimes called a *superblock* because it is equivalent to eight Class A address blocks. Such an enormous address block is not made available for end-user organizations on the Internet. Instead, a /5 might be allocated to a regional registry for use in providing IP address block assignments to service providers and/or large end-user organizations in the registry's home region.

Backward Compatibility with Classical IP

Backward compatibility is always a critical issue whenever a technological advancement is proposed. CIDR was no exception. You know, based on your reading thus far in the book, that Classical IP has become obsolete. However, CIDR represented more of an extension of Classical IP than a complete rewrite. The backward compatibility was almost complete: The entire 32-bit address space was preserved, as was support for all previously assigned IP addresses. The notion of splitting an address into host and network address subfields was also retained. As you'll see throughout this chapter, CIDR represented nothing more than a complete legitimization of the classical form of VLSM. The degree of backward compatibility with Classical IP ensured CIDR's success. The classes themselves were abolished, yet the address space survived.

Symmetry of CIDR Notation

The binary mathematics of the IP address space creates a marvelous natural symmetry in CIDR-compliant addresses. What at first glance appears to be an unmanageable jumble of numbers is actually a remarkably logical system. The key is remembering that the binary number system works based on powers of 2. For each bit you move to the left, you double the bit's value. For each bit you move to the right, you halve the bit's value. These facts help you better appreciate CIDR's /number notation. For example, if you halve a bit's value by moving to the right, you can logically assume that the entire string of bits that follows the bit in question is also halved.

Look at Table 6-2 to see how this works. In this table, we'll look at a real /24 network address block and then figure out how many /25 networks it contains. Logically, a /25 features a network prefix that is exactly 1 bit longer than a /24, and that bit comes from the right. So you can expect that a /25 is exactly half the size of a /24, but let's prove it. Table 6-1 dissects 192.1.64.0/24. The bits that represent the extended network prefix are indicated in bold. I've indented both of the /25s to indicate that they are actually subcomponents of the /24 address space.

Table 6-2   *Symmetry of CIDR Notation*

Decimal Address	Binary Address
192.168.64.0/24	**11000000.10101000.01000000**.00000000
192.168.64.0/25	**11000000.10101000.01000000.***0*0000000
192.168.64.128/25	**11000000.10101000.01000000.***1*0000000

As is evident from Table 6-2, when you borrow a single bit from the host octet of the /24 network, you create exactly two /25 networks. That's because you are borrowing only a single bit, and that bit can have only two possible values: 0 and 1. Thinking about this a little more, you can see that this borrowed bit is in the leftmost position of its octet. This bit carries a decimal value of 128. Thus, the initial value of the last octet in the second /25 network must be .128. Logically, then, the highest-value host address in 192.1.64.0/25 must be .127. Converting the binary string 01111111 to decimal yields exactly 127. This value serves as the broadcast address for that network and cannot be assigned to any endpoint.

This symmetry works on any bit boundary. Table 6-3 shows how exactly two /24 network blocks can be created from a /23. It uses the same address block as the preceding example so that you can see the progression of the addresses as subblocks are created.

Table 6-3   *Creating /24 Networks from a /23*

Decimal Address	Binary Address
192.168.64.0/23	**11000000. 10101000.0100000***0*.00000000
192.168.64.0/24	**11000000. 10101000.01000000**.00000000
192.168.65.0/24	**11000000. 10101000.01000001**.00000000

Table 6-4 shows how this pattern progresses even further. If two /25 networks can be created from a single /24, there must also be two /26 networks in each of those /25 networks, for a total of four /26 networks in each /24. The next logical conclusion is that each /24 network can be used to create exactly eight /27 networks, because Base2 has eight unique numeric combinations ranging from 000 through 111. This is what you see in Table 6-4. Focus on the bold italic numbers, and you can see how you are counting in binary. This "counting" is obvious only when you look at the value of the last octet in binary. In decimal, you can see the incrementation, but it occurs in increments of 32, which is the value of the least-significant of the 3 bits borrowed from the host field to create the /27 networks.

Table 6-4   *Creating /27 Networks from a /24*

Decimal Address	Binary Address
192.168.64.0/24	**11000000. 10101000.01000000**.00000000
192.168.64.0/27	**11000000. 10101000.01000000.***000*00000
192.168.64.32/27	**11000000. 10101000.01000000.***001*00000

Table 6-4   *Creating /27 Networks from a /24 (Continued)*

Decimal Address	Binary Address
192.168.64.64/27	11000000. 10101000.01000000.*01*000000
192.168.64.96/27	11000000. 10101000.01000000.*011*00000
192.168.64.128/27	11000000. 10101000.01000000.*10*000000
192.168.64.160/27	11000000. 10101000.01000000.*101*00000
192.168.64.192/27	11000000. 10101000.01000000.*11*000000
192.168.64.224/27	11000000. 10101000.01000000.*111*00000

This pattern can get quite tedious to fully examine using just mathematics. If you tend to learn best visually, refer to Figure 6-1. It demonstrates the hierarchical and mathematical relationship between network blocks. Space constraints prevent the creation of this type of chart for the entire IP address space, but this small sampling from /24 through /27 should adequately demonstrate the pattern.

Figure 6-1   *The Mathematical Relationship Between Network Block Sizes*

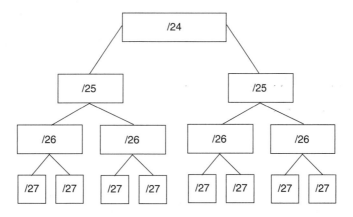

If you understand this basic symmetry, and you adhere to it when creating subnets in your network, you shouldn't experience any problems—unless, of course, you fail to keep good records! My point is simple: Understanding the bit boundaries and nested symmetries found in CIDR lets you properly create subnetwork addresses. Some examples presented in Chapter 4, "Variable-Length Subnet Masks," violated this principle. Now you can better appreciate why those examples were suboptimal. Reviewing the tables in that chapter, you will see that subnets often started outside conventional bit boundaries.

Violating bit boundaries has its consequences, but they are not necessarily fatal. For example, a network can function quite well with a poorly designed address space. The two main consequences of poor address space implementation are

- Confusion as to which hosts fit in which subnet

- Creating inefficiency and possibly unusable addresses, because one subnet boundary might overlap with another

Although none of these consequences will kill a network, they tend to be very persistent. Most address schemes take on a life of their own after they are implemented. You would be surprised at how difficult it can be to correct past mistakes in an address space that is in daily use.

Other consequences of a poorly designed addressing scheme require a finer appreciation of just how useful CIDR's symmetry really is. The next two sections look at how CIDR blocks are designed to be aggregatable and subdividable.

From Symmetry Comes Aggregatability

Under the rules of Classical IP, there was at best a weak, positive correlation between network addresses and geography. Thus, two numerically adjacent network addresses of any class could be on opposite sides of the world. From a router's perspective, even though these two network blocks are numerically contiguous, they *must* be regarded as completely and utterly unrelated! Logically, if they are on opposite sides of the world, you probably will take different routes to get to each one. Thus, routers throughout the Internet would have to remember a separate route for each router. This is the opposite of aggregatability, and it can quickly spell death for a network's performance simply by consuming more and more of a router's finite memory and CPU resources.

Aggregatability: What a Concept!

Aggregation of addresses is nothing more than the inverse of subnetting on a large scale. Subnetting lets you take a single network address block and carve it into smaller subnetwork blocks. Aggregation is taking several network addresses (also known as prefixes), lumping them together, and advertising just one network prefix to other networks. Several critical assumptions are buried in this simple explanation. The two most important are as follows:

- Network prefixes must be numerically similar, if not contiguous, to enable identifying them via a unique network prefix.

- Networks using those prefixes should be close enough geographically to be able to use the same ISP for their connectivity to the Internet.

From an ISP's perspective, numerically similar network addresses should be aggregated. For example, let's say that an ISP has been given a Class B-sized network address (a /16 network prefix). An address block of this size can support 65,535 endpoints. The ISP isn't too likely to encounter any single customer that requires all this address space. Instead, it is much more likely that the ISP will have dozens or hundreds of customers that each require a small number of addresses.

Without trying to chart an entire /16 network's potential allocation scheme, let's just agree that it would be to everyone's benefit to be able to just tell the rest of the Internet about the /16 network address. This simplification relieves you of the burden of having to communicate explicitly about each /27 or /24 or /20 network address that might have been created from it. All those subnetworks begin with the same 16 bits anyway. Thus, they can—and should—be aggregated and advertised to the Internet as a single network prefix. The subnetworks' longer bitstrings are of use only within that service provider's network. In this sense, aggregatable network addresses function precisely like subnets created from a single network address.

Unfortunately, not all the Internet's address space can be aggregated to any appreciable degree. Benefiting from CIDR's aggregatability means that you have to start handing out network address blocks based on geography. During the Internet's early days, any organization could request its own address space. Such requests were satisfied as they were received, and the actual range of addresses allocated to that organization depended only on the size of the request. Thus, there was no attempt to correlate geography and IP network addresses. This policy enabled the notion of an IP address space being portable from ISP to ISP but effectively defied the promised benefits of aggregatability. IANA and the IETF countered by effectively declaring address space given to ISPs to be nonportable. We'll revisit this volatile issue in the last section of this chapter, as well as in subsequent chapters.

Aggregation Versus Subnetting

CIDR introduced mechanisms designed to enhance aggregatability. The first and foremost of these mechanisms was simply the ability to define network addresses on any bit boundary instead of on every eighth bit boundary. VLSM had previously demonstrated the wisdom of this bitwise approach. Despite the handicaps of not being routable and, therefore, of only local significance, VLSM had a dramatic positive impact on the efficiency with which IP network blocks could be used.

CIDR built upon this approach by implementing subnet masks as routable information. That's a point that often creates confusion, even among experienced network engineers! For many years, subnets were limited to local use. The distinction between subnets and network addresses was reinforced by the routability of only those addresses that conformed to Classical IP's octet boundaries. Networks created along other boundaries (such as a /23 or a /25 instead of a /24) couldn't be routed. Thus, they were deemed useful only locally. CIDR changed that by doing away with the old routable classes. Under CIDR's rules, anything from a /5 to a /32 prefix could be routed. Thus, the old, easy delineation between a subnet and a network was rendered obsolete. The difference between a subnet and a network address is now just semantic.

A practical implication of this evolutionary step is that now you *must* pass subnet mask information explicitly as part of the routing information. Thus, masks are still essential! If anything, the term *subnet mask* has become a misnomer that only contributes to confusion. It is properly termed a *network mask*. In fact, the shorthand convention of a slash followed by the number of bits used to identify the network address is intended just for human use. When configuring routers, you are still expected to enter the subnet mask in good old-fashioned dotted-quad style. Thus, instead of specifying a /23 route, you must enter a mask of 255.255.254.0. In binary, that translates into

> 11111111.11111111.11111110.0000000

Without the mask, it would be impossible to determine how many bits of a CIDRized IP address were used to identify the network versus the hosts within that network.

CIDR obviously had a dramatic impact on routers and routing protocols. It required a comprehensive upgrade to the Internet's infrastructure before it could be implemented and supported. Despite the logistics and cost of this migration, CIDR became an unqualified success.

Supernetting

Arguably the single most powerful advance experienced by the IPv4 address space is the capability known as *supernetting*. Before we delve too deeply into this topic, let's dispel a very popular misperception. Supernetting was *not* introduced with CIDR! It was first specified in June 1992 in RFC 1338 as a standalone strategy for improving the aggregatability of IP address blocks. The fact that I'm including it as a subtopic in a chapter on CIDR should tell you something about how pervasive this myth has become. Yet the facts remain publicly available: Supernetting was introduced 15 months before CIDR. However, CIDR made supernetting infinitely more useful simply by creating a classless IP address space. Thus, supernets could be created on any bit boundary, as opposed to the class-based octet boundaries that constrained the authors of RFC 1388.

Supernetting is the concept of taking two or more numerically contiguous network address blocks and consolidating them into a single, larger network address. Thus, if you had a pair of /25 networks that happened to be numerically contiguous, you could *probably* aggregate them into a single /24 network. This would free you from having to route between the two /25 address spaces. Supernetting would also let you advertise just one network block (the /24) to the world instead of two distinct /25 network addresses.

I say probably because certain rules and limitations apply. Just because two network blocks are numerically contiguous doesn't mean that they can be supernetted. However, if they are not numerically contiguous, they absolutely cannot be formed into a supernet. The next section looks a bit more closely at some of the rules that govern the creation of supernets.

The Rules

Supernetting, like many other topics indigenous to the IP address space, gets a bad reputation for being complex and difficult to understand. That's unfortunate, because supernetting is one of CIDR's most important features. More importantly, it can be remarkably easy to understand if it is explained properly. I have already given you a thumbnail sketch of the supernet function. Now it's time to look at the provisos. There are only three basic rules for supernet creation:

- Numeric contiguity
- Even divisibility
- Single interface

Each of these is examined in the following sections to help you better appreciate their impact on supernetting an address space.

Numeric Contiguity

In order for supernetting to be possible, network addresses must be numbered consecutively. This rule is probably the one that is the most intuitive of the three rules for creating supernets. If two network address blocks are not numerically adjacent, attempts to join them must necessarily include all the addresses that keep them apart. You can more completely understand what that means by looking at an example and learning from it. Table 6-5 demonstrates a /24 network block that has been subnetted into eight fixed-length subnets using a mask of 255.255.255.224. That mask, if you'll refer back to Table 6-1, equates to a /27 CIDR network.

Table 6-5   *Numeric Contiguity of Subnets Within a /24*

Subnet Number	Decimal Address	Contiguous With Which Numbers
Base	192.168.64.0/24	Not applicable
Subnet 0	192.168.64.0/27	1
Subnet 1	192.168.64.32/27	0 and 2
Subnet 2	192.168.64.64/27	1 and 3
Subnet 3	192.168.64.96/27	2 and 4
Subnet 4	192.168.64.128/27	3 and 5
Subnet 5	192.168.64.160/27	4 and 6
Subnet 6	192.168.64.192/27	5 and 7
Subnet 7	192.168.64.224/27	6

The third column of Table 6-5 identifies the direct contiguity of each of the eight defined subnets. Subnet 0 is numerically contiguous only with subnet 1, and subnet 1 is numerically contiguous with both subnets 0 and 2. This much should be fairly obvious. Getting back to my point about nonadjacent addresses, suppose you want to supernet subnets 1 and 3. You can't do that directly because subnet 2 (with its 32 addresses) lies between them. However, it might be possible to create a much larger subnet by integrating subnets 1, 2, and 3. However, we still have two more rules to examine before we can state with authority that such a supernet is technically feasible!

Even Divisibility

The next test to determine the supernetability of an address space is even divisibility. This test is designed to ensure that network addresses end on the correct bit boundaries to preserve the symmetry of a CIDRized address space. Even divisibility is determined by dividing the octet that contains the boundary between host and network address fields by the number of networks you are trying to supernet together. For example, if you were to combine two /24 networks, the third octet of the first network address must be divisible by 2. If you wanted to combine eight /24 networks, the first network's third octet would have to be divisible by 8.

In essence, the first network block in a supernetted group of addresses forms the base address of the new, larger address block. Everything else in the supernet is built from it. Thus, it is imperative that this initial address block conform to CIDR bit boundaries.

Table 6-6 helps you better understand why this is the case. This table builds on Table 6-5 by showing both the numerically contiguous subnets and whether the appropriate octet is evenly divisible. I have used bold to indicate which octet of each address you look at to make this determination.

Table 6-6   *Numeric Contiguity and Even Divisibility of Subnets Within a /24*

Subnet Number	Decimal Address	Contiguous With Which Numbers	Even Divisibility of Third Octet?
Base	192.168.64.0/24	Not applicable	Not applicable
Subnet 0	192.168.64.**0**/27	1	Yes
Subnet 1	192.168.64.**32**/27	0 and 2	Yes
Subnet 2	192.168.64.**64**/27	1 and 3	Yes
Subnet 3	192.168.64.**96**/27	2 and 4	No
Subnet 4	192.168.64.**128**/27	3 and 5	Yes
Subnet 5	192.168.64.**160**/27	4 and 6	Yes
Subnet 6	192.168.64.**192**/27	5 and 7	Yes
Subnet 7	192.168.64.**224**/27	6	Yes

Let's look at some of these individual base addresses a bit more closely so that you can better appreciate the logic behind the rule of even divisibility. Table 6-7 shows the binary mathematics that underlie the test of even divisibility. The 2 bits that are critical to determining even divisibility for our supernet example are shown in bold italic.

Table 6-7   *Binary Mathematics of Even Divisibility*

Decimal Address	Binary Address
192.168.64.**32**/27	**11000000**. **10101000.01000000**.*00I*00000
192.168.64.**64**/27	**11000000**. **10101000.01000000**.*01*000000

In effect, this proposed supernet reduces the size of the network's mask from 27 bits to 26 bits. For the symmetry of the address space to be conserved, that 26th bit must start at 0. In Table 6-7, 192.168.64.32/27 and 192.168.64.64/27 are supernetted together and are advertised as 192.168.64.32/26. In binary math, the next increment above 00 is 01. Thus, the two /27 network blocks can both be referenced by the same 26-bit network address.

The next example does not conform to symmetry and doesn't work as expected. Although in binary math 01 increments to 10, the increment requires you to reset the least-significant bit to 0 and then increment a more-significant bit (the leftmost of the two number columns) to 1. Thus, the bitstring differs for the two subnets, and they cannot be supernetted together. Table 6-8 shows you how this bitstring differs. The bits significant for supernetting are in bold italic.

Table 6-8   *Binary Mathematics of Uneven Divisibility*

Decimal Address	Binary Address
192.168.64.**95**/27	**11000000**. **10101000.01000000**.*01*011111
192.168.64.**128**/27	**11000000**. **10101000.01000000**.*10*000000

Table 6-6 shows that the only subnet that can't become the base of a two-network supernet is subnet 3. Its final octet is an odd number—95. Now you know why. All the other subnets can become the base of a two-network /26 supernet. Thus, of all the potential combinations for supernetting, the only set that doesn't meet both the criteria (even divisibility and numeric contiguity) is the pairing of subnets 3 and 4.

Single Interface

The last critical precondition for supernetting is that the two or more network blocks that are to be aggregated must be connected to the same interface. Otherwise, why bother? If they are connected to different interfaces, you must route between the two networks. In practical terms, this rule does not preclude you from creating a supernet from two networks that are connected to different router interfaces. However, this rule forces you to reconfigure your physical topology so that the combined supernet connects to only one interface.

Figures 6-2 and 6-3 better demonstrate how the single-interface rule can have a physical impact on a network's topology. Together they demonstrate the before-and-after perspective of supernetting.

Figure 6-2   *Before: Two /27 Networks Routed Together*

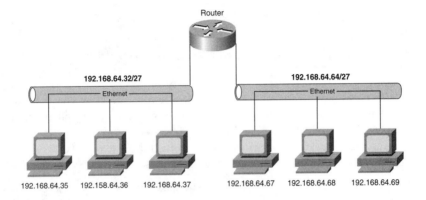

Figure 6-3 shows a network after supernetting. Two small LANs are routed together; all traffic flowing between them must be routed.

Figure 6-3   *After: Two /27 Networks Supernetted to Form a /26*

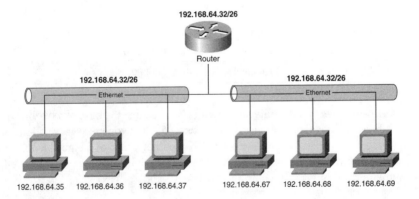

Obviously, this criterion adds a physical element to the purely mathematical requirements of supernetting's first two prerequisites. You must accept the fact that, unless a pair of subnets are physically constructed such that they can be interconnected, and then use the same router interface, they cannot be supernetted. This is true even if two or more subnets pass the criteria for contiguity and divisibility. Thus, the actual number of supernets that can be formed is a subset of those that are mathematically feasible. It is impossible to determine which subnets are supernetable without physically examining each subnetwork.

Aggregation Versus Supernetting

Supernetting and aggregation are extremely similar concepts, especially mathematically. It is how they are implemented that makes them distinct. Aggregation is what routers to do reduce their workload. They try to shorten network prefixes to minimize the total number of prefixes that must be advertised externally either to the rest of the network or to the Internet. Supernetting, by virtue of its single-interface rule, requires physical consolidation of networks as opposed to just a logical consolidation of the network addresses into a smaller prefix.

Figures 6-4 and 6-5 better demonstrate aggregation versus supernetting.

Figure 6-4   *From the Internet's Perspective, a Pair of /24 Networks Are Aggregated as a /23*

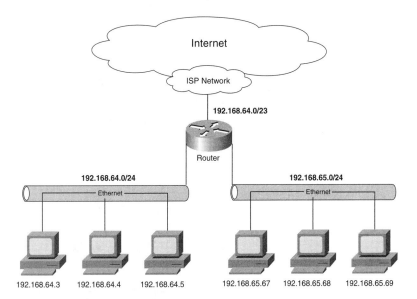

In Figure 6-4, you can see that interconnectivity between the two /24 networks is achieved via the same router. This router recognizes that the two networks are numerically contiguous, and it advertises just a single /23 network prefix to the Internet. Thus, the Internet can reach both networks using just 23 bits of their network addresses. Inbound packets get only as far as the router shared by the /24 networks. That router must then examine the destination address of each inbound packet to determine which of its two /24 networks the packet is destined for. Making such a determination requires the router to make a routing decision based on all 24 bits of the two network prefixes.

This captures the essence of aggregation, albeit on a very small scale. There is a strong correlation between geographic distance and the number of bits you need in order to reach any given destination. A good way to think about how this works is navigating your way to your favorite restaurant. If that restaurant is located in Kansas City, Mo., your initial directions can be as simple as "Go west" if you are located east of the Mississippi River. However, after you reach that city, you need much more precise information in order to find your way through the complex network of streets and storefronts in order to find your destination. IP-based networks are no different. Precision is just defined in terms of how many of the network prefix's bits you are looking at.

Figure 6-5 shows the same network topology and also advertises just a single /23 network prefix to the Internet. However, that's where the similarities end. The two /24 networks have been integrated into a /23 network. This network requires only a single connection to the router. More importantly, the router need not look at the 24th bit of an inbound packet to figure out what to do with it: All inbound packets can be forwarded using just the /23 network. The individual /24 networks have, in effect, ceased to exist. In their place is a single, larger network.

Figure 6-5 *The Pair of /24 Networks Are Supernetted into a /23*

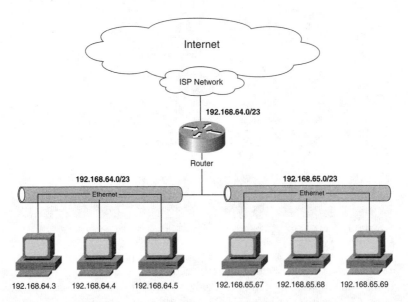

This pair of examples use a limited scale to demonstrate aggregation versus supernetting. In reality, aggregation can occur on a very large scale. In fact, ISPs might aggregate hundreds or thousands of customer networks into just one network prefix that gets communicated to the entire Internet. This, of course, raises an issue. Is it possible to overaggregate? In other words, which is better: longer or shorter network prefixes?

Which Is Better: Longer or Shorter?

Under CIDR supernetting rules, no distinction is made between network and subnetwork addresses. Both are regarded as a network prefix to a host address, and routing decisions *can* be made on the entire prefix. I say "can" because it isn't mandatory.

We tend to take the Internet for granted. Everything we could ever hope to find is always right at our fingertips. At least, that's how it seems! However, if you look a little deeper, you discover a concept known as *reachability*. Reachability is a general term that describes whether any given destination can be reached through the Internet. The very fact that such a term exists should tell you that reaching intended destinations is not necessarily guaranteed. Which ISP networks you need to traverse to satisfy any given communication request across the Internet, and which approaches those ISPs use for routing, can have a huge impact on the reachability of destination networks. This is a by-product of network aggregation.

NOTE   A /20 is considered the smallest network size for global routability. That's not to say you couldn't advertise a smaller block, such as a /24 network. Smaller blocks run the risk of not being accepted *universally* throughout the Internet simply because each ISP sets its own policy as to how long a prefix it will support. Ideally, there won't be any standalone /24 network addresses; all should be created from within much larger ISP network address blocks and be advertised to the Internet as those larger blocks.

Each ISP decides how it will route across its own network. There are many different approaches, one of which is based on the principle of the longest numeric "match." Having examined how supernetting and CIDR were intended to improve route aggregation across the Internet, you can now better appreciate the pros and cons of network prefix length. It's a concise debate. Longer prefixes are much more precise. But they result in the need to track a greater overall number of routes than if you abstract a smaller network prefix from among a larger number of more-specific prefixes.

The aggregatability of the CIDR IPv4 address space gives you the best of both worlds: You can use very long (and therefore very precise) network prefixes where you have to, and very short, less-precise network prefixes where you can. Ostensibly, the closer you are in an internetwork to the destination network, the greater the precision you require of the network address. The farther you get from that destination, the less precise the network prefix can be. In this manner, routes can be generalized, with specificity increasing with proximity to the destination. In simpler terms, and as discussed earlier in this chapter, you might be able to accurately route an IP packet to a service provider network using just 16 network address bits. Then you can look at additional bits to figure out what to do with that packet after it's on the service provider's network.

The bottom line is that both longer and shorter prefixes play an important role in the proper functioning of an IP network. This works due to the concept of aggregation.

Summary

CIDR had a rather inauspicious beginning; it was originally designed as yet another in the IETF's bag of short-term tricks to buy time for IPv6 to be developed. It's been successful beyond its developers' imagination. CIDR has not only successfully staved off address space depletion, but it has also enabled Internet routing to become much more efficient through a greater degree of aggregation. This efficiency simply was not possible under Classical IP rules. For all its benefits, CIDR was less revolutionary than might be suspected. It was directly based on VLSM and, for that reason, was readily understood and accepted by the Internet community.

CHAPTER 7

Private Addresses and NAT

Two of the more-significant technologies in IPv4's evolution were created separately but were clearly made for each other. These technologies are private addresses and Network Address Translation (NAT).

This chapter explores the private address space that was reserved by the IETF in RFC 1597 and then affirmed in RFC 1918. This chapter then looks at how NAT makes private addresses practical, useful, and, in some situations, superior to directly registered IP addresses.

Private Address Spaces

After the Internet became commercialized, its popularity soared. More importantly, so did the popularity of TCP/IP and its addressing architecture and space. Seemingly overnight, software engineers embraced the TCP/IP communications protocol suite and it became the de facto standard for networked communications between applications. As a direct result of this trend, many organizations began implementing TCP/IP to support their base of applications even though they might not have needed or wanted access to the Internet. Implementing TCP/IP absolutely requires that you also implement the Internet's addressing scheme, regardless of whether you intend to actually use the Internet.

In March 1994, the IETF released RFC 1597. This document acknowledged that many organizations were using TCP/IP and IP addresses but remained isolated from the Internet. This was perfectly acceptable in the days before commercialization, because the installed base of TCP/IP networks was relatively low. But the commercialization of the Internet threatened to rapidly deplete the IP address space.

The theory behind RFC 1597 (and its update in RFC 1918) was that a block of addresses could be reserved for use in private networks. This afforded a legitimate mechanism for networks that needed IP for application support but did not want or need to access the Internet. Such a mechanism would serve a twofold purpose.

First, it would mitigate the demand for new IP addresses. This would help make the remaining address blocks last a little longer. The downside is that these addresses cannot be routed over the Internet.

Second, this approach would help keep down the swelling of the Internet's routing tables. Reserved address blocks cannot be routed through the Internet and are limited to local use.

NOTE	The addresses reserved in RFC 1918 are sometimes called *nonroutable addresses* because they cannot be routed across the Internet. However, that does not mean that they can't be routed! Quite the contrary: Many a private IP WAN has been built successfully using these so-called nonroutable addresses. The reserved addresses can be routed—just not across the Internet.

The Mathematics of Private Addressing

One very common misperception about RFCs 1597 and 1918 is that these documents reserved an entire Class A, an entire Class B, and an entire Class C network address space. People who think this either don't really understand the IP address architecture or haven't read the RFCs. Probably both. Table 7-1 lists the address blocks that were reserved in RFC 1597 (and reinforced in the updated RFC 1918, which is still Internet Best Current Practice #5) for use solely in private networks.

Table 7-1   *RFCs 1597 and 1918 Private Address Spaces*

Network Address Size in Bits	Base Address	Terminal Address
/8	10.0.0.0	10.255.255.255
/12	172.16.0.0	172.31.255.255
/16	192.168.0.0	192.168.255.255

A quick glance at Table 7-1 should demonstrate that entire blocks of Class A, B, and C network address space are indeed not reserved! In fact, if you read those RFCs, you'll see that only the address block taken from the Class A space matches the classical boundary for that address. Thus, the space reserved from the Class A address space by RFC 1918 is, in fact, an entire Class A address space. 8 of its address bits are used for network identification. That leaves 24 bits for host addresses. For this reason, the RFC refers to this reserved address block as the *24-bit address*. This is in stark contrast to the popular convention of explicitly identifying the number of bits in a network address.

The others don't follow the classical boundaries so neatly. The address block reserved by RFC 1918 within the Class B address range, for example, is actually a block of 16 numerically contiguous Class B spaces. If you plotted this out in a binary string, you would see that the Class B RFC 1597 space offers 20 bits for host addresses (rather than just 16, as is found in a Class B network). Thus, in the RFC, this address type is called the *20-bit address*. As I mentioned before, this is very confusing and is contrary to the established conventions.

Table 7-2 shows you the binary and decimal limits of this reserved address space. The network mask is indicated in bold so that you can more easily see that this network block uses 12 bits.

Table 7-2   *Mathematical Limits of the 172.16 Reserved Space*

	Decimal	Binary
Base address	172.16.0.0	**10101100.0001**0000.00000000.00000000
Terminal address	172.31.255.255	**10101100.0001**1111.11111111.11111111

The Class C network space is equal in size to a set of 255 numerically contiguous Class C network addresses. If you think about this, and visualize it in binary, you will realize that this reserved address space offers 16 bits of host addresses. Thus, the block reserved from the Class C address space is identical in size to a Class B network block. Table 7-3 shows the actual reserved range of addresses. Again, for your visual reference, the bits used to identify the network are indicated in bold. The other bits are used for host addressing.

Table 7-3   *Mathematical Limits of the 192.168 Reserved Space*

	Decimal	Binary
Base address	192.168.0.0	**11000000.10101000.**00000000.00000000
Terminal address	192.168.255.255	**11000000.10101000.**11111111.11111111

Benefits and Drawbacks of Private Addressing

Having waded through the mathematics of reserved private address blocks, it's probably appropriate to look at some of the operational impacts of private addressing. In other words, let's look at the benefits and limitations of this tool.

Benefits

The greatest benefit of using private address space is that the global Internet address space is conserved for use where it is really needed. Although this is a noble goal, the benefits are distributed externally: The organization implementing private addressing is helping the Internet community at large, but not necessarily itself, in the process—at least, not if this were the only benefit.

One other benefit, perhaps the most compelling of all, is that you don't need permission to use these addresses. They were created explicitly to be unique per network but nonunique globally. As you saw earlier in this chapter, one of the more effective ways that IANA's pool of available addresses was protected was by rationing them carefully. Gone are the days when address blocks were handed out to anyone who asked. With the introduction of RFC 1466, a stringent standard of justification was imposed on anyone asking for address space. Even service providers had to pass stringent criteria to justify being assigned more address space. So, here was the classic carrot and stick: Use the RFC 1597/1918 addresses hassle-free, or butt heads with the Keeper of Unassigned Addresses in an almost-always-futile attempt to procure your own addresses.

Another, more-subtle reason to use private addressing is that the network becomes inherently more secure. Because private address spaces are not valid routes across the Internet, a network that used them couldn't be hacked via the Internet. Of course, such a network would have a difficult time communicating with the Internet if it had those addresses in the first place, but hopefully you get my point.

Drawbacks

The drawbacks of using the private address space reserved in RFC 1918 are relatively easy to enumerate. There's exactly one. That first, last, and only drawback is that these addresses cannot be routed across the Internet. But they *can* be routed internally within a private network. You're probably thinking that this isn't a flaw; it's a feature. And you're right. But this becomes a problem if your requirements change *after* you implement RFC 1918 addresses. For example, if you suddenly find that your users require connectivity to, or accessibility from, the Internet, this limitation can become quite problematic. Quite literally, if you try to connect to the Internet using RFC 1918 addresses, you won't be able to communicate at all. The ISP you are connecting to won't recognize your address space (identified in each of your IP packets via the source address field) as routable, so no inbound packets will be able to reach you. That includes packets generated in response to your queries!

That's not to say that using RFC 1918 addresses is risky. In fact, if you have no plans to connect to the Net, RFC 1918 is perfect for you.

When requirements change like that, you aren't necessarily facing an address migration. This is where NAT can be extremely useful.

NAT

Network Address Translation (NAT) was developed specifically to counter the lone weakness inherent in the private addresses of RFC 1918. That's not to suggest that it makes those nonunique addresses globally routable, because it doesn't. Rather, it lets you translate those nonunique addresses to unique and routable addresses at the edge of your network. This permits access to and from the global Internet. In other words, you operate with two sets of addresses: You would have your private RFC 1918 addresses configured on endpoints throughout your network, and then a globally routable block of addresses would be configured on your NAT device. NAT would be responsible for correlating the internal and global addresses and translating as needed to support communications.

Originally described in RFC 1631 in May 1994, NAT was originally conceived as yet another of the stopgap measures to shore up the flagging IPv4 address space. If you take the time to read this document (www.ietf.org/rfc/rfc1631.txt), you will see that the IETF was absolutely counting on IPv6 to save the Internet from its impending address crisis. This document explicitly identifies the two biggest problems facing the Internet as a shortage of

IP addresses and the scalability of routing across the Internet. In Chapter 5, "The Date of Doom," we looked at how these two are really different perspectives on the same problem, so their appearance in RFC 1631 shouldn't be a startling revelation.

What *is* startling is the explicit admission that at least some parties within the IETF were concerned that CIDR (then under development) might not buy enough time for IPv6 to be completed. That's a staggering statement! CIDR was initially conceived as just another stopgap tool to buy time for the new IP protocol and addressing system to be developed. This fear became the motivator for the development of NAT.

Framing the Problem Statement

The authors of RFC 1631 apparently believed strongly enough in their proposal to say the following:

> It is possible that CIDR will not be adequate to maintain the IP Internet until the long-term solutions are in place. This memo proposes another short-term solution, address reuse, that complements CIDR or even makes it unnecessary.

With the benefit of hindsight, that remarkable statement is both amusing and illuminating. As late as the middle of 1994, there was still great debate as to whether a migration to a classless IP address system was even needed. This is significant because CIDR was stipulated in a series of RFCs published in September 1993, 8 months prior to the release of RFC 1631 NAT! If nothing else, this should give you some indication that there was little consensus on anything other than three basic facts:

- The IPv4 address space, in its class-based configuration, was about to break.

- The correct way to solve the problem was to make a completely new Internet Protocol (eventually named IPv6).

- Something needed to be done immediately to forestall the impending collapse of the classful system long enough to roll out the new version of IP.

Beyond these three basic facts, consensus broke down. Nobody really knew the correct approach to take, so the IETF attacked in all directions. The development of NAT capability was aimed at enhancing the usefulness of the RFC 1918 addresses. One of the single biggest "traps" inherent in the use of nonunique addresses was the inability to convert them to routable addresses. Should requirements change, and Internet connectivity become necessary, anyone using RFC 1918 addresses would face a painful address migration. In comparison, address translation seemed like a welcome alternative.

As significant as NAT has become, it is almost laughable to think that at its inception it was being bandied about as an alternative to CIDR. With hindsight, it is remarkably obvious that CIDR and NAT are different tools intended for different uses. Both technologies were also so successful at buying time for IPv4 that they are still in active use.

Technical Overview

Before we get too caught up in technical details, one salient point to understand is that NAT is a router-based function. It was designed to provide hosts on a private network with a means of communicating transparently with destinations outside that network, and vice versa. Traditionally, NAT has been used in conjunction with RFC 1918 addresses (specifically designed for use in addressing private numbers), but that is not a mandate. NAT can be used to translate unique addresses into other unique addresses, too. Either way, it enhances security by hiding addresses within a private network from the outside world. Thus, NAT can be highly appropriate for securing a network, regardless of what kind of IP addresses are in use.

The way this works is actually quite simple. A gateway router (one that sits at the border of two different networks) functions as an address translator between two neighboring networks. This translation means that a NAT network has different types of IP addresses, each serving a slightly different purpose. Before we venture too far ahead, you need to understand the subtle distinctions between these address types. If you assume that an enterprise is using NAT to establish communications with the Internet, this helps you establish a frame of reference for understanding the differences between the address types. The original specification for NAT had two address types:

- **Inside local (IL) address**—This is the address of a host *inside* an enterprise's network *as it is known within that network*. The IL may be globally unique (either obtained from the ISP or directly registered to the enterprise), or it may be selected from an RFC 1918 reserved range. Communications within a network may occur directly using IL addresses, without the need for translation.

- **Inside global (IG) address**—This is the IP address of a host *inside* an enterprise's network *as it appears to the Internet*. That last phrase is the critical distinction between an IG and an IL address. IG addresses must be globally unique, regardless of whether they were obtained from the ISP or directly registered to the enterprise. It is important to recognize that the IG address is advertised to external networks and is used for routing to the internal network. Thus, RFC 1918 private addresses cannot be used as IG addresses.

Together, these address types let a network communicate with other IP-based networks without having to reveal its internal addresses. That's a key statement, because so many people think that the only reason NAT exists is for use with RFC 1918 addresses. The truth is, it can be used with any network address and may be implemented to enhance a network's security regardless of whether it uses private or globally routable addresses.

The NAT router must keep a table—known as an *address translation table* (no acronyms, please)—that correlates these different address types. How this correlation works depends on whether we are talking about packets coming into, or going out of, that private network. We'll look at both traffic types in the next section.

Over time, NAT has become much more sophisticated and feature-rich. Today's NAT can translate external as well as internal addresses and can even translate TCP port addresses. Later in this chapter we'll look at some of the technological advances that NAT has benefited from. For now, let's continue with our examination of the basic NAT specification. This will give you a context within which you can better appreciate the enhancements made to NAT since RFC 1631.

Operational Mechanics

NAT is a router-based function that must reside at a network's border. For the purposes of explaining how a NAT works, let's start with a very basic implementation topology. Take a look at Figure 7-1. This figure shows a simple stub network that consists of just one local-area network. This LAN uses private addresses in the 172.16.9.0/24 block. NAT is performed at the gateway router between that network and the Internet. This connection is the only egress point for this network.

Figure 7-1   *NAT Translates Nonunique and Unique Addresses at the Border of a Stub Network*

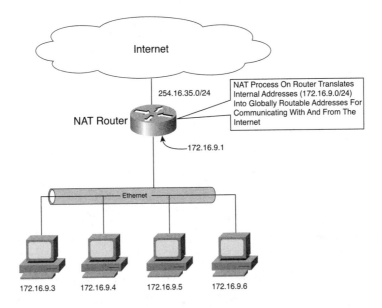

For now, let's make the simplifying assumption that the end user entered an IP address as opposed to a host and domain name string. This lets you focus on the mechanics of NAT without the added complexity of translating a name into an IP number. We'll look at how that is done in Chapter 9, "IP Multicasting." Given this simplifying assumption, when an endpoint on that LAN tries to access a host that resides outside its boundaries, the request can't be resolved locally, and the gateway router accepts it. That router has only two interfaces configured: the LAN and a serial connection to the Internet. Because it is seldom useful to send a datagram or packet back through the interface it came in on, the router has only two choices — drop the packet or send it out the other interface. Using the other interface requires that some work be done to the datagram, because that is the interface where NAT resides.

The first thing NAT does is check the header of that packet to determine its source IP address. The packet is coming from an endpoint located somewhere within the network, so the source IP address is an inside local address. NAT won't permit such addresses to pass into an external network. NAT searches its address translation table for this address. If no entry is found that corresponds to that destination address, the packet is simply discarded. If a match is found within the address translation table, the corresponding inside global address is retrieved from the table and is used in lieu of the inside local address in the packet's source address field.

Table 7-4 summarizes this gateway router's address translation table. For the sake of example, let's pretend that the globally routable address is in the 254.16.35.0 range. That address is not a valid address. In fact, it's a part of the reserved Class E address space. But I am extremely reluctant to use "real" IP addresses in an example.

Table 7-4 *Stub Network's Address Translation Table*

Inside Local Addresses	Inside Global Addresses
172.16.9.0/24	254.16.35.0/24
172.16.9.1	254.16.35.1
172.16.9.3	254.16.35.3
172.16.9.4	254.16.35.4
172.16.9.5	254.16.35.5
172.16.9.6	254.16.35.6

After a packet's source address field is updated with the appropriate inside global address, the packet can be launched out the router's interface and into the foreign network that lies beyond. Although that's a brief-enough synopsis of how NAT treats outbound packets, it is also necessary to see how NAT supports address translation for incoming packets.

Very generally speaking, there are two basic reasons for packets to be inbound to a NAT network:

- Responses to a session generated from within the NAT network
- Sessions that originate from external hosts

Regardless of the variety, packets that are inbound to a NAT network pass through the same process. Such packets are sent to machines bearing inside local address types. As such, they must be intercepted by the NAT for translation of the destination address to an inside global address.

The process by which NAT translates IG addresses to IL addresses is exactly the reverse of the one we just looked at. An incoming packet is accepted by the NAT (which could be a process configured on a router interface, firewall, or other specialized network appliance), and its destination address is examined and hashed against the address translation table for a matching record. If the destination address (really an IG address) is known, the corresponding IL address is then substituted in the packet's destination address, and the packet is launched into the private network. If the destination IG address isn't known, the packet is discarded.

Implementation Topologies

Although NAT was originally conceived for a single purpose (staving off address-space depletion), it has proven itself remarkably versatile. Today, NAT can be used to support numerous, vastly different network topologies. In addition to the simple stub network connected to the Internet (as you saw in Figure 7-1), some of the more common implementation varieties include the following:

- Private network with multiple egress points
- Partitioned-backbone stub network
- Using NAT for a subset of IP addresses in a network

We'll look at each in a bit more detail throughout this section.

NOTE   Since its inception, NAT has become almost synonymous with the nonunique private IP addresses reserved in RFCs 1597 and 1918. However, nothing in any of the NAT RFCs requires the use of these nonunique IP addresses. Thus, you can use NAT to simply "hide" globally routable IP addresses from external networks. In and of itself, that would tend to improve the security of the networked computing assets behind the NAT router.

A Network with Multiple Egress Points

Two implementation varieties are very similar but have a single, significant difference. These varieties are a network with multiple egress points, and a multihomed network. *Egress* is a networking term that indicates a way off a network. In simpler terms, it is a connection to a different network. Both varieties are topologically similar in that they feature two or more connections from the private network to the "outside."

The key difference between these two varieties lies in how you define "outside." A network with multiple egress points enjoys redundant connections to an external network. A multihomed network also enjoys redundant connections, but with an added measure of fault tolerance. This additional fault tolerance derives from connecting to two or more external networks.

Redundant Connections to an External Network

Figure 7-2 demonstrates a simple network with multiple egress points. For the sake of this example, assume that both connections run to the same Internet service provider. In other words, this is just a network with multiple egress points, as opposed to a multihomed network.

Figure 7-2   *NAT Translation Tables Must Be Kept Consistent in Networks That Have Multiple Egress Points*

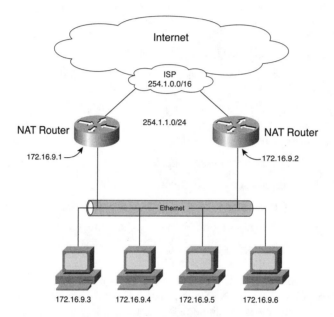

In this case, you have multiple connections to the same ISP network, and you use their address blocks as inside global addresses. As shown in Figure 7-2, both egress connections go to the same external network, and they both use inside global addresses that were created from that service provider's large block of addresses. The enterprise network uses 254.1.1.0/24 as its network address. That block was carved from the service provider's 254.1.0.0/16 block. So, all route advertisements to the Internet are simply aggregated up to the /16. No smaller or more-specific route advertisements are needed. In more practical terms, the entire Internet can access all the destinations within the ISP's customer base just by remembering a route to 254.1.0.0/16. That ISP then assumes responsibility for remembering more-specific routes within its network to each destination network created from this large address space.

The only subtle issue in this type of topology is that there are multiple address translation tables. Specifically, there is one per NAT interface. Given that each redundant NAT interface supports the same base of internal devices, it is imperative that the tables be kept consistent with each other. In practice, this can become tedious and time-consuming. Yet it is the price that must be paid for redundancy in a network that must connect externally without the benefit of globally routable IP addresses.

NAT in Multihomed Private Networks

Multihoming is another one of those concepts that made more sense for end users of the Internet than it did for the entities responsible for maintaining its technology base. At its simplest, a multihomed network is one that enjoys two or more connections to another network. Those connections would most likely run to different locations, and probably even to different service provider networks. That greatly complicates routing across the Internet, because it creates two very different, but valid, paths to the same destination. There are other issues too, but they're strictly tangential to our discussion of NAT. We'll come back to multihoming issues in Chapter 12, "Network Stability."

For now, it is sufficient just to know that multihoming greatly complicates internetworking. However, it is highly desirable to end-user organizations for the functionality it brings. Potential benefits of multihoming include reducing and/or eliminating downtime and load balancing. Both are highly attractive to any organization that relies on its network for commercial purposes. But multihoming makes network operations "interesting," and supporting NAT in a multihomed environment is no exception.

For the purposes of this book, let's assume that external network is the Internet. Figure 7-3 gives you a relatively simple topology of a multihomed private network. We'll use this to further explore and explain the vicissitudes of supporting NAT with multiple egress points.

The first thing that a multihomed network needs, like any network, is an address space. Without it, communication is not possible. There are several options for obtaining valid inside global addresses in multihomed configurations. Using Figure 7-3 as a guide, these options are as follows:

- Use a directly registered address space.
- Accept a range of addresses from both ISP #1 and ISP #2 and use them both.
- Accept a range of addresses from ISP #1.
- Accept a range of addresses from ISP #2.

The first option almost doesn't make sense in a NAT implementation. If you could obtain your own IP address space from your regional registrar, you would probably just implement that space and forget about address translation.

Figure 7-3 *Multihomed Private Network*

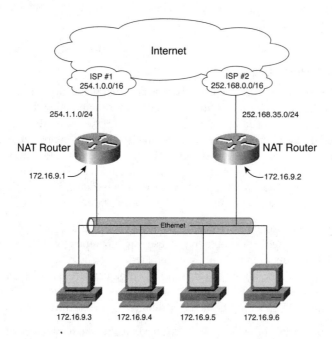

The other three options warrant an explanation before we look at them because they are different ways of solving a common problem. When NAT is introduced in a multihomed network, an added complexity is introduced in the form of a dual set of inside global addresses. Each set of inside global addresses is maintained in its own address translation table. Thus, in a network with multiple egress connections, you have multiple address translation tables to keep synchronized. If those connections go to different networks, you have created the potential for a single internal host to be known externally via two different inside global IP addresses.

So, the challenge in a dual-homed network is figuring out how to keep such a conflict from occurring. The key is carefully managing your inside global addresses. Think about it: Inside local addresses are strictly local. Therefore, who cares what they are! The only addresses that are visible are the inside global addresses maintained by each NAT.

With that brief explanation of the underlying problem, the second, third, and fourth options for obtaining IP addresses raise different sets of issues that need to be examined in more detail.

Option 2

Figure 7-3 demonstrates a multihomed network that uses two different sets of inside global addresses. Two different global addresses identify each of the internal networked devices on the Internet. The correlation between the single set of inside local addresses and the two different sets of inside global addresses is explained in Table 7-5.

Table 7-5   *Address Translation Tables in a Multihomed Network with Redundant Inside Global Addresses*

Inside Local Addresses	Inside Global Addresses (ISP #1)	Inside Global Addresses (ISP #2)
172.16.9.0/24	254.1.1.0/24	252.168.35.0/24
172.16.9.1	254.1.1.1	252.168.35.1
172.16.9.3	254.1.1.3	252.168.35.3
172.16.9.4	254.1.1.4	2592.168.35.4
172.16.9.5	254.1.1.5	252.168.35.5
172.16.9.6	254.1.1.6	252.168.35.6

Options 3 and 4

Options 3 and 4 are variants of the same solution. In effect, you are accepting a block of addresses from one service provider and using them as the only valid addresses for accessing your network. You could just implement them directly within your network and avoid NAT entirely. But if you wanted to change service providers, you would have to surrender those addresses. Thus, it makes much more sense to think of such "borrowed" addresses as fodder for translation.

Those ISP-provided addresses would serve as inside global addresses, and you would probably rely on the address blocks reserved in RFC 1918 for your inside local addressing. Migrating to a different service provider would be neatly accomplished just by reconfiguring your NAT routers' translation tables. This is illustrated in Figure 7-4. As with previous examples, all addresses shown are from RFC 1918 rather than using any particular organization's IP address blocks.

In this example, the address block obtained from ISP #1 is used for both connections to the Internet. This forces ISP #2 to accept and advertise a route for a network address that does not belong to it. But there's no guarantee that any given service provider will support a different service provider's addresses. That's a very complex issue, and we'll come back to it in Part IV of this book. For now, let's just continue with the simplifying assumption that the two ISPs won't let you advertise your inside global addresses using a different ISP's address block. That leaves us with few good options for configuring NAT to work in a multihomed environment. This is where RFC 2260 comes in.

Figure 7-4 *Using One Service Provider's Addresses in a Multihomed Network*

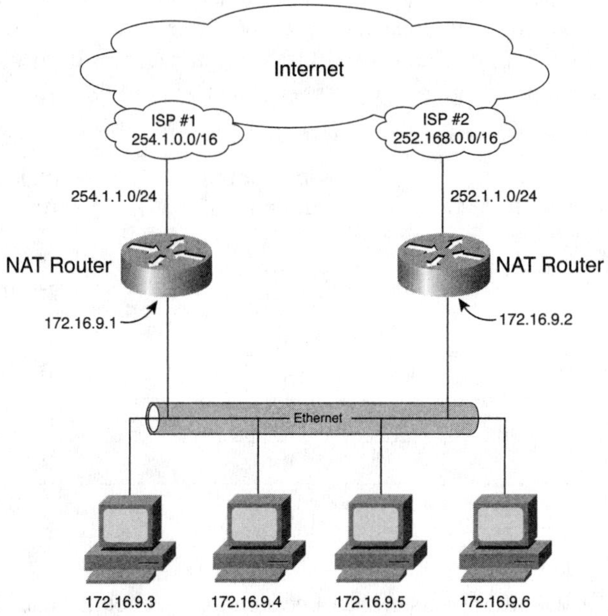

RFC 2260

RFC 2260 spelled out a proposed update to NAT specifically designed for enterprises that were multihomed to the Internet via different ISPs. The address allocation and routing scheme described in that document has the potential for tremendous scalability, because it balances traffic loads across multiple Internet connections. The load balancing is achieved by statically configuring which endpoint address uses which Internet connection. Anything statically configured is not flexible and requires manual intervention to change. To better appreciate how RFC 2260 advocates implementing static load balancing of the address translation function, see Figure 7-5.

As shown in Figure 7-5, the multihomed private network consists of two LAN environments. Each of those LANs connects to the Internet via a NAT router. Rather than trying to keep a pair of address translation tables synchronized, the hosts within the enterprise are arbitrarily divided into two groups. The hosts numbered 176.16.9.3 and 176.16.9.4 use ISP #1, and the hosts numbered 176.16.9.5 and 176.16.9.6 use ISP #2. This has the added value of improving performance by minimizing the size of each address translation table.

Figure 7-5   *Static Load Balancing in a Multihomed Private Network*

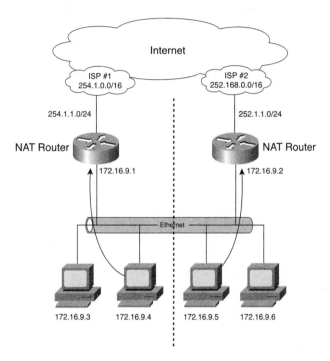

Anyone who's ever spent any time running a network knows one basic fact: Traffic loads are highly dynamic. Although you can discern some basic pattern over time, loads and flows vary continuously. Given this fluidity, it doesn't seem to make much sense to statically configure a load-balancing mechanism based solely on IP address. Quite simply, you are locking yourself into a rigid and inflexible load-balancing scheme despite the fact that traffic loads are anything but rigid and inflexible.

Perhaps the best way to explain this incongruity is to point out that RFC 2260 wasn't specifically designed to balance traffic loads across diverse network egress connections. It was designed to balance the workload imposed by the NAT function in a multihomed network. That's a subtle distinction, but it should help you set a more realistic expectation of what load balancing means in the context of this RFC.

NAT for a Subset of Addresses at a Single Location

Another variety of NAT implementation is to implement it for just a subset of hosts within a private network. The key to making NAT work well is to minimize the size of the address translation tables. Thus, it makes sense to implement NAT for just those hosts that require communication with the external network.

Figure 7-6 shows a stub network that has developed a *demilitarized zone (DMZ)* in its network. This DMZ is a semisecured network region that contains the company's commercial Web site. The computer that hosts this Web presence is the only device in the entire network that requires communication with devices outside the confines of that network. As such, it is the only device that requires an entry in the address translation table. Although all the networked devices use the RFC 1918 address space, only 172.16.9.65 and 172.16.9.66 are serviced by the NAT.

Figure 7-6   *Using NAT for a Subset of Hosts in a Stub Network*

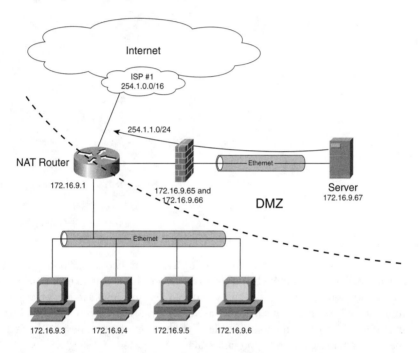

Limiting the address translation table to just this one device offers two main benefits. First, because the translation table is kept to a minimum, the load that supporting NAT would otherwise impose on the router is also kept to a minimum. Second, because the other hosts in the company are kept hidden from the Internet, they are inherently more secure than if the entire network were accessible to the Internet via NAT.

Although this is an extreme example in that just one host requires Internet access, it isn't an unrealistic example. It also nicely demonstrates another use for NAT.

Partitioned Backbone Stubs

If you read RFCs long enough, eventually you'll come across a new term. That's what happened to me when I was doing the research for this chapter. The term that caught me by surprise was *partitioned backbone stubs*. RFC 1631 explains that one of the more "sophisticated" uses of NAT would be to let an enterprise outsource its backbone to an ISP. Each of that enterprise's locations would be connected to the ISP's network. This topology is shown in Figure 7-7.

Figure 7-7   *Using NAT to Partition an Enterprise's Network Backbone*

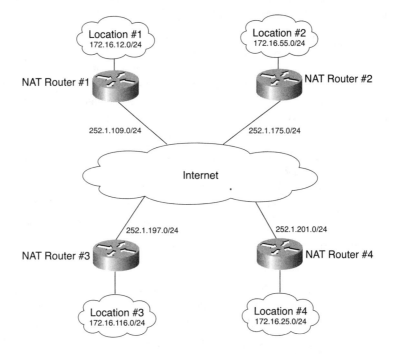

Figure 7-7 shows a company with four locations interconnected via a backbone owned and operated by an ISP. The inside local addresses are indicated inside each of the clouds that represent the network in each of the company's locations. The outside global addresses are indicated outside the NAT router facing the Internet. (Again, these network addresses are nonroutable, but let's pretend that they are for the sake of example.) Each location runs NAT at its border router. This allows that company's locations to use private addresses yet still communicate through another network. But there is a price to pay for this capability. The company's "backbone network" is a virtual one: Each location is a stub that hangs off someone else's network—hence the term *partitioned backbone stub*.

The original NAT concept called for a one-to-one mapping of IL to IG addresses. In large networks, or in networks in which a large percentage of the inside local host addresses needed to communicate with external networked devices, that one-to-one mapping between the different address types resulted in large address translation tables. Large tables directly translated into quite a bit of time added to any communication session that required address translation. But this configuration doesn't and shouldn't enable any-to-any connectivity. If you were responsible for this sample network, you wouldn't want other companies connected to the same service provider to enjoy access to your inside hosts.

Thus, it seems logical that the routers in each of the partitioned stubs should keep track of routes to the local address spaces of every other partitioned stub in the company's network. But you wouldn't want the routers in the ISP's public network to maintain routes to any of the local addresses. If they did, your "private" network wouldn't be very secure.

The only logical explanation is that the border routers (the ones that, by the way, also run NAT) must tunnel through the public backbone. Tunneling is a complex topic, but in its simplest form, it is a way of wrapping an IP packet with another IP packet. The external packet is intended solely for transporting the internal packet through an untrusted, unsecured, or technologically different network. In this particular case, wrapping a packet with a packet lets you forward packets of data to hosts in a different partition even though that partition uses RFC 1918 addresses that can't be routed globally.

The way this works is simple. The network topology for a partitioned backbone stub network can be used as an example to demonstrate NAT tunnels. Each NAT router is required to set aside one inside global address for tunneling. NAT uses encapsulation to transport IP packets that aren't considered globally routable (due to their RFC 1918 addresses) through the ISP network. Each NAT router's reserved global address becomes both of the following:

- The source address of IP packets outbound from that router

- The destination address of all IP packets destined for the stub network hiding behind each individual NAT router

To better understand how this works, consider the following list. Using Figure 7-7 as a guide, in a typical sequence of events, the steps are as follows:

Step 1   A host in network 172.16.12.0/24 needs to communicate with a host in network 172.16.25.0/24.

Step 2   The packets from this communication session can't be satisfied within network 172.16.12.0/24. They are accepted by that network's gateway router (NAT Router #1 in Figure 7-7) for delivery to an external network.

Step 3   Router #1 examines each packet's destination IP address field and recognizes that the addresses aren't valid in the local network. Thus, it must find an acceptable address to use for transport on the Internet. This is where the NAT function is used. The destination address, such as 172.16.25.68, isn't valid globally.

Step 4   Gateway router #1 wraps the host's IP packets with another IP packet that contains the corresponding inside global address reserved by the NAT at the destination network's edge. In this case, the "routable" destination address is 252.1.201.68. For the sake of example, each stub network in our example uses IG addresses provided by the ISP. Those addresses are known to—and are routable by—that ISP's network.

Step 5   The wrapped packet is launched into the service provider's network, where it is forwarded to its destination.

Step 6   When the IP packet reaches its destination, the recipient NAT router, #4, unwraps (or *decapsulates,* to use the proper technical term) the packet. The wrapper, having fulfilled its mission, is discarded. What remains is the original IP packet, complete with the private address of its destination host. This private address can now be directly used to forward the IP packet to its intended destination.

In this manner, each NAT router correlates one destination address with an entire block of addresses that lie within each partition. Absent of any other considerations, this represents a tremendous reduction in the size of each NAT router's address translation table. The reduction in size pays dividends in the form of decreased processing time per packet.

You might wonder why anyone would build a network in this fashion instead of just directly interconnecting the locations. Without getting too far off topic, suffice it to say that treating each networked location as a stub off someone else's network is a way to provide interconnectivity without all the costs normally associated with a private network. As the telcom and Internet industries continue to commoditize, outsourcing a private backbone becomes increasingly attractive financially.

This concept led to the development of other, more-significant enhancements to NAT. They are explained in the next section.

Updates and Enhancements

NAT was created specifically to mitigate, at least in some small way, the impending IPv4 address-space crisis. Over time, it has evolved with the Internet and now is much more than its creators ever envisioned. The part about making CIDR unnecessary never really came to fruition, but NAT has seen numerous enhancements and updates since its original description back in 1994. The current NAT has been stretched to accommodate scalable routing and load distribution in multihomed networks, coexistence with IPSec, and compatibility with IPv6, to name just a few of its newer capabilities. Each of these enhancements was documented in an RFC.

These RFCs include the informational documents listed in Table 7-6.

Table 7-6 *Additional NAT RFCs*

RFC	URL	Topic
2663	www.ietf.org/rfc/rfc2663.txt	Standardizing NAT terminology
2694	www.ietf.org/rfc/rfc2694.txt	DNS extensions to NAT
2709	www.ietf.org/rfc/rfc2709.txt	Implementing NAT with tunnel-mode IPSec
2766	www.ietf.org/rfc/rfc2766.txt	IPv4-to-IPv6 NAT protocol translation
2993	www.ietf.org/rfc/rfc2993.txt	NAT's architectural implications
3022	www.ietf.org/rfc/rfc3022.txt	Introduction of TCP and UDP port number translation by NAT devices
3027	www.ietf.org/rfc/rfc3027.txt	NAT's architectural implications, updated

NAT has become a complex and sprawling array of capabilities rolled up and regarded euphemistically by a single name. The multitude of NAT-specific RFCs and other documents can be confusing. Table 7-6 presents some of the more salient documents for your later perusal. These documents are a combination of informational documents published to decrease the potential for confusion and important new extensions to NAT. Each merits examination, but such examination would detract from the primary topic of this book. For example, entire chapters could be devoted to IPSec and NAT, IPv6 and NAT, and port-address translation with NAT. Although each is significant and worth examination, they are advanced topics. As such, they are poor candidates for inclusion in a book on the fundamentals of IP addressing.

Problems with NAT

Although NAT might sound like the perfect answer to virtually any scenario that involves a private network with Internet connectivity, it isn't a panacea. In fact, it wouldn't be very difficult to find knowledgeable network engineers who regard NAT as akin to crabgrass or kudzu, to name a pair of human-induced agricultural disasters.

NAT, by its very nature, conceals source and/or destination IP addresses. Many problems can emanate from that basic, inescapable fact. You can categorize these problems by their impact area:

- Technical incompatibilities
- Scalability and network performance issues
- Logistical difficulties

Each of these is examined briefly in the next sections.

Technical Incompatibilities

The most egregious problem is that NAT breaks any network-based application that requires end-to-end session integrity. This is a direct result of NAT's interception of inbound and outbound IP packets and rewriting their headers to achieve the desired address translation.

Some of the specific technologies that are at least partially incompatible with NAT include SNMP, IPSec's authentication and encryption technologies, and the emerging Mobile IP. Many network engineers believe that NAT is directly responsible for the inability of IPSec and Mobile IP to achieve any meaningful degree of market acceptance.

Scalability

Other problems with NAT have nothing to do with technical incompatibilities. For example, NAT imposes a potentially substantial overhead on any router that supports the translation function. This overhead can be substantial enough, depending on the configuration, to prevent graceful scalability. Hardware-based appliances have appeared on the market to prevent such adverse effects on your network, but not everyone who needs to implement NAT can afford to purchase another device. Consequently, the point about NAT's impacts on router performance remains valid.

Another problem is that the probability of experiencing address problems increases greatly with NAT. The problem becomes worse, not better, with each additional translator you configure in your network. Think about it: The more translation devices you have in your network (ideally, you'd have one for each egress point), the more address tables you would have. Keeping them synchronized can be challenging, time-consuming, and onerous.

Logistical Challenges

There are logistical challenges, too, with a NAT network. For example, security is a double-edged sword. This chapter has treated NAT's privacy-enhancing aspect as a positive attribute. However, that capability also has a dark side. Debugging a problem or chasing a hacker can run into a brick wall at a NAT simply because the true source IP address is hidden from destinations. Although such challenges aren't showstoppers, they are just some of the little "gotchas" that await any network administrator who must implement and use NAT.

In all honesty, NAT has become an unavoidable part of the Internet technology base. Recent policy changes regarding the availability of directly registered address space (as discussed in earlier chapters) have made it all but necessary for many organizations that no longer qualify for their own address space. Regardless of how you feel about it, NAT is here to stay!

Summary

Private addresses and NAT are a near-perfect pair of complementary technologies. Together, they have done wonders to stave off the Date of Doom and the collapse of the Internet's address space. I say near-perfect because there have been many unanticipated side effects. We examined some of the more prominent technical implications in this chapter. There has been political fallout, too. For example, it is now nearly impossible for a private enterprise to convince the various regional registries of the need for directly registered address space. Organizations that try are usually informed that their needs would be better met with RFC 1918 addresses and NAT. Part IV of this book looks a bit more closely at the implications of this policy shift.

In Chapter 8, "Internet Names," we'll look at a different aspect of IP addressing: how it relates to domain and host names.

PART III

Advanced IP Topics

CHAPTER 8

Internet Names

As you have seen in previous chapters, the Internet's addressing system is what makes its destinations accessible and usable. Without IP addressing, you couldn't use the Internet or any other IP-based network. Despite this, it's a rare geek who actually uses IP addresses directly. It can be done, but it would take a better man than I am to remember all the numeric addresses of the hosts I need to access. More important than facilitating access to known hosts, mnemonic names greatly increase your chances of discovering new hosts. Although there are many tools for finding desired destinations, including search engines and hyperlinks, guessing at a domain name remains a very useful and expedient technique. Thus, mnemonic names are absolutely essential to making the Internet, and all IP-based networks, usable and useful.

This chapter traces the emergence of names as an informal and local-use mechanism, through its standardization across ARPANET (the Internet's predecessor) and its maturation into a standardized and hierarchical system that can reliably translate user-friendly names into numeric addresses.

Introduction to Internet Names

There was a time when names were somewhat arbitrary (if not outright capricious) and less-than-universal in their use. In the very beginning of the Internet, there were only hundreds of computers, and each one could be accessed using a mnemonic that was locally created by network administrators. This led to the inevitable: one destination computer that was known by a myriad of names that varied by location. Although there was merit in having such mnemonics, the administrators agreed that consistency of nomenclature would be even better. What was originally a convenience for a small cadre of network and host administrators evolved into a system that became the single most enabling mechanism that opened up the benefits of the Internet to nontechnical users.

This original system was simply a loose agreement among network/host administrators on a set of mnemonic names that correlated to numeric IP addresses. This agreement formalized an existing practice. These administrators had already realized that their user communities either couldn't or wouldn't use numeric addresses to access specific hosts. Thus, virtually all of them had deployed a scripted function that allowed their users to use mnemonic names for host access. Their scripts checked those names against a small but ever-growing list of known host addresses and provided an automatic translation between names and numbers.

Because this function was highly localized, there wasn't much consistency from network to network with respect to host naming conventions. After all, this was a localized translation function; the names used didn't need to be the names used by those remote hosts' administrators. They could be somewhat arbitrarily selected. For example, a name could be the local user's nickname instead of the host's official name. Needless to say, this had the potential to create great confusion. More importantly, given the highly decentralized nature of maintaining such local lists, the probability of disseminating information about moves, adds, deletes, or other changes quickly and evenly throughout the ARPANET community was slim to none. Thus, you could reasonably expect connectivity problems caused by this attempt at simplifying host access for users. Life is full of delicious irony!

hosts.txt

Fortunately, these sage administrators communicated with each other and often published documents requesting comments (ARPANET's RFCs) from other administrators. Together, they realized that it was critical to standardize on a format for naming hosts as well as a set of names for known hosts. To ensure future scalability, they further agreed to have this list managed centrally to ensure that it remained as up-to-date and evenly distributed as possible. This mechanism became known as the hosts.txt file. The Stanford Research Institute maintained the hosts.txt file via its *Network Information Center (NIC)* and transmitted to known hosts using the *file transfer protocol (FTP)*. RFCs 952 and 953 spelled out the details of this update mechanism and procedure in October 1985.

NOTE   A vestige of the original hosts.txt file and the mind-set that led to its creation remain in evidence even today. Most operating systems support the creation of a file that correlates IP addresses with mnemonics that are of local significance only. For example, UNIX systems contain an etc/hosts file to support this function.

The idea was simple enough: maintain a list of all known hosts, as well as certain other data that would be useful in deciphering the list. This list would be nothing more than a flat text file that was pushed to all administrators in the network on a regular basis. Updating local lists was up to each administrator. Failure to do so meant that their users did not have access to the most current information about known hosts.

Although it might sound foolish to try and track all known hosts in a single flat file, you must remember that this dates back to RFC 606, published in December 1973. The ARPANET was using IP, but the IPv4 address scheme had yet to be devised. The address space was still only 8 bits long. Mathematically, there couldn't be any more than 255 hosts.

Problems with Flatness

The hosts.txt file approach worked well for a couple of years. However, several inherent problems threatened the usefulness of this mechanism as the Internet continued to grow:

- **Collision of host names**—Locally defined host names create the possibility of a single character string being used to identify two or more different end systems. This is known as name collision, and it can result in an inconsistent translation of names to numeric addresses.

- **A limited number of mnemonically useful names**—A finite number of useful and meaningful character strings can be used to name hosts. Imagine, for example, that only one host in the world could have the name klingon. Absent a hierarchical naming system, the first Trekkie who gave his or her computer that name would prevent anyone else in the world from using it.

- **Timeliness and uniformity of implementing updates**—The "official list" couldn't be updated in real time, so a batch-oriented approach was required. In other words, changes, deletes, and additions to the hosts.txt file would be batched and then sent out periodically. Depending on how frequently the updated list was sent out, a host could be online but still inaccessible. An additional time lag could be experienced if network or host administrators did not promptly process the newly received hosts.txt file.

- **The lack of a name dispute resolution mechanism and authority**—Some mechanism is needed to reconcile cases in which two or more people select the same name for their box. In the days of the hosts.txt file, there was no way to resolve such disputes aside from embracing a first-come, first-served philosophy. But even that approach wasn't perfect, because updates were done in a batched manner.

Generally speaking, these problems were rooted in the flatness of the address space. Flatness in this particular case means the absence of a hierarchical structure. That by itself limited the number of meaningful names that could be assigned to hosts. Each name could be used only once throughout the world—at least the parts of the world that interconnected via the Internet! Although the NIC was responsible for tracking hosts on the Internet, it had no authority to resolve disputes over names. Thus, a chronic problem became the collision of names. In a flat environment, host names had to be unique.

You could cope with this lack of hierarchy by assigning pseudo-random strings of letters to substitute for names. That could help ensure uniqueness for a very long time, but it utterly defeats the intent behind having a mnemonic name that users can understand and remember better than pseudo-random strings of numbers.

Aside from the limited number of names that could be both useful and usable, the notion of sending out a flat file periodically to update distributed tables meant that there would be a gap between when a host came online and when distributed users would know it existed.

The largest problem with the hosts.txt approach was its inability to scale upward. As more hosts on more networks came online, the challenge of keeping them up-to-date in the file grew immeasurably. Not only were there more hosts to keep track of, each of them also had to receive the hosts.txt file. After a while, just updating the file of known hosts became almost a full-time job.

By September 1981, with a mere 400+ hosts on the ARPANET, it had become painfully obvious that there had to be a better solution. A series of RFCs began emanating from the technical constituents of ARPANET calling for a hierarchical approach to Internet names. Although each examined the same problem from a different perspective, the prevailing theme remained the need for a hierarchical namespace. Over time, these disparate RFCs coalesced into a distributed, hierarchical system that became known as the *Domain Name System (DNS)*.

DNS: The Hierarchical Approach

DNS is a remarkably complex system—one that many fine books are entirely dedicated to explaining. I won't try to explain the intricacy and nuance of the system's operational mechanics in a single chapter. My intent is to simply provide you with an overview of the system as it relates to Internet names and numeric addresses.

The basic concept of DNS was spelled out in RFCs 882 and 883, which were published in November 1983. Numerous updates have been made to this basic description (including RFCs 1034 and 1035) in the nearly 20 years since they were published, but the core of DNS has remained. At its simplest, DNS is a hierarchical, distributed database. The two key aspects of DNS are

- Hierarchical namespace
- Distributed server-based architecture to perform name-to-number conversion

Together, they enable a robust, reliable, and highly scalable mechanism for translating unique names into unique numeric addresses. This chapter is entirely focused on the namespace itself, including its hierarchy, uses, and even controversies. The physical architecture that supports name-to-number and number-to-name translations is addressed (if you'll pardon the double entendre!) in the next chapter.

Hierarchical Namespace

The hallmark of the DNS is its hierarchical namespace. Much like numeric host IP addresses, which can be duplicated across different network IP addresses, the introduction of levels of domain naming enabled the reuse of many common host names without compromising the uniqueness so critical for reliable name-to-number translation.

At this stage in the evolution of the Internet, it is difficult to imagine anyone who is not familiar with its namespace. With that familiarity comes an implicit understanding of Internet name construction and use. Such an understanding forms the basis of guessing URLs—a common practice among Internet users.

NOTE A URL is a uniform resource locator. Most people know what it is instinctively even after browsing the Internet just once, even if they don't know the term. However, there is a subtle distinction between a URL and a *Fully Qualified Domain Name (FQDN)*. For example, people can logically guess that the Cisco Systems Web site is www.cisco.com. That string is an FQDN. When you preface an FQDN with protocol-level commands, you get a URL. For example, www.cisco.com is a protocol-level command that uses the *Hypertext Transfer Protocol (HTTP)* to access the computer that hosts the Cisco Systems Web page.

A URL is a good example to use, because it requires the user to be able to recognize and follow the basic rules governing the Internet's hierarchical namespace. For example, a high school student trying to research colleges might spend an afternoon surfing the Net. One guess might be www.lehigh.edu. This name does, in fact, resolve into the external Web site of my alma mater, Lehigh University. More significantly, it demonstrates a three-level address that adheres to the convention that is broken down in Table 8-1.

Table 8-1 *Construction of a Hierarchical Internet Name*

Host Name	Subdomain	Domain
www	.lehigh	.edu

As is evident in Table 8-1, the groupings become larger as you move to the right. The .lehigh domain contains numerous hosts; this one just happens to be named www. Similarly, the .edu domain contains innumerable academic institutions. As such, .edu functions as an aggregator for related entities. In the parlance of the Internet, .edu is a *top-level domain (TLD)*. There are numerous TLDs, and all share a common root. The Internet naming system's root is usually denoted with a "**.**". This hierarchical effect is best appreciated visually. Figure 8-1 demonstrates the relationship between the root and the Internet's TLDs.

Figure 8-1   *Hierarchical Arrangement Within .edu*

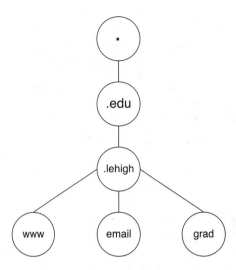

If this illustration looks familiar, don't be surprised. It is exactly how you would map out the relationship between files, directories, and drives on a computer. In fact, the hierarchy used for the Internet's naming system was based on UNIX concepts, so the similarities are inescapable even though the terminology might differ. For example, the field identified in Table 8-1 as the domain is more precisely identified as a top-level domain, or even a first-level domain. The subdomain is more commonly known as a *second-level domain (SLD)*.

The Internet's hierarchical domain namespace, just like UNIX operating systems, begins with *root* and branches out in a tree-like manner. This enables the creation of subdivided namespaces within higher-level domain names. The concepts of TLDs and SLDs are further explored in the next few sections.

Top-Level Domains

Jon Postel, the guiding light responsible for so much of the foundation upon which today's Internet was built, issued RFC 1591 in March 1994. Titled "Domain Name System Structure and Delegation," this document focused on TLDs and their administration. Administration of SLDs and host names was regarded as the purview of other entities.

The top-level domain was deemed to have certain generic domains that would be of worldwide applicability. These generic TLDs and their intended roles as listed in RFC 1591 are described in Table 8-2.

Table 8-2   *Some TLDs and Their Intended Uses*

TLD	Description
.com	Intended as a broad category for all commercial entities, .com has become the single-most immediately recognizable TLD.
.edu	Originally created for all academic and educational institutions, it is not uncommon to find universities, colleges, schools, and even organizations only marginally related to education contained in this domain.
.net	Designed for providers of Internet services, the .net domain has become an unruly collection that almost rivals .com in its breadth of registered names.
.org	Organizations that don't quite fit into any of the other categories need an area of their own. These organizations aren't commercial in nature, aren't educational institutions or government/military agencies, and aren't international. This might sound like a sketchy, poorly conceived basis for a domain, but that is why it was developed!
.int	Probably the least-recognizable TLD, the .int code is reserved for use by organizations established by international treaty or for international databases. One example is www.redcross.int, which is the Web site of the International Red Cross. Many entities that qualify for this domain also supplement their reach with domain names from the more-recognizable TLDs.
.gov	A mnemonic abbreviation of "government." It is reserved for use by the U.S. Federal Government and its subagencies.
.mil	A mnemonic abbreviation of "military." It is reserved for use by the U.S. Armed Forces.

The list presented in Table 8-1 is not comprehensive. Several new TLDs have recently been added, and almost every country enjoys its own unique *country code TLD (ccTLD)*. These are just the more commonly encountered TLDs. The new generic TLDs are examined later, in the section "Newly-Created TLDs."

Figure 8-2 demonstrates the relationship between root and the Internet's generic TLDs.

Sharing a common root can easily be taken for granted. However, you must realize that if TLDs didn't share a common origin, each of them would be an island. That is, they would be isolated and separate systems that would be required to resolve names within each TLD. Thus, a common root means that a single hierarchical system (albeit with widely distributed servers) can satisfy name resolution for the entire Internet.

Figure 8-2   *Root and the Generic TLDs*

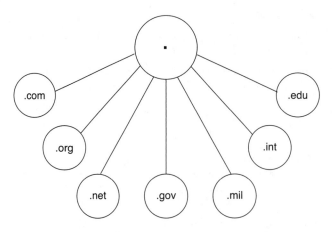

A Special Purpose

It is important to realize that each of these domains was conceived for a specific purpose. The notion of a charter for each domain was never formalized outside the RFC process, and no policing mechanism was ever developed. With the exceptions of .int, .gov, and .mil, virtually anyone could register a name in any TLD. The price of entry was limited to just paying the annual fee for the name registration. Consequently, the original intent became occluded over time—particularly after the Internet commercialized. At that point, it seemingly became standard operating procedure for companies to register themselves, and all their trademarks, trade names, brands, and so on, in each of the available TLDs. Although this completely violated the original intent of the TLDs, it ensured that no one could defraud the Internet community by pretending to be someone they weren't. This touched off a debate that still rages between technologists and intellectual-property lawyers. For more on this debate, see the sidebar near the end of this chapter.

Global Expansion of the TLD

If you detected a strong U.S. bias in the TLDs outlined in Table 8-1, you are correct. The bias begins with the abbreviations themselves—they are all mnemonic, but only in the English language. Even more obvious is the reservation of two generic TLDs just for the U.S. Government. In short, these domains reflect the evolution of the ARPANET into the Internet, which was predominantly a U.S.-based internetwork. Clearly, some work needed to be done to ensure the Internet's global scalability.

RFC 1394, published in January 1993, correlated TELEX answer-back codes to international Internet domains. This RFC formed the basis for TLDs to be assigned to each country. The result was an extensive list of ccTLDs. Despite this effort to ensure global consistency of TLDs, problems with the system remain:

- Trying to achieve consensus on what a country is
- Lack of standards for subdomains in ccTLDs

These issues are discussed in the following sections.

What's a Country?

Although it might seem simple, and even noble, to ensure that every country gets its own ccTLD, this is deceptively difficult. For example, it isn't difficult to find governments that are recognized as a "country" by some nations but not others. Sometimes the world community is split almost down the middle on this subject, with some countries backing one faction while others back another faction, regardless of who is in power. Thus, it is easy to forgive Internet Corporation for Assigned Names and Numbers (ICANN) for taking the easy way out of this conundrum. They are not in the business of bestowing political recognition on emerging nations. For that reason, it was decided to use standard ISO-3166 from the International Organization for Standardization (ISO) to establish the Internet's country codes.

Standards for SLDs?

The second concern is that there exists only a general sense of cohesiveness with respect to the conventions used to create subdomains inside each ccTLD. The ccTLD operators were left to their own devices when it came to how to use their country code. Given this, it shouldn't be surprising that there is disparity across the ccTLDs. Instead, it should be absolutely stunning that there is any consistency at all!

Some ccTLD operators have mimicked the generic TLDs of the Internet and have created .edu, .com, .net, and so on within their country code. Thus, to access a university in Australia, you would use anycollege.edu.au. Other country code operators have opted to conserve characters by carving out two-letter subdomains that reflect the same functional groupings. For example, Japan uses .co instead of .com and .ac (for academic) instead of .edu. Other subdomains that are frequently encountered within the ccTLDs include .go (government) and .re (research). To continue our fictitious example of anycollege, its domain name in Japan would be anycollege.ac.jp. This example is mapped out in Table 8-3.

Table 8-3   *Construction of a Hierarchical Internet Name*

Host Name	Subdomain	Second-Level Domain	Top-Level Domain
www	.anycollege	.ac	.jp

This example is important because it demonstrates that international users of the Internet have proven the viability of four-part FQDNs. The lack of absolute standardization for SLDs within ccTLDs hasn't hindered acceptance and/or use. A larger potential flaw lies tacitly in the fact that the very creation of ccTLDs implied that the generic TLDs were all but officially reserved for entities in the United States. Evidence of this bias can be seen in the relatively underutilized .us ccTLD.

The Case for Strong SLDs in the U.S.

Internet users in the United States have become accustomed to three-part addresses (hostname.SLD.TLD). Thus, within each generic TLD is a remarkable flatness—the very thing we were trying to avoid. This flatness would be OK if it weren't for the lack of enforcement of the original intent. Lacking any enforcement mechanism, the result has been a chaotic and extremely problematic pattern of market behaviors. These behaviors include the following:

- **Financial speculation on domain names**—Immediately after the Internet was commercialized, individuals began speculating on the future value of specific domain names. For a mere $35 annual fee, risk-taking individuals could reserve well-known names such as Pepsi, BMW, or any other globally recognizable brand name. The individual would gladly surrender the domain name to anyone willing to pay him or her lots of money. No laws prohibited this. This practice has become known as *cybersquatting,* and the people who do it are *cybersquatters*.

- **Defending against name/trademark infringement**—A slightly more insidious game that was often seen amounted to little more than trademark infringement. Entrepreneurs would reserve a well-known name and then use it for their own purposes. Today, it is still quite easy to find online gambling, pornography, and other seedy uses of the Net operating behind domain names that are intentional misspellings of famous names.

- **Defending against name/trademark speculation**—Owners of famous names and trademarks have found it necessary to proactively defend against the type of abuses just described. Consequently, it is not uncommon to find some large companies that have registered dozens of domain names across the spectrum of available TLDs to protect their image and brands.

The combination of these three forces has resulted in an absolute dearth of good domain names within the generic TLDs. Given the flatness of those TLDs, the result is a general lack of available names.

Follow the Better Example

Other countries have made much better use of their ccTLD and have avoided the flatness trap. Operators of ccTLDs have alleviated global name collisions by carving out the functional equivalents of .com and .edu among other generic TLDs within their ccTLD. For example, a company's domain name in Japan would be mycompany.co.jp rather than simply mycompany.com. More importantly, the same locally-recognized name (mycompany, in this example) could be reused without worry, because .co.jp is a different domain than .com. Alternatively, different companies with the same name could take advantage of the segmentation afforded by this extra hierarchical layer. In effect, the same name is used in different parts of the world without fear of a name collision. This example is shown in tree format in Figure 8-3.

Figure 8-3   *Hierarchical Structure of a Domain Name Within a Typical ccTLD*

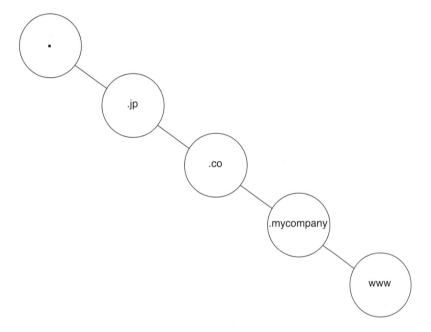

The original generic TLDs made sense. They were neither arbitrary nor capricious, and they served admirably as a logical grouping—at least, they did until people stopped following the intent behind their mnemonics. Thus, a credible argument could be made in favor of embracing these generic TLDs as SLDs within the .us country code and then enforcing their original intent.

The .us ccTLD, in comparison to other ccTLDs, is underutilized. You could argue that the cultural reliance of Americans on the generic TLDs has prevented the .us ccTLD from becoming as well-developed as other ccTLD namespaces around the world. Alternatively, you could place the blame squarely on RFC 1480, which was published in June 1993, as the reason for the underutilization of the .us ccTLD. The next section discusses RFC 1480.

RFC 1480

RFC 1480 is remarkable in that it specified a substructure for .us. Other ccTLDs have had no such structure dictated, but it was recommended that the mnemonic functionality of the original generic TLDs be replicated within each ccTLD. In and of itself, this reinforces the parochial thinking of the early Internet and demonstrates just how U.S.-centric it was! This RFC called for the .us ccTLD to be carved up geographically rather than functionally. Thus, it contained more than 50 SLDs—one for each state, plus a few others.

Furthermore, RFC 1480 called for a complex array of additional levels of subdomains. Including host names, an FQDN that fully complies with the hierarchical scheme posited in this document can result in a name that contains five or six names! The best way to understand this complex structure is to take it one layer at a time. For the sake of consistency, variable subdomain names appear in parentheses, and constants are explicitly identified.

Table 8-4 identifies SLDs that are direct children of .us. As such, they are parallel to the state's SLD. This relationship to .us and the Internet's root is depicted in Figure 8-4.

Figure 8-4 *Hierarchical Structure of SLDs Within the .us ccTLD*

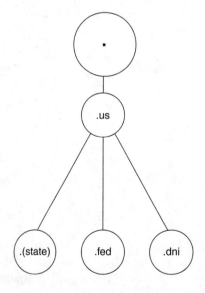

Table 8-4   *SLDs Within .us and Their Intended Uses*

TLD	Description
.fed	Despite the fact that there is already a .gov TLD, RFC 1480 called for the creation of an SLD under the .us TLD that would be reserved for use by the U.S. Federal Government and its myriad branches. A fictitious example (I don't know of any real ones!) is www.fedbranch.fed.us.
.dni	This SLD was created for distributed, but national, institutes within the U.S. Such organizations would span multiple states, municipalities, and so on. Although I can understand why someone would have thought this important, dni is hardly mnemonic, and I can't think of a single example that would showcase this SLD.
.(state)	Each state was given its own SLD, identified by postal abbreviations. For example, PA is Pennsylvania, NY is New York, and so on. This SLD branches into a complex array of subdomains that extend for several levels.

Of the various SLDs within .us presented in Table 8-4, the most interesting and complex is the .(state) variable name. The .(state) subdomains are explained in Table 8-5, and their hierarchical relationship is shown in Figure 8-5.

Table 8-5   *Subdomains Under .(state).us and Their Intended Uses*

TLD	Description
.state	Just to make things challenging for newbies (OK, so maybe it just feels that way), a .state subdomain was created under the .(state) SLD for use by that state's government branches. To better illustrate this, Pennsylvania's official state Web site is www.state.pa.us. The .(state) SLD is a variable; in this example it takes the value of .pa. Directly below .pa is the subdomain with the constant name of .state. This naming convention applies for all 50 states. This naming convention, though counterintuitive, complies with RFC 1480. Anyone accustomed to thinking logically would presume that pa is a subset of state.us rather than state's being a subset of pa.us.
(locality)	A wildcard subdomain of .(state) is .(locality). Not every government branch is part of the state government. There are county, municipal, and city government branches. These can be identified explicitly under .(state) directly, rather than appearing as a child of .state.
	Valid "localities" can include cities, counties, parishes, and townships. An additional sublayer of domain names exists in the form of the reserved names .ci and .co. These names are constants, just like .state, and they let city and county government agencies be explicitly identified in an FQDN. A fictitious example that identifies the Web site of the police department of the city of Easton, Pennsylvania might be www.police.ci.easton.pa.us.
	Alternatively, a county might be too rural to support well-developed cities. Another fictitious example of a police department in Pike County, Pennsylvania might be www.police.co.pike.pa.us.

continues

Table 8-5 *Subdomains Under .(state).us and Their Intended Uses (Continued)*

TLD	Description
.(locality) (*Cont.*)	The real question is, does the specificity afforded by these types of hierarchical names provide value to the organizations that the hierarchy was developed for? The answer appears to be no. Those organizations appear to prefer shorter, more-succinct, but less-specific domain names.
.gen	Conceived as a catchall for any organizations that don't fall neatly into any of the other RFC 1480 domains or subdomains, .gen refers to *general independent entities*. I have never been able to find any domain names created within this subdomain. If there were such a name, the domain name for Acme Products (I always root for the Coyote) in Arizona would be acme.gen.az.us.
.lib	Libraries, too, were given a reserved subdomain under .(state).us. Not many libraries use the .lib.(state).us domain. One library that does is the Hunterdon County Library in New Jersey. Its URL is www.hunterdon.lib.nj.us.
.cc	The .edu TLD has had a checkered past. It was originally set aside for all educational organizations, but then it shifted to just colleges and universities in the U.S. that conferred baccalaureate and/or masters degrees. This left out community colleges! Ostensibly, this was done to minimize the potential for name collisions among U.S.-based institutions of higher learning, but it relegated two-year schools to a subdomain under the .us ccTLD. Under this scheme, Raritan Valley Community College (another of my alma maters!) would have a Web presence at www.rvcc.cc.nj.us.
	Although this isn't a terrible domain name, it is much more difficult to remember than www.raritanval.edu (the actual Web site). Over time, U.S. colleges have demonstrated their preference for shorter, less-complex domain names by registering for mnemonic names in the .edu TLD.
.tec	Similar to community colleges, vocational and technical schools were also given a subdomain of their own. A typical school in New York might use the Web site www.vo-tech.tec.ny.us. Then again, they would be more likely to just register a domain name in .edu!
.k12	Yet another branch of education is kindergarten through 12th grade. In theory, schools in this category can register domain names in this subdomain. A fictitious example might be www.(school-name).k12.nj.us. Some public schools use this branch of the .us ccTLD, but you would have to search to find them.

Given this convoluted structure, the mnemonic nature of domain names becomes lost. Names defined inside .us have the potential to be up to six levels deep. At that level of complexity, you're better off just using raw IP addresses! OK, so maybe IP addresses are a bit of a stretch, but the fact remains that the .us ccTLD is underutilized. Entities that qualify for names within its stipulated substructure prefer shorter, more mnemonic names within the .org, .com, and even .net TLDs. Only government agencies seem to still use the structure set forth in RFC 1480. Even those agencies don't completely use the .us TLD. It is relatively easy to find such agencies with domains in .edu, .gov, .org, and even .com.

Figure 8-5   *Hierarchical Structure of Subdomains Within the .(state).us Domain*

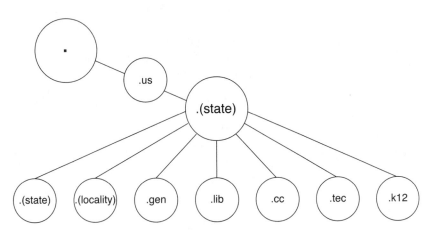

The irony hidden in the wreckage of RFC 1480-inspired domain names is that technological advances have diminished the significance of names as a means of accessing Internet sites. Search engines and sophisticated algorithms for gathering, categorizing, indexing, and keyword searching make it easier than ever to find information on the Internet, regardless of how simple or convoluted a host's domain name might be.

A recent interesting development that might obsolete RFC 1480 and rejuvenate the .us namespace is that Neustar, Inc. (www.neustar.com/) was recently awarded a contract to manage the .us namespace. Neustar has proposed expanding the .us ccTLD to allow registrations of domain names in the second level of .us. Simultaneously, they have proposed opening this namespace for competition between registrars. Together, these efforts are intended to create a more meaningful use of this namespace. Whether it will be successful remains to be seen.

Newly-Created TLDs

After a protracted debate, ICANN accepted a recommendation to expand the Internet's TLD namespace. Numerous issues were explored, but all parties generally agreed that there was pent-up demand for additional namespace. The areas of disagreement tended to be the following:

- Which new TLDs would generate the greatest benefit for the Internet's user community

- Who gets granted the right to sell names in any given new TLD and how that is decided

- How to protect the trademarks, trade names, and other publicly visible forms of intellectual property owned by any given company in an expanded Internet namespace

After vigorous, and thorough, debate, the working group assigned by ICANN to explore this issue offered a recommendation to expand the Internet's namespace with seven new TLDs. Of these seven, three would be *sponsored*. That is, they would be intentionally designed to serve a specific niche, and appropriate mechanisms would be developed to ensure that people and/or organizations attempting to register any names within that sponsored TLD met the criteria set forth in advance.

Table 8-6 identifies the new TLDs, specifies whether they are sponsored, and describes their intended purposes.

Table 8-6   *Newly-Sanctioned TLDs*

TLD	Sponsored?	Purpose
.aero	Yes	Air-transport industry
.biz	No	Businesses (an alternative to .com)
.coop	Yes	Cooperative organizations
.info	No	Not defined or restricted
.museum	Yes	Chartered museums only
.name	No	Individual people and families
.pro	No	Professionals such as accountants, lawyers, physicians, and so on

Not all of these currently can accept name registrations. Over time, all are expected to become operational. For more details, and up-to-date information on the status of these TLDs, refer to www.icann.org/tlds.

Sponsored Versus Unsponsored

The notion of a sponsored namespace actually isn't a very new concept. The original, generic TLDs were selected for specific niches, albeit very broad ones. In other words, they had a charter. Unfortunately, no one enforced their charter, and they became increasingly generalized over time. Many of the problems that have directly contributed to the near-depletion of meaningful names in the original generic TLDs can be attributed to the lack of enforcement mechanisms.

A direct corollary can be seen in the telephone system. The 800 toll-free number range was nearing depletion, so a plan was formulated to deploy 888 as an additional range of toll-free numbers. Unfortunately, many companies and organizations that had an 800 number (along with a fair bit of money invested in its advertisement) felt compelled to protect their investment by claiming the same number in the new range. Thus, the new range was nearly depleted shortly after it was put into service. Consequently, the 877 number range was opened for the same purpose, but it too suffered a similar premature depletion. Recently, 866 was assigned for toll-free calling. It seems likely that duplication of numbers from 877, 888, and 800 will prematurely exhaust even this new supply of numbers.

The same problem awaits TLD expansion. The only way to avoid this is to craft TLDs for a narrow, specific purpose and have a highly mnemonic name. Yet even this won't completely mitigate the problems that plague the Internet's namespace. Additional protective measures must include sentinels that watch over each portion of the namespace. Such sentinels, better known as sponsors, enter into agreements with ICANN for specific TLDs and operate them in a manner consistent with ICANN's goals. TLDs that lack sponsorship will continue to experience the same set of cybersquatting versus counter-cybersquatting market dynamics that have plagued the original generic and unsponsored TLDs.

Clever ccTLD Reuses

ccTLDs offer some potential for clever dual uses. Moldava, for example, uses the .md ccTLD. This character string lends itself nicely to the medical field in English-speaking parts of the world. It doesn't take tremendous imagination to see why a physician would prefer a domain name within .md as opposed to the same name in .pro or even .com. Simply stated, .md immediately, specifically, and unambiguously conveys their profession.

Another ccTLD that enjoys a highly mnemonic character string is Tuvalu. That country uses the .tv ccTLD, which also suggests a dual use in the Anglo-speaking world. The television industry could benefit tremendously from registering certain names within that country code.

Carving out mnemonic niches can be a potential source of revenue for emerging countries via the use of an underutilized asset. Linguistic differences also likely mean that the opportunity for name collisions to occur is remarkably small despite the domain's dual use. Unfortunately, the mnemonic value of a ccTLD varies greatly from country to country. Thus, not every nation recognized with a ccTLD will be able to successfully remarket name registrations to specialty niches.

Obtaining Your Very Own Namespace

Thanks to the mechanics of a free-market economy, obtaining your own namespace has never been easier. Your friendly neighborhood Internet service provider (ISP) can usually accommodate your request for a domain name on your behalf.

Alternatively, numerous entities are willing to sell the rights to use a namespace (caveats!) directly to you on an annual basis. Frequently, a valid credit card lets you complete this process online. ICANN currently recognizes about 90 legitimate registrars around the world. Dozens more companies have completed the accreditation process but have not yet become operational as domain name registrars. For a complete list of registrars, visit www.icann.org/registrars/accredited-list.html.

Be careful when selecting a registrar—they are not functional clones. Some registrars are chartered for only certain countries, and others are limited to selling namespace within specific top-level domains. Thus, it is imperative that you understand your particular needs and then conduct some research before attempting to register your own namespace.

Resolving Conflicts

Unfortunately, conflicts over name ownership happen far more often than I care to admit. Only in rare cases does a domain name actually reflect a truly global brand name that is so recognizable as to defy infringement. For example, Coca-Cola, AT&T, and IBM are well-recognized brand names in all corners of the world. Other names, such as "White House," are much more ambiguous. This can identify everything from the building located at 1600 Pennsylvania Avenue in Washington, DC to a fruit juice maker to an Internet pornographer. The question is, who has the legal right to the Internet name? This remarkably simple question is excruciatingly painful to answer.

Boiled down to its simplest, "White House" is a fictitious name under which an entity seeks to do business. Fictitious name registrations are obtained from the state within which a U.S.-based company is incorporated or headquartered. Those local government branches only verify that the name is unique within their purview; they do not attempt to establish a name's global uniqueness before granting the local rights to use it.

In the old days (before Al Gore invented the Internet), this made perfect sense. Today, however, even small companies can legitimately have global aspirations. So who gets whitehouse.com? And should that entity also have dibs on every possible permutation of that name? Would white-house.com, whitehouse.net, or even whithouse.com be confusing? (Note that last intentional misspelling. Many Web site operators intentionally select SLD names that are a simple typo away from large, well-traveled sites in the hopes of luring unsuspecting visitors.) Could someone claim brand infringement? Again, these are easy questions to ask, yet they all but defy answering.

ICANN has bogged down under the crushing weight of the legal and political entanglements of these superficially simple questions. It has embraced a *Uniform Domain-name Dispute-Resolution Policy* (UDRP). (OK, so the acronym doesn't quite fit the name. I didn't make it up!) This policy, although not intended to obviate conflicts over names, provides a framework for resolving the inevitable conflicts. Essentially, it placates owners of trademarks and other famous names by protecting them from cybersquatters. ICANN's policy can be found at www.icann.org/udrp/.

Nonstandard Internet Names

In this great age of open standards, virtually every company is tempted to re-create the benefits of closed and proprietary systems through private extension of the open standards. Even the Internet's domain naming system is not immune. Numerous private companies have sought to capitalize on ICANN's inability to quickly agree on an expansion of the Internet's namespace.

Expanding the Internet Namespace: The Good, The Bad, and the Ugly

The great debate about whether and how to expand the Internet's namespace transcends technical arguments. In fact, the technical aspects of any proposed expansion border on the trivial. Yet the debate has meandered through virtually every possible argument for and against expanding the Internet's namespace by increasing the number of TLDs.

The emergence of so many rogue registrars would seem to prove the economic viability of TLD namespace expansion. ICANN's inability to provide a quick answer to the popular clamor for new namespaces created an opportunity for entrepreneurial entities who weren't afraid to operate outside the Internet's standards by offering proprietary and nearly unlimited SLD/TLD combinations. Even a cursory examination of the whois database containing names "sold" by such registrars reveals an interesting phenomenon: Virtually all the names registered fall into just two small categories.

The first category is pornographic. Sad to say, this category represents the vast majority of SLD/TLD combinations registered via the rogues. Perhaps the best thing you can say about this is that capitalism is alive and well on the Internet, and this is an aspect of the Net that has proven itself commercially.

The second category is even more disconcerting. It can best be described as being illicit attempts at extortion. The game harks back to the very beginning of the Internet's commercialization. Many savvy individuals registered well-known names but did not develop any Web site or other Internet presence for those names. Such individuals merely waited until the legal owner of that well-known name (ostensibly a very large and well-funded company) became aware of the Internet's potential and sought to establish its own presence. At that point, the company either had to settle for a less-than-obvious domain name or had to negotiate with the "owner" of its Internet domain name. A modest annual fee had the potential to generate millions for those who had the foresight to see this opportunity and the willingness to play chicken with large corporations.

Despite the various *Acceptable Use Policies* (AUPs) and legal precedents established since those halcyon days, the other significant set of customers patronizing rogue registrars appears to be those bent on perpetuating that old game. Virtually every conceivable SLD/TLD combination for any given major corporation has been registered. This has given the large and well-funded corporations of the world adequate reason to staunchly oppose any expansion of the Internet's namespace. Such expansion, they argue, directly increases opportunities for infringement on their trademarks, brand names, and reputation.

As one of AT&T's two representatives on ICANN's Working Group C, I became intimately familiar with both sides of the debate. The sad conclusion I reached was that both sides were correct! There was, and remains, a tremendous need to improve the Internet's usefulness and scalability by increasing the number of available TLDs. However, that also increases the burden on virtually any company (regardless of size) that places any value on its trademarks, brand names, and so on. Failure to aggressively defend such property can be interpreted in the courts as an abandonment of that property. Thus, AUPs are of little consolation, and the cost of defending property only increases with each expansion of the TLD namespace if the new TLDs aren't carefully chartered and that charter rigorously enforced by an official sponsor.

ICANN chartered Working Group C to evaluate the desirability and feasibility of expanding the Internet's TLD namespace. Work in this group quickly got bogged down in politics and splintered into numerous factions. The great, and severely protracted, debate over whether to expand the number of available TLDs created an opportunity that has been exploited. Several "creative" organizations began offering virtually unlimited namespaces for an annual fee.

For example, the generic TLDs include .com, .net, .edu, .org, .gov, and .mil. Additionally, there are more than 100 country codes, such as .ca (Canada), .jp (Japan), and so on.

The rogue name registrars allow virtually any alphanumeric string to be assigned and used. Thus, even though sportack.com is already taken (and by a legitimate business, I might add), I could secure the rights to the mark.sportack namespace should I choose to patronize a rogue registrar. In such a case, mark would be the secondary domain and sportack the TLD. Obviously, such a TLD would have limited usefulness but would be very valuable to a very small number of people or organizations. This would be particularly true of famous names that are instantly recognizable globally without the context of a meaningful TLD. For example, Coca-Cola is a famous brand. You could argue that it is more famous than virtually any other registered domain in the .com TLD. Such a brand might benefit from being separated from the .com riffraff by having coca.cola as its domain name.

This approach heralds a dramatic departure from the original intent, and current usage, of top-level domains. TLDs offer a logical but extremely broad grouping for a very large collection of otherwise unrelated second-level domains. This is self-apparent in their names (commercial, education, organization, government, military, and so on).

Hcatcd arguments have been made both for and against such unconventional namespaces. Those in favor claim that they make the Internet truly user-friendly by removing the pigeon-holes that otherwise constrict name creativity. Those against claim that they lose the benefits of well-known TLDs that would let users make logical guesses at the name of a site they hadn't previously visited. I won't presume to judge the merits of such names, but I will point out that because they don't conform to Internet standards, they cannot be ubiquitously useful. That, in and of itself, limits their value.

Using Proprietary Names

To use these namespaces, you must point your browser to use their proprietary DNS. DNS is a networked application that automatically translates or resolves mnemonic names into IP addresses that network devices can understand and process. Such proprietary name resolvers support the full Internet namespace and also provide resolution of nonconforming proprietary names. Typically, the entity that "sells" you the annual rights to the use of a nonconforming name also supports that name in its DNS. Unless you are using their DNS, you cannot use that proprietary name. The name won't be recognized by conventional DNS resolvers and will generate an error message.

For a proprietary DNS to be successful, it must also conform to and resolve all the standards-compliant names in use throughout the Internet. The operators of such name-selling services understand that, and they ensure that their DNS is an extension of the standard Internet names. However, it is important to note that ubiquitous resolution currently is impossible, because the myriad rogue registrars do not cooperate with each other. Thus, yourcompany.yourcompany is an SLD.TLD pairing that might resolve to different sites, depending on whose proprietary DNS you are using.

Subdomains Within Private SLDs

There is yet another option for creating a somewhat proprietary namespace. It is technically possible for an individual or organization to register a domain name under one of the existing generic TLDs and then use it to create subdomains for sale to other organizations. For example, if you were astute enough to register eateries.com, you could conceivably sell the rights to subdomains created within that domain to virtually any restaurant operator. For example, "Eat at Joe's" could register the subdomain eatatjoes for an FQDN of eatatjoes.eateries.com. The URL would be www.eatatjoes.eateries.com. The overall effect is a longer domain name, but one that is highly mnemonic. In this manner, usability is enhanced by the creation of a more mnemonic SLD within an overly broad or generic TLD.

Summary

The use of mnemonic names instead of raw IP addresses dates back to the very beginning of the Internet's precursor. Since the beginning, this concept has depended on cooperation and collaboration to ensure the ubiquitous consistency of name-to-number translations. Although many helpful advances have been made, and DNS continues to evolve into an increasingly useful and dynamic tool, some members of the Internet community are dissatisfied with the pace of this technology's evolution. Consequently, the temptation—and the reward—of stepping outside the bounds of standardization have only been heightened by the Internet's commercialization. The only way to avoid the pitfalls of such entrepreneurial initiative is to be aware of them.

Having thoroughly examined the names and naming systems used in the Internet, you should be adequately prepared for the next chapter, which explores the structure and mechanics of today's DNS.

IP Multicasting

One of a network's most useful functions is multicasting. Not surprisingly, multicasting can be supported only if a network's addressing system has mechanisms that let it be supported, and only if those mechanisms are activated. IP multicasting at its simplest is a means of sending data from one device to many other devices simultaneously. Although nothing in IP prevents any particular end system from communicating with several other end systems, it is *how* communications occur that makes IP multicasting brilliant from the perspective of the astute and confusing for the uninitiated.

This chapter looks at the basic concept of IP multicasting, how it was implemented in the IPv4 address space, and some of the ways in which multicasting is supported.

The Concept of Multicasting

The basic concept of multicasting is simple enough: Reduce the total amount of bandwidth you consume by forwarding a single stream of IP packets to multiple recipients simultaneously. That was easy enough to say, but several assumptions and concepts that require further scrutiny are submerged in that definition.

The first assumption is that multicasting implies a type of communication in which two or more recipients want to receive the same data at the same time. You might wonder why you would want to send the same stream of packets to more than one destination. What practical purpose could that serve? From the perspective of the nontechnical end user, it can be difficult to imagine a scenario in which you would benefit from sending the same stuff to multiple recipients. These are all fair questions, and we'll make sense of all of them.

Another issue with multicasting is how you address an IP packet that is to be simultaneously delivered to multiple, specific destinations. Each IP packet has room for only one destination IP address in its header, so it is safe to assume that you need some mechanism in the IP address system that can accommodate this type of requirement.

This section examines some basic communications paradigms, including some examples of when each would be appropriate. This will help you better appreciate the niche that multicasting fills in an IP network.

Different Communications Paradigms

The Internet and other IP-based networks feature any-to-any communications. With the exception of local permissions, which may be configured by network administrators, this means that any system can communicate with any other system, provided that they are interconnected either directly or indirectly.

Perhaps the best way to demonstrate multicasting is to show you what it is not. There are three distinct paradigms for networked communications:

- Unicasting
- Broadcasting
- Multicasting

By examining them in the proper sequence, you can develop a better appreciation of multicasting. After a little thought, you should be able to quickly recognize which types of applications or network functions are good candidates for multicasting and which are not. Besides, as you'll see later in this chapter, broadcasting can be a very effective multicast mechanism if used properly.

Unicasting

Unicasting is a fancy way of saying one-to-one communication. This is how most Internet users communicate and interact with other users, systems, and applications. At its simplest, a single user communicates across a network or internetwork with another, singular system. That destination system could be someone's personal computer or a content-bearing server.

Many types of communications feature this type of one-to-one correlation between source and destination machines. Here are some quick examples of one-to-one communication:

- Sending a print request to a networked printer
- Sharing MP3 files with a friend across the Internet
- Using an IP-based e-mail system
- Pulling down stock quotes from the web

None of these are good candidates for multicasting, because a single, specific host is communicating with a single, specific destination. More subtly, communications must flow in both directions for each of these types of sessions to be successful. Any networked application that requires either reliable delivery of information or bidirectional communication is not a good candidate for multicasting.

Figure 9-1 illustrates unicasting between two specific end systems across the Internet.

Figure 9-1   *Unicast Datagrams in an IP Network*

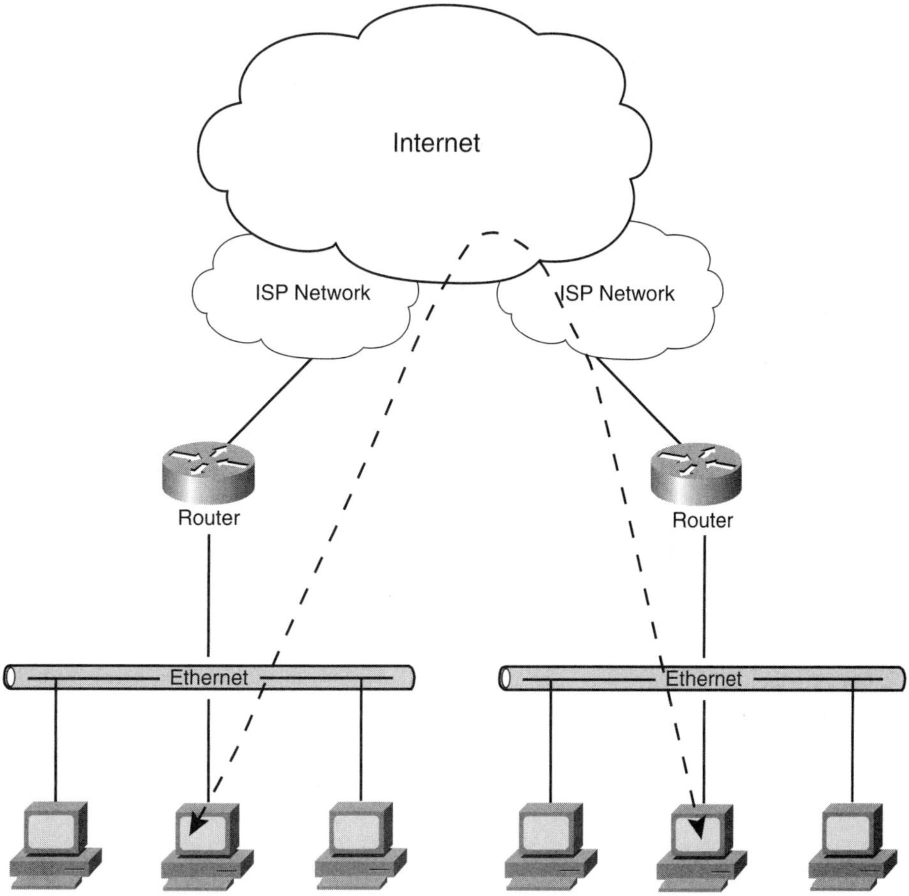

Broadcasting

The next type of communication is known as *broadcasting*. Broadcasting features one-to-all communication. In an internetwork the size and scale of the Internet, one-to-all communication doesn't make much sense. But on a more localized level, such a communication mechanism is ideal for many network-based functions.

Figure 9-2 illustrates the one-to-all form of communication that is broadcasting. The heavy dotted lines indicate the flow of broadcast datagrams. As evidenced in the figure, the router does not forward LAN broadcasts. The router's LAN interface is a part of the LAN community, and it must accept LAN broadcasts just like any other device in that LAN. Those broadcasts, however, are not forwarded.

Figure 9-2   *Broadcast Datagrams in an IP Network*

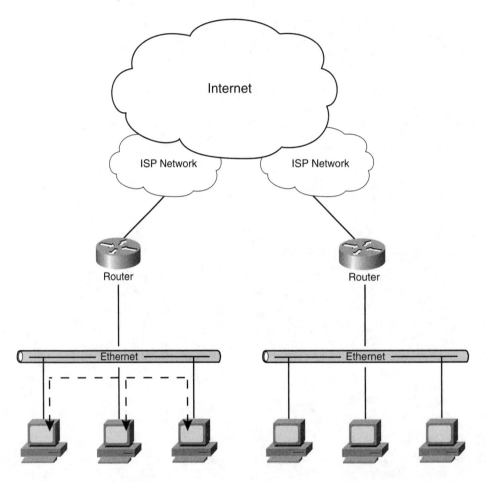

Broadcasting by its very nature isn't the type of communication that typifies end-user
communication across a network. Few, if any, end users need to communicate with every
other known endpoint connected to their network. Instead, broadcasting has become
extraordinarily valuable as a supporting mechanism for many vital network functions,
including routing table updates, and networked devices using address resolution protocol
(ARP) to build a table that correlates known MAC addresses (Layer 2) with their IP
addresses (Layer 3).

If nothing else, these two examples should demonstrate that broadcasting is a phenomenon of networking and not a feature of any particular protocol or technology. It is used in both LANs and WANs. There might be many different ways to implement and use broadcasting, but the fundamental paradigm of one-to-all communication remains constant.

Multicasting

This is another type of communication that can best be described as a one-to-many paradigm. With multicasting, a single specific host initiates a communication session. Each IP packet within that session is sent simultaneously to multiple recipients. The catch is that those recipients are quite specific; you don't just dump packets at random. For example, some online games need to work this way. The game server transmits the same packetized data to all active players. Obviously, this means that the players are participating in the same game. Otherwise, different data streams would be required!

In the absence of multicasting capabilities, this type of communication session would require the originating machine to generate a separate stream of packets for each machine it needed to communicate with. This isn't a very scalable approach in terms of either the bandwidth required or the resources required within the originating machine. From the perspective of the gamer, excessive loads on either the game server or the Internet are unacceptable.

Although this might seem like a trivial example, it is a real one. Internet-based games have become quite popular. Although many continue to feature unicasting, this genre of applications appears uniquely positioned to benefit from multicasting technology. In Figure 9-3, the communication stream is delivered very particularly to specific destinations, rather than being flooded to all systems within the targeted network.

That ability to target specific destinations is the very heart of multicasting. The key to achieving this selective delivery lies in being able to keep track of your intended destination machines and correlate that list with a single IP address that is placed by the originating machine into the IP packet's header. Each router would have to be configured to support multicasting.

Figures 9-1 through 9-3 all assume communication between end systems. Although they adequately demonstrate the distinctions between unicasting, multicasting, and broadcasting, they were designed solely to whet your appetite for multicasting. Multicasting can be, and is, supported in a variety of configurations, including communication between end systems and communication between routers. These are best thought of as different multicasting applications, because they both use the same set of multicast mechanisms.

Figure 9-3   *Multicast Datagrams in an IP Network*

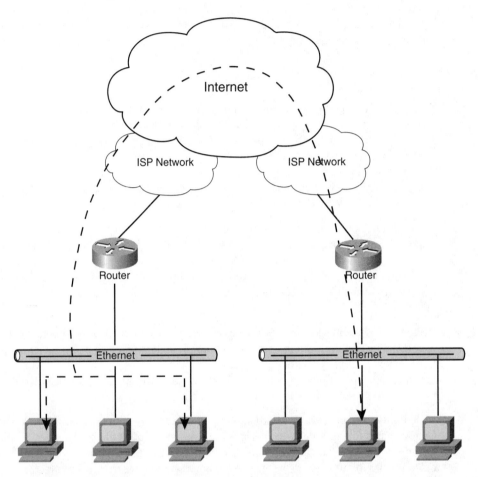

It is important to note that multicasting uses only User Datagram Protocol (UDP) as opposed to Transmission Control Protocol (TCP). Both are protocol suites that complement IP, but they function very differently. TCP is reliable in that it keeps track of individual packets sent and received (it must receive an acknowledgment of each packet received) and automatically puts received data back in its original sequence if it was received out of order. TCP can also determine if a segment of data is missing and can automatically retransmit it. UDP is a much less complex protocol. It offers a best-effort, unreliable transmission. If the data arrives at its destination, great. If not, live without it. Don't get the impression that TCP is better than UDP. They are different tools intended for different purposes. Knowing that multicasting uses UDP should tell you something about the intended field of use. Multicasting is a niche capability. It is invaluable for satisfying certain unique network requirements, but it is not a capability that can be used for every need. For example, if you needed to set up a streaming video session to transmit your company president's speech, you would find multicasting perfect. Streaming video is highly time-sensitive, so the additional overheads of TCP's reliable delivery mechanisms are not only unnecessary but antithetical to your needs. If a packet gets delivered late, just get rid of it. UDP's frugal overheads are ideal for supporting this type of application.

The next section thoroughly examines the multicast addressing mechanisms of the IPv4 protocol suite.

IPv4 Multicasting Mechanisms

Figure 9-3 should have raised a question in your mind. Although it demonstrated how a single flow of communications from one device conserves bandwidth by being forwarded to multiple destinations simultaneously, you should be asking how that can happen. After all, each IP packet has room for only one source address and one destination address. So how can you forward a packet with just one destination address to a limitless number of destinations, each with its own IP address? The answer is remarkably simple: Use a fictitious address that correlates to a list of real IP addresses. Such fictitious addresses are known as *multicast addresses*. The fictitious nature of such addresses sometimes results in their being called *multicast codes* instead of addresses. Both terms describe the same thing, but they are properly called addresses.

IANA (the Internet's authority for assigned names and numbers) controls the assignment of IP multicast addresses. Originally, the Class D address space was reserved for supporting multicast communications. The Class D address space was identified as all IPv4 addresses that begin with the binary string 1110. The remaining 28 bits were used to uniquely identify multicast groups. Mathematically valid addresses are in the range 224.0.0.0 through 239.255.255.255. These addresses are used individually as destination addresses and are explicitly carried as such in each multicast IP packet's destination address field. The source IP address used in the header of IP multicast packets is always the source address of the machine that originates the multicast.

Our review of IP addresses up to this point in the book should leave you secure in the knowledge that end systems can't be configured with an IP address greater than 223.255.255.255. Recall from Chapter 2, "Classical IP: The Way It Was," that this address was the mathematical upper boundary of the former Class C address space. Addresses above that were reserved for a variety of uses, including multicasting.

If an address is reserved, and it can't be assigned to an endpoint (much less multiple endpoints), how can it be used to communicate through a network? The answer is deceptively simple: The address corresponds to a list of unique destinations that were previously identified as belonging to a group that wants to receive multicast messages. These groups are the multicast groups we've been talking about.

Types of Multicast Addresses

Having seen how multicasting works, it's time to start looking a bit more closely at some of its specialized implementations. Multicast addresses are not created equal, or so it seems when you examine their prescribed functionality. Some addresses are limited in their effective scope to LANs, whereas others are global in scope. Others might be limited to just within a network operator's autonomous system. The four main types of multicast addresses are

- Global addresses
- Limited-scope addresses
- GLOP addresses
- Reserved addresses

A brief look at each of these multicast address types will help you better appreciate some of the capabilities and uses of multicasting.

Global Addresses

Some multicast addresses are truly global in their scope. This means that they are valid around the world and should be supported globally. Whether they are might depend on your service provider's position on multicasting. Without getting into that, just accept that some multicast addresses are supposed to be globally routable. As such, multicast groups whose individual members are scattered around the world, or even just across different networks regardless of their geographic location, must use global multicast addresses.

Limited-Scope Addresses

Another type of multicast address is the *limited-scope address*. Limited-scope addresses are typically valid only within a specific and finite scope, such as within a single LAN or WAN. This class of multicast addresses lets you satisfy local requirements for multicasting without adding to the burden of the Internet's routers.

A more subtle implication of limited-scope addresses is that they do not have to be globally unique. Much like the nonglobally routable addresses reserved by RFCs 1597 and 1918, limited-scope multicast addresses can be reused within different networks without a problem. Two examples of multicast addresses that are limited in scope are the reserved addresses 224.0.0.1 and 224.0.0.2. The first one is used to communicate with all systems on a subnetwork, and the second one is limited to all routers on a subnetwork.

GLOP Addresses

The next form of multicast address worth mentioning is the *GLOP address*. No, I didn't make up that name! RFC 2770, published in February 2000, proposed an experimental protocol for use in supporting multicasting across the Internet. A range of Class D addresses was reserved for use by this experiment. This range was termed *GLOP addresses* without any explanation of the apparent acronym. I like the name; I just can't explain its significance.

An output of the IETF's Multicast Deployment working group (MBONED), RFC 2770 was specifically designed to provide a static mechanism for assigning multicast addresses to protocols and/or organizations. Traditionally, multicast addresses were assigned from the available pool of addresses on an as-needed basis and then were reclaimed when the need expired. For example, a company might want to use multicasting for a new marketing promotion, such as live videocasting of a fashion show. When the show ends, the multicast code would be reclaimed.

Although that works well enough, it leaves the Internet without a really coherent approach to supporting long-term multicasting requirements. Dynamic allocation serves sporadic requirements, but as the Internet's user base matures, a more persistent mechanism will likely be required. That's where GLOP comes in.

The way GLOP works is simple: You embed a network operator's autonomous system number (ASN) into the second and third octets of an IP multicast address in the 233.0.0.0/8 address block. After having learned about Class D addresses in Chapter 2, you might be wondering about the /8 suffix. After all, these are *not* blocks of network addresses. Each multicast address uses all 32 bits for identifying unique groups. In this case, the /8 suffix identifies a group of addresses, as opposed to identifying the number of bits that routing decisions are based on. That leaves 24 bits for identifying unique multicast addresses within the 233.0.0.0/8 range.

Perhaps an example will help make this concept a bit more understandable. The example used in RFC 2770 uses ASN 5662. Expressed as a binary number, 5662 is 1011000011110. If you used this value as part of an IP address, you would have to pad it with three leading 0s. Mathematicians love to suppress leading 0s, but for reasons explained in Chapter 2, you can't do that for the subfields of a 32-bit IP address without fundamentally changing the overall address. Thus, expressed as a 16-bit binary number, 5662 translates into 0001011000011110.

Given that IP addresses are chopped into four 8-bit binary components, this 16-bit string must be segmented into two 8-bit strings. These strings are 00010110 and 00011110. Translating each to decimal yields 22 and 30. Thus, if the network operator that owned ASN 5662 obtained a GLOP address, it would be assigned 233.22.30.0. The fourth octet is available to that operator for specifying up to 255 multicast groups within its autonomous system.

NOTE   Some sources of technical literature insist on walking you through hexadecimal numbers when calculating a GLOP address. Whether you go directly from Base 10 to Base 2 and then to dotted-quad IP address notation or from Base 10 to Base 16 to dotted-quad is up to you. The mathematics of either operation yield the same result. Given that IPv4 is inherently binary as opposed to inherently hexadecimal, it makes sense to me to simply avoid the Base 16 number system in this case.

In theory, individual network operators reserve a numerically contiguous GLOP addresses for use within their respective routing domains. I say "in theory" because this is still just an experimental technology. Whether it becomes a permanent part of the Internet's technology base remains to be seen. I've included it in this chapter because it is an interesting proposal that seems to nicely fill a technological void. As such, I wouldn't be surprised if it advanced beyond the experimental stage.

Reserved Addresses

One of the more clever applications of multicasting is its use to satisfy locally bounded broadcast needs of specific technologies. In simpler terms, many niche network functions require one-to-many communications. Previously in this chapter, we assumed that one-to-many was defined globally. On that scale, one-to-all communications would be impractical. However, on a smaller scale, one-to-all communications are highly desirable and useful. When you think about it, a localized one-to-all communication session is actually one-to-many from a global perspective.

Reserving link local addresses enabled the implementation of localized one-to-all multi-casting. You know that IANA reserved a block of IPv4 address space (known collectively as the Class D address space) for multicasting purposes. However, less well-known is that specific addresses within that reserved block were then reserved for use in performing specific network functions. Table 9-1 contains a small sample of reserved multicast addresses.

NOTE   Multicast group codes are not reserved in any one particular place. Rather, the way they are used can be highly application-specific. As a result, reservations are made in a startlingly large number of documents. In no particular order, some of these documents include RFCs 1112, 1119, 1045, 1075, 2328, 1190, 1723, 1884, 2114, 2365, and 2730, among others. For a complete list of multicast address assignments and reservations, refer to www.iana.org/assignments/multicast-addressesIf you read through this listing, you will notice that specific applications use a specific multicast code. In that regard, multicast addresses can be reserved much like well-known TCP/UDP port numbers.

Table 9-1   *Sample of Reserved Multicast Addresses*

Reserved Address	Function
224.0.0.1	Broadcasts to all *systems* on *this* subnet
224.0.0.2	Broadcasts to all *routers* on *this* subnet
224.0.0.5	Reserved for use by OSPF routers in flooding Link State Advertisements throughout any given area, as per RFC 2328
224.0.0.6	Reserved for use by OSPF *designated* routers, as per RFC 2328
224.0.0.9	Reserved for use by routers running the RIPv2 routing protocol
224.0.0.10	Reserved for use by routers running Cisco's IGRP routing protocol
224.0.0.12	Reserved for use by DHCP and other relay agents
224.0.0.102	Reserved for use by Cisco's Hot Standby Router Protocol (HSRP)
224.0.1.1	Network Time Protocol (NTP)

Reserved multicast addresses number in the hundreds, if not thousands. This listing is just a concise sample to give you an idea of some of the uses of a multicast address. If you followed the link mentioned in the preceding Note to IANA's list of reserved multicast addresses, you would see an interesting pattern in the data. Most of the reserved addresses are used by network layer utilities, but some blocks are set aside for generic use in supporting voice and video communications.

NOTE   Multicast IP addresses function much like individual host addresses. For example, if you issue a **ping** command using a multicast address, each host that belongs to the multicast group identified by that address is compelled to reply.

A third, important use of multicasting is also evident in that list of addresses. Many companies reserve multicast addresses to directly support their online commercial operations or services. Two examples are Internet gaming and music services. This is an interesting contrast to a multicast address being reserved for use by specific network protocols.

Operational Mechanics

Having seen the various types of multicast addresses, the next logical step is to see how a router handles IP packets bearing a multicast address as the destination. From a router's perspective, *the destination of a multicast address is an interface, not an end system.* At the risk of greatly oversimplifying a complex and critical function, routers deploy a variety of mechanisms to discover other routers in a network or internetwork. After discovery, routers communicate with each other to share what they know about known destinations, possible routes to those destinations, and some measure of the efficiency of each possible route.

This information is stored on each router in a routing table. A routing table correlates a destination with the router's interface that should be used to reach end systems within that destination network. Usually, but not always, this destination is a network IP address. To better illustrate this point, look at the network diagram shown in Figure 9-4. This network features a single router that interconnects three LANs. Each host that belongs to the multicast group supported in this network is identified, and separate arrows demonstrate how datagrams are propagated in support of multicasting.

Figure 9-4   *Multicasting in a Small Network*

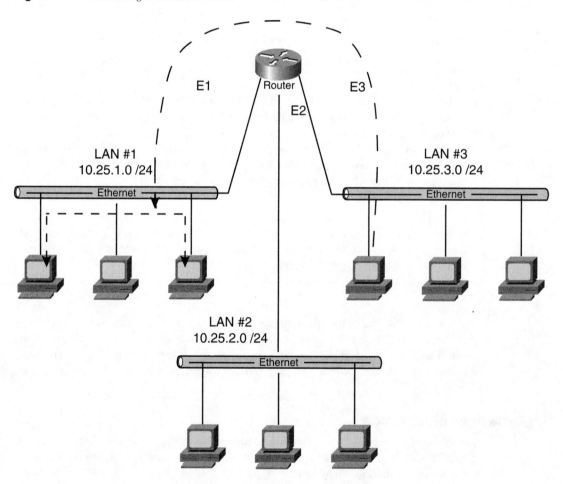

The router in Figure 9-4 would have a remarkably small routing table. Table 9-2 shows a very sanitized form of the theoretical contents of this router's routing table. For the sake of simplicity, we'll assume that only one routing protocol is in use. Each routing protocol maintains its own routing table, so this assumption lets us use a single routing table.

Table 9-2   *Routing Table Contents*

Destination Address	Corresponding Interface(s)
10.25.1.0/24	E1
10.25.2.0/24	E2
10.25.3.0/24	E3
224.0.0.3 (multicast address)	E1, E3

This routing table demonstrates just four entries: one for each of the three interconnected LANs, plus another entry for a locally supported multicast group. Given this simple network topology and routing table, you can see that the router does not attempt to forward packets to specific destinations. Instead, it forwards multicast addresses out the appropriate interface or interfaces. The onus is then on the downstream hosts to determine whether they are the intended recipients of a multicast stream of packets.

The next piece of the multicast puzzle lies in managing multicast addresses—or, more precisely, managing the groups of IP addresses that join a *multicast group*.

Group Management

It goes without saying that chaos would reign if there were not some central way to manage global multicast groups. Without such regulation, there exists the probability of two or more multicast groups using the same multicast address. The mechanism is known as Internet Group Management Protocol (IGMP). IGMP was first stipulated in RFC 1112, which has subsequently come to be known as IGMP Version 1, or IGMPv1 for short. An update that came about with RFC 2236 is known as IGMPv2. Both are designed to manage multicast groups by providing mechanisms for hosts and routers to share information about multicast group membership.

NOTE   From the perspective of IGMP, all members of a group are created equal. Thus, no mechanism inherent in the protocol enforces the role of sender versus recipient. The IP multicast model calls for all members of a multicast group to receive any datagrams addressed to that group's address. *You do not have to belong to a group to send datagrams to that group.*

IGMPv1

IGMPv1 manages multicast traffic using just two data structures: query packets and report packets. Query messages are used to poll network devices to determine whether they are members of a multicast group. Report packets, logically, are messages sent by network devices in response to queries. Reports notify the querying device of the host's membership status.

Responsibility for managing a multicast group's membership falls to the router. Routers configured to support multicasting generate query packets addressed to the all-hosts multicast address 224.0.0.1. In the case of the network shown in Figure 9-4, the router must generate two of these packets—one for each interface that supports multicasting. LAN #2 (10.25.2.0/24) does not support multicasting, and its interface on the router is not configured for this capability. Consequently, such queries are sent only to LAN #1 and LAN #3.

IGMP lets individual hosts dynamically register with specific multicast groups on their LAN. Hosts achieve this by sending IGMP messages to their local router. This router must be configured to support multicasting. Otherwise, it won't accept or act on any messages sent to the all-routers multicast address.

Joining Groups Using IGMPv1

Hosts must have some mechanism to notify their upstream router of their membership in a multicast group. Otherwise, that router won't know to forward multicast data streams to that host. Remember that the router doesn't track individual host membership in multicast groups, but it must track which of its interfaces have downstream devices that are members of particular multicast groups.

The way a host joins a multicast group is simple. In fact, there are two options. First, that host can wait for a query packet and then respond. Or it can simply generate a report packet without waiting for a query. Either way, the report packet lets a host identify itself as belonging to a specific multicast group or groups. The report packet must be sent to the all-router multicast group code 224.0.0.2.

Leaving Groups Using IGMPv1

IGMPv1 did not stipulate any specific mechanism for leaving a multicast group. Consequently, multicast members using this protocol leave groups passively. That is, they don't provide any explicit notification to their upstream router of their departure. Instead, such hosts simply cease responding to queries from their upstream router. The router builds its membership list based on responses, not nonresponses. So a host's failure to respond equates to a passive exit from a multicast group.

IGMPv2

IGMPv2 came about with the publication of RFC 2236. It is remarkably similar to its v1 counterpart, but it features numerous subtle improvements designed to improve operating efficiency by minimizing lag times for joining and leaving groups. IGMPv2 isn't quite as concise a protocol as IGMPv1, but it achieves its operating efficiency with just four packet types that are used for host-to-multicast-router communications:

- Membership query
- Version 1 Membership report
- Version 2 Membership report
- Leave report

In case you wonder why there are two types of membership reports, the answer is simple: It affords backward compatibility with IGMPv1-only machines. The version 2 Membership report differs slightly from the version 1 report in header structure and functionality. The version 1 header contains a field for explicitly identifying a protocol version number as well as an unused field that is set to a pattern of 0s.

The version 2 header replaces both of these fields with just a Type field (which identifies which of the four message types is contained in the packet) as well as a Maximum Response Time field. The Maximum Response Time defaults to 10 seconds, but you can change it manually in 1/10 second increments. Its function is to lower the time delay for joining groups by setting a maximum limit on how much time can elapse before a response is sent to a membership query. Implicit in this description is the fact that this field is meaningful only in a membership query. Membership reports and Leave reports cannot use this field.

The process of joining a group using IGMPv2 does not differ from that used in IGMPv1. However, the creation of a Leave report means that hosts using IGMPv2 can leave a multicast group immediately. Using the IGMPv1 protocol, such departures are passive rather than active, which translates into a longer interval before the multicast router recognizes the change in membership.

Summary

IP multicasting is one of those quixotic topics: absolutely indispensable, yet only selectively so. Only a fraction of the networked applications and functions that use IP can benefit from multicasting capabilities. However, that small subset runs the gamut. Uses range from critical router-level functions such as routing table updates in certain routing protocols to some of the Internet's more lighthearted uses, such as music distribution and online gaming.

Despite its reputation, multicasting is not some arcane form of sorcery. It is a logical extension of the capabilities of the IP suite, and it takes advantage of a reserved block of addresses. These reserved addresses can be used to support the development of local and/or global groups of addresses for multicast purposes. Having examined the multicast group addresses, as well as how those group addresses are translated into unique IP addresses, should have helped remove some of the mystery of multicasting.

Strategies for Network Stability, Scalability, and Performance

CHAPTER 10

Networking with IP

Up to this point in the book, we've focused on the IP address space—its theories, mathematical mechanics, and even some of its more advanced topics such as NAT. But it is imperative to realize that an IP address is much more than just an arbitrary number that gets configured on a network-attached device. An IP address is an active and dynamic part of the network and is used in support of numerous critical functions.

Its role is that of an intermediary. People who use IP-based networks are inclined to use mnemonic Internet names (such as www.mycompany.com) to access resources. Thus, it is imperative to correlate IP addresses to names. But LANs don't use IP addresses; they use MAC addresses. It is equally imperative to correlate IP addresses to MAC addresses. This chapter looks at how all this fits together in the context of a typical networked communications session.

Dissecting a Typical Communications Session

A "typical communications session" is a vague phrase that almost defies description. Depending on where you work and what technologies have been implemented, the typical network can have seemingly infinite variety. For the sake of example, let's assume that our network consists of Ethernet LANs that communicate via the TCP/IP protocol suite. We'll dissect this communications session within this technical context to better appreciate the active role of IP addresses.

We'll use a simple example throughout this chapter to demonstrate how the various network components interact and culminate in a successful communications session. The example uses Hypertext Transfer Protocol (HTTP) to access the website of a nearby host.

An Example

It's sometimes difficult to remember that there are other communications protocols besides TCP/IP. The successful commercialization of the Internet has made TCP/IP so ubiquitous as to make all other communications protocols seem superfluous. Given that the title of this book is *IP Addressing Fundamentals,* we'll limit our discussion of "a typical communications session" to IP. A scan of desktop settings reveals all sorts of IP and IP-like addresses.

Some of these numbers include the computer's own IP address, a Domain Name System (DNS), default gateway, and subnet mask. All this information is provided via an IP address, range of IP addresses, or IP-based mask and is intended to facilitate communications using that protocol.

That shouldn't be too surprising. The surprise comes when you stop to think about the layers of communications protocols in a "typical" communications session. Each layer requires its own addressing system. The TCP protocol suite uses protocol-specific addresses called port numbers to identify specific applications per host. IP uses numeric machine-level addresses to identify endpoint devices on a network. Also, LANs typically use physical machine addresses that are burned into the firmware of their interface cards to uniquely identify endpoint devices. To make matters worse, humans tend not to like using IP addresses. Instead, they vastly prefer human-friendly mnemonics such as www.mycompany.com in order to reach their own website, or jane.doe@mycompany.com to send an e-mail message to a coworker. Each of these examples of a mnemonic address represents a completely different paradigm for networked computing. That's symptomatic of networked computing in general. Networked applications have matured to the point that applications follow no single paradigm.

Given that caveat, we'll use a simple HTTP example to demonstrate the key concepts presented in this chapter. In our example, a human (John Smith) manipulates the keyboard of his desktop computer to view the website on a colleague's (Jane Doe) desktop computer. Their respective HTTP utilities appear to be communicating directly with each other to facilitate this transfer of web content. This perception is known as *logical adjacency*. Figure 10-1 depicts a somewhat abstract perspective of what happens in this sample communications session.

Figure 10-1   *The Logical Perspective: John Smith Accesses Jane Doe's Website, www.jane.doe.mycompany.com*

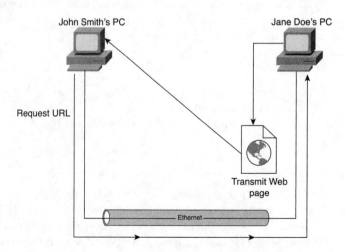

Layers of Protocols

So much for the logical perspective. Now let's consider what really happens by investigating the various layers of protocols that interoperate in support of a communications session. The communications session in our example uses HTTP. That protocol must reside on both devices in order for the session to be successful. Both devices must be able to communicate with each other, which means they need a network interconnecting them, as well as a networking protocol. The next thing we need is an address, or the two computers won't know how to reach each other.

John Smith is the one who initiates the session, so he must have the correct address. The address of Jane's website is www.janedoe.mycompany.com. This address is known as a uniform resource locator (URL). The URL is actually several bundled addresses. www is the name of specific web content, which is typically accessed using HTTP. That utility uses TCP's well-known port 80. In other words, it corresponds to an application-level address. The next portion, janedoe, is the name of a host within the mycompany.com domain. Logically, because janedoe is a host, it must have a unique IP address. That address is created from the IP network address block assigned to mycompany.com.

This nested series of addresses might initially appear to be everything you need to get the communications session going. You have an application port number, a machine name, and a domain name. But that's still not enough. Application-level addresses are valid only at the application level. That might sound a bit trite, but think about it. Even the most sophisticated and powerful software can't function without support from other mechanisms such as a network. Thus, you must conclude that the URL is really only an indirect means of identifying an addressee, not the last piece of information that is required to complete the delivery. If you stop to think about that for a while, you will realize that some means of correlating indirect application-level addresses with network-level addresses must exist. Otherwise, networked applications would have a very tough time functioning properly.

Figure 10-2 takes the simple topology of a web-browsing session and dissects it into its functional layers. This helps you better appreciate the sequence of events that are requisite to a successful communications session.

Figure 10-2 *The Layered Perspective: John Smith Accesses Jane Doe's Website, www.jane.doe.mycompany.com*

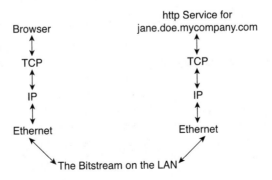

This session requires reliable delivery of data and uses the TCP/IP communications protocol suite. That protocol suite consists of two sets of protocols, with each set focused on different functions. TCP stands for Transmission Control Protocol. IP stands for Internet Protocol. It is a lower-layer suite of protocols responsible for getting data through networks.

TCP works in conjunction with IP. Each set of protocols is responsible for different, but highly compatible, functions. That shouldn't be too surprising, especially when you consider that they were made for each other. TCP, generally speaking, focuses on interactions with applications, including handling application data, and preparing that data for transport via IP. IP, generally speaking, focuses on getting packetized application data to the stipulated destination. Thus, IP is more network-oriented than application-oriented.

NOTE   TCP isn't the only suite of protocols designed for use with IP. Other classes of protocols include User Datagram Protocol (UDP) and Internet Control Message Protocol (ICMP). Although they are not quite as visible as TCP (and, consequently, are not as well-known), both UDP and ICMP are critical components of the comprehensive suite of communications protocols that has come to be known generically as TCP/IP, or simply IP.

But merely encapsulating data for transport across a network isn't equivalent to transporting it across a network. Thus, IP must rely on other mechanisms for transmission and local delivery. These mechanisms are provided courtesy of a LAN—Ethernet in this example.

This example nicely exhibits the interaction of the IP address space with other mechanisms both above and below it in the stack of communications protocols. We'll come back to this example and use it to demonstrate the interactions and correlative mechanisms that regulate hand-offs between the stacked protocols.

NOTE   The phrase "stack of communications protocols" implies two concepts:

- More than one communications protocol is required to support networked communications between devices on a network.

- Those communications protocols have a logical order or sequence.

Given these two points, it seems logical that a reliable mechanism, or set of mechanisms, is required to track the correlation between all these addresses. More importantly, you need to keep them synchronized in an environment that can be highly dynamic. The best way to explain this is to introduce, or reintroduce, the concept of a model that maps out the logical sequence of events in a communications session. It seems as if every communications protocol has its own model to explain how it works. We'll use the ubiquitous seven-layer Open Systems Interconnect (OSI) Reference Model.

The OSI Reference Model

The International Organization for Standardization (or ISO, as it prefers to be called) regulates global standards for a wide variety of technologies. When it comes to data communications, ISO tends to embrace and adopt standards established at either the national level (such as the American National Standards Institute [ANSI]) or the industry level. Consequently, the ISO isn't regarded as a powerhouse authority in any one field. Perhaps its greatest contribution to the field of data communications is its reference model that describes the sequence of events that are prerequisite to a successful data communications session.

The OSI Reference Model, shown in Figure 10-3, organizes all the requisite steps in a data communications session into seven layers that dictate the necessary sequence of events. Included in this figure is how TCP/IP and Ethernet fit into the model. This helps make the stacking relationship between these protocols more clear.

Figure 10-3 *The OSI's Seven-Layer Reference Model as It Relates to Commonly-Used Network Protocols*

OSI Reference Model Layer Description	Layer Number	
Application	7	
Presentation	6	
Session	5	TCP
Transport	4	
Network	3	IP
Data Link	2	Ethernet
Physical	1	

As is evident in Figure 10-3, TCP correlates loosely with Layers 4 and 5 and is responsible for interfacing with networked applications such as e-mail and HTTP. IP is distinctly a Layer 3 protocol. It provides all the mechanisms and functions necessary to transport application data across networks. All varieties and speeds of Ethernet occupy Layers 1 and 2. All these layers (and functions) are necessary to support a communications session.

The way they interoperate to form the logical adjacency between peer processes is simple: Data is passed from one layer to the next and, typically, is encapsulated. To illustrate this point, an application passes data to TCP. The TCP suite of protocols segments the data into more manageable chunks for transport across the network. Each chunk is numbered so that data can be put back into the proper order at its destination. Each data chunk is also given an application address (a port number) so that it can be delivered to the proper application. The TCP data segments are then passed on to IP. IP wraps the segments with packets. Packets bear the IP address of both the source and the destination machines engaged in the communications session. But packets are a Layer 3 construct, not a Layer 2 mechanism, so they must be handed off to a Layer 2 protocol for further processing. In this case, Ethernet accepts the IP packets and encapsulates them with a frame. The frame must also use source and destination addresses, but those are MAC addresses, not IP addresses. This structure can be transmitted one bit at a time on the LAN.

NOTE   TCP is the "reliable" transport protocol used in conjunction with IP. Being a reliable protocol isn't easy. It means that you have to guarantee not only that IP packets get to their destination, but also that they can be put back together in the right order after they arrive. To do all this, TCP relies on features such as sequence numbers and delivery acknowledgments. Such features are not necessarily a trait you find in all Layer 4 transport protocols.

When the data arrives at its intended destination, the encapsulation process is reversed. The Ethernet network interface card strips off the frame to reveal the IP packet entombed within. It then hands off that packet to IP. IP then removes the IP packet to reveal the TCP segment. The segment is passed on to the appropriate application based on the port number indicated in the segment's header. The net effect is that each layered mechanism logically appears to be communicating with its peer process on the other machine it is communicating with.

Identifying the Points of Translation

From the preceding discussion of logical adjacency, it should be somewhat obvious that there are a number of points at which a handoff is made between two dissimilar protocols or technologies. Identifying these points of translation is the first step in understanding them.

The two key points at which translation must occur are

- Translating mnemonic names into IP addresses
- Translating IP addresses into MAC addresses

Figure 10-4 shows where these translations occur in the stack of communications protocols.

These two translation functions are performed through separate mechanisms. Mnemonic names are translated into IP addresses via DNS. IP addresses are translated into MAC addresses through Address Resolution Protocol (ARP). We'll look at how each works throughout the remainder of this chapter.

Figure 10-4 *Points of Translation Relative to the OSI's Seven-Layer Reference Model*

OSI Reference Model Layer Description	Layer Number
Application	7
Presentation	6
Session	5
Transport	4
Network	3
Data Link	2
Physical	1

Mnemonics to IP Address

IP Address to MAC Address

Domain Name System

The Internet's addressing system is what makes its destinations accessible and usable. Without IP addressing, you couldn't use the Internet or any other IP-based network. Despite this, it's a rare geek who actually uses IP addresses directly. It can be done, but it would take a better brain than I have to remember all the numeric addresses of the hosts I need to access.

Another subtle benefit of mnemonics is that they greatly increase your chances of discovering new hosts. Although there are many tools for finding desired destinations, including search engines and hyperlinks, guessing at a domain name remains a very useful and expedient technique. Such a heuristic approach to finding content is much more productive than trying to guess the IP addresses of Internet sites you think you'd like to visit. Mnemonic names are absolutely essential to making the Internet, and all IP-based networks, usable and useful.

Chapter 8, "Internet Names," traced the emergence of names as an informal and local-use mechanism, through its standardization across ARPANET (the Internet's predecessor), and its maturation into a standardized and hierarchical system that can reliably translate user-friendly names into numeric addresses. We stopped just shy of showing how DNS fits into the larger context of an IP-based communications session.

We'll begin our exploration of the hierarchical nature of DNS by looking at how servers are distributed throughout the Internet to support name-to-number translations. As you might expect in a global network, the DNS is deployed in a highly distributed manner.

Unlike some other network functions that must be built and supported for each network, DNS can work across networks. As a result, many end-user organizations choose not to build their own DNS. Instead, they use their service provider's DNS.

Distributed Architecture

The distributed nature of DNS is a function of the Internet's namespace architecture. Thus, exploring the namespace architecture is a great way to understand DNS. The Internet's namespace is subdivided into mnemonic domains known as top-level domains (TLDs). Although the original mnemonic intent of the TLDs has become greatly diluted through misuse, the resulting hierarchy of TLDs still provides a marvelous mechanism for subdividing name resolution across the Internet. The Internet has only one root (the proverbial "dot" discussed in Chapter 8), and all the TLDs are subordinate to that root. In practice, the Internet has become so large and heavily used that it is not feasible or desirable to use just one name server for this root. More than a dozen servers back each other up and function as the place to start when you're seeking to resolve a name. For now, let's regard this root name service as a single, logical entity.

Under the root are the TLDs. Each TLD has its own name server. These servers are TLD-specific; they cannot resolve names that lie in the others' domains. For example, the .com name server cannot resolve example.net. Nor does the root name server expect it to do so. Consequently, the root name server only refers queries about names within the .net TLD to the .net name server. In industry parlance, the .net name server is authoritative for the .net TLD. Figure 10-5 shows the distributed nature of name servers within the Internet on a very limited scale.

NOTE   Consider the example shown in Figure 10-5 as illustrative only. In reality, the .net and .com namespaces share a single authoritative name server.

Figure 10-5 *The Distributed Architecture of Name Servers Within the Internet*

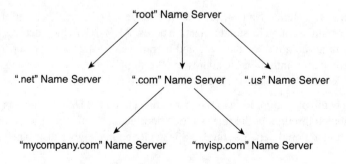

Individual companies, including end-user organizations and service providers, may operate their own name servers. These servers also fit into the hierarchy. They are authoritative only for the domains run by that company.

The operational implication of this distributed architecture is that you can minimize the burden of each name server in the Internet's myriad networks. A name server doesn't have to know every name defined across the Internet; it just has to know the name and address of a name server that does. To borrow a sporting colloquialism, DNS plays zone defense. The namespace is carved into zones. Responsibility for these zones is clearly defined among the various DNS servers that track Internet names and answer queries within their assigned zone.

Zones Versus Domains

The Internet's DNS uses decentralization to maintain acceptable levels of performance for name resolution. One such approach to decentralization is to carve the namespace into zones based on domain names. The result is that a given name server may be authoritative for a specific domain but not for the entire top-level domain. That probably sounded a bit vague, so let's look at a figure that helps reinforce that point.

Chapter 8 showed how TLDs are carved into second-level domains (SLDs) and subdomains. There's no need to rehash things completely, so let's just focus on a TLD carved into a couple of domains. Figure 10-6 shows an example. Superimposed over the domain levels are dotted lines that show the zones of authority.

Figure 10-6 *Zones of Authority Relative to Domains and Subdomains*

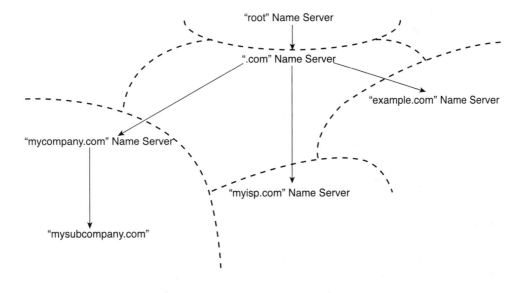

Figure 10-6 shows how zones can be created within a namespace. A separate name server can be deployed for each zone. Each name server can answer questions about names and numbers for servers defined within its domain or subdomain. The only subdomain in evidence is mysubcompany.com, which is a subsidiary of mycompany.com. The subdomain mysubcompany.com does not have its own name server. It relies on the mycompany.com name server. In other words, the name server is authoritative for that subdomain. For names that are outside its zone, the name server can figure out whether the query is of a higher or lower level relative to itself in the hierarchy. Based on that determination, the name server knows which other name server either has the right information to answer the query or is the next server in the hierarchy that gets the query closer to resolution.

Resolving a Name

The preceding two sections looked at how the hierarchy of the Internet's namespace influenced the distributed nature of DNS. We touched on the concept of name servers but skipped the process of translating mnemonic names into numeric IP addresses. Translating a name into a numeric address breaks down into two distinct functions. We've already looked at the name server. The other service is known as the *resolver*. We'll cover both the name server and the resolver in more detail in the next two sections. By way of exploring the functions of these two servers, you can also see more precisely how name resolution fits into the context of an IP communications session.

Name Servers

You've seen a bit of how the name servers are arranged hierarchically and are given authority over a specific zone. What you haven't seen is how that hierarchy of authority actually works.

The name server keeps a table of all names defined in the Internet's various domains. When queried, the name server replies. The distributed nature of DNS means that you can config-ure certain name servers to be authoritative for their zone. When queried, the name server responds with the appropriate IP address for the mnemonic being queried *if it resides within the name server's authoritative zone*. If the mnemonic lies outside the name server's authority, the name server is obligated to respond with the IP address of the next name server in the hierarchy that it believes is the next step closest to the host name being queried. In this manner, a name server might not be able to answer your questions, but it gets you closer to the answer.

Resolvers

A resolver is a computer that receives requests from applications, which might reside on different computers, such as end-user workstations. The resolver then polls its list of name servers to retrieve the needed information. After receiving that information, it interprets it to see if it looks valid or erroneous. If the information is valid, the resolver responds to the requesting application. Some versions of resolver software are more sophisticated and can build a cache of names that have been resolved. This has the significant benefit of reducing the amount of time and resources required to resolve names. You still have to go through the process of contacting name servers to get an answer the first time, but subsequent queries can be satisfied by checking the cached table of names and addresses.

It is important to note that having resolvers doesn't necessarily displace the burden of resolution. Indeed, the name servers are still ultimately responsible for resolving a name into an IP address. The role of the resolver does, however, mitigate the workload placed on name servers by intercepting requests and by chasing down the correct answer to the query. The next section shows the interaction between an end user, the resolver, and the hierarchy of name servers.

Walking Through the Process

Unless the resolver knows that the name being queried is within its domain, or already has it cached, the resolver starts at the top of the appropriate domain name tree and follows the hierarchy of authority.

If we go back to the example of John Smith accessing a website on Jane Doe's desktop, we can walk through the process. Assuming that both people (and, more saliently, their computers) reside within the same domain and share a common name server that is authoritative for that domain, the example is relatively straightforward. John Smith attempts to establish an HTTP session with Jane Doe's computer by feeding his browser the address www.jane-doe.mycompany.com.

Although that address might satisfy the requirements of the application software, it doesn't fly as far as TCP/IP is concerned. That protocol suite must seek a translation of janedoe.mycompany.com into an IP address before it can do anything else. In this example, we've conveniently located a DNS name server on the same LAN as both John's and Jane's computers. The IP address of that name server is statically configured on each computer in that network, so they all know where to go to get a good name-to-number translation. Figure 10-7 shows the steps required for that translation.

John Smith's computer sends a request to the name server. Because this is a small environment, the load on the server isn't great. Thus, the decision was made to not purchase and install a separate machine to specialize as a resolver. The name server can step up to the extra work. The name server recognizes that the host name lies within the mycompany.com domain and that it is authoritative for that domain. As a result, no referrals or recursive queries are needed. The name server simply looks up janedoe in its table and replies to John Smith's computer with the IP address that corresponds to janedoe. Now John Smith's computer knows how to get the website hosted by that computer.

Figure 10-7 *Resolving a Name Within the Same Domain and Zone of Authority*

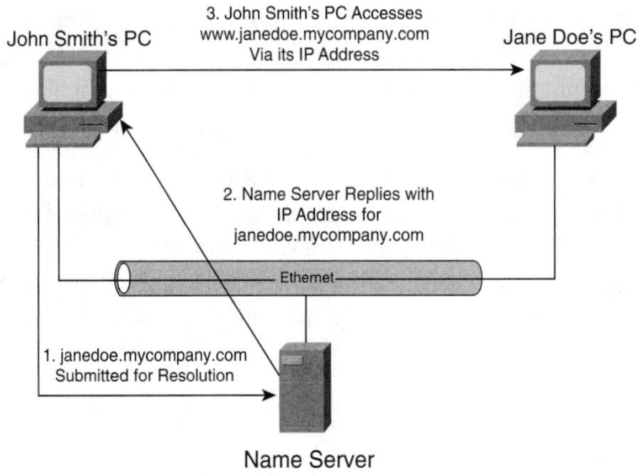

This example is almost too simple. Yet it shows how things work locally. Let's stretch the example and assume that John Smith is at home and connects to his colleague's desktop website from a different domain. Suspend your belief in proper network security for the sake of this example, and just assume ubiquitous connectivity without the complexity of firewalls, demilitarized zones, or other defenses against unwanted access to a private network. That doesn't make for the most realistic of examples, but it makes the mechanics of the basic process easier to follow.

Given this example, there are two approaches for resolving names: iterative and recursive. They differ only in their mechanics and where the burden of processing lies rather than in their results. We'll look at both using the example.

Iterative Queries

An iterative query is one that is completed in stages or iterations. In other words, the machine you query might not have the answer to your query, but it knows where to look for the answer. It chases down your query, getting ever closer to the answer, until it finds it.

Figure 10-8 shows John Smith accessing Jane Doe's website via his local ISP. As a result, the two computers lie within the same TLD (.com) but different SLDs (mycompany.com versus myisp.com).

Figure 10-8 *The Iterative Process of Resolving a Name Via a Resolver That Proxies the Request to Name Servers*

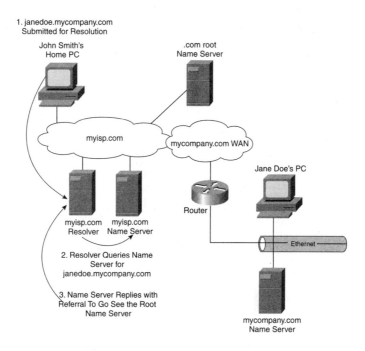

The first big difference from Figure 10-7 is that the ISP has configured a resolver. That machine becomes John Smith's first stop in trying to resolve www.janedoe.com into an IP address. The resolver accepts his query and, in turn, queries the myisp.com name server. That name server is not authoritative for the SLD being queried. Consequently, it can't provide an answer to the query. Because the resolver issued an iterative query as opposed to a recursive query, the name server simply refers the resolver to the next-closest machine to the zone of authority in which it believes the jane.doe machine resides. In this case, it refers the myisp.com resolver to one of the Internet's root name servers.

NOTE   The concept of iterative querying assumes that the resolver is intelligent enough to process a referral. Not all resolvers have this capability. Some, referred to as stub resolvers, can only issue queries.

The resolver must then query the root name server for an IP address for mycompany.com. The root name server, however, tracks only TLDs. mycompany.com is an SLD, not a TLD. Thus, the root name server, too, must provide a referral to the resolver instead of an answer to the query. It refers the resolver to the name server that is authoritative for the .com TLD.

The resolver must then query the .com name server. Unfortunately, it also doesn't know the IP address for janedoe.mycompany.com, but it does know the IP address of the name server that is authoritative for mycompany.com. It provides the resolver with that address. Armed with this information, the myisp.com resolver finally can translate John's (remember him?) request into an IP address. Figure 10-9 shows the final steps in using the iterative process to resolve a name.

Figure 10-9 *The Final Steps in Iterating Toward Resolving a Name*

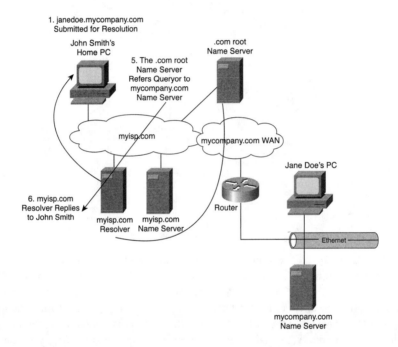

As long and painful as this process might sound, the hierarchical arrangement of zones results in a remarkably efficient distribution of workload. Provided that there are no congested areas of the Internet, or other problems, the total time to translation can be remarkably quick. I offer as proof the fact that everybody uses DNS, but few people complain about it (unless, of course, a name server is down or there are other network-affecting problems).

Recursive Queries

The recursive approach to resolving names is very similar to the iterative approach. It must be, due to the hierarchically distributed nature of DNS. Using the same example, let's look at the steps involved in a recursive query. John's computer queries the myisp.com resolver, looking for an IP address to janedoe.mycompany.com. That resolver begins by issuing a recursive query to the myisp.com name server.

The fact that it is a recursive query obligates that name server to keep digging until it comes up with the answer. The resolver either does not or cannot accept referrals. That subtle difference in query type from the resolver to the name server determines where the burden of the search is placed. As you saw in the iterative query, the burden was placed on the resolver. In this case, the resolver places the burden on the name server. This is illustrated in Figure 10-10.

Figure 10-10   *The Recursive Process of Resolving a Name Via a Resolver That Proxies the Request to Name Servers*

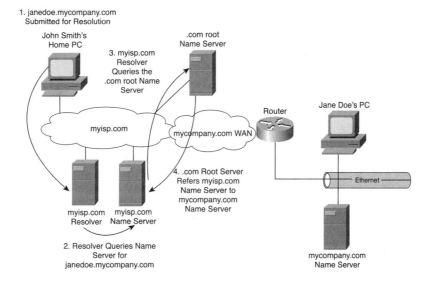

The myisp.com name server must go through the same sequence of events as previously described. If mycompany.com buys access and other services from myisp.com, the two name servers probably are linked hierarchically. If that's the case, the myisp.com name server can resolve John's request by querying the mycompany.com name server directly. Otherwise, the myisp.com name server knows that it isn't authoritative for the mycompany.com domain, so it issues a request to the root's name server. The root responds by referring the myisp.com name server to the .com name server. The myisp.com name server must then query the .com name server, which, in turn, recognizes that it is not authoritative for the domain being queried. But it refers the myisp.com name server to the mycompany.com name server. The myisp.com name server finally gets the answer that the myisp.com resolver is looking for when it queries the mycompany.com name server.

The myisp.com resolver completes its mission by replying to John's computer with the IP address of Jane's desktop computer. John's browser can then retrieve the information it is waiting so patiently for. This is illustrated in Figure 10-11.

Figure 10-11 *The Last Steps in Using the Recursive Approach to Resolving a Name*

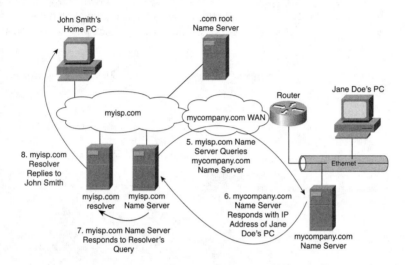

It is important to realize that we skipped a step in the two iterative name-resolving scenarios we just examined. That step is converting IP addresses to physical or MAC addresses. Overlooking that little detail greatly simplified our scenarios and made it possible to focus on the role and mechanics of name servers and resolvers. The next section rounds out your appreciation of IP-to-MAC address translation by looking much more closely at the processes and mechanisms that enable that translation.

The Dubious Benefit of Reverse DNS

Although DNS is one of those functions you can't ignore, it has a sibling that you almost don't notice. That sibling, Reverse DNS (RDNS), is one of those quirky utilities that most people never even know exists. It is, as its name implies, the opposite of DNS. DNS facilitates human usage of IP networks by allowing them to access hosts using user-friendly names for both hosts and domains. Although these two fields might not necessarily translate cleanly into numeric host and network addresses, they usually translate reliably. RDNS lets you find domain names when all you have to work with is an IP address. RDNS is a search utility that reflects the registration information for each network address block, whether it was directly registered to a company or assigned for temporary use and recorded via the SWIP process.

RDNS also is implemented by some applications as a crude substitute for authentication. For example, some FTP programs attempt to authenticate a user's host name with his or her IP address by checking RDNS to see if they match.

As I said before, this is almost never of value, and the vast majority of IP network users never even hear of RDNS. The few who do are almost exclusively hostmasters or technical personnel who work for an ISP. Such personnel are keenly aware of their employers' identity, and they want to make sure that if someone enters his IP network address in an RDNS search utility, he comes back with the right name.

This leads us to the one dubious benefit of RDNS. A fair number of CIDR address blocks that I have had ex-customers try to walk away with have come to my attention via trouble tickets opened by those ex-customers. Logically, anyone astute enough to appreciate the value of a directly registered network address space would also appreciate the value of correct RDNS information. When those ex-customers call and complain that their RDNS doesn't work right, I'm more than happy to tell them, "Of course it doesn't!" But thanks for letting me know you've taken some of my address space!

Translating IP Addresses into MAC Addresses

The second of our two original translation requirements was translating IP addresses into MAC addresses. Network devices really communicate via physical addresses. Physical addresses, although they are typically globally unique, are valid only for communications within a single Layer 2 domain. In the world of Ethernet and other networks standardized via the IEEE's 802 family of network protocols, physical addresses are known as *MAC addresses*.

Previous chapters of this book have conveniently overlooked that point in order to focus on IP addresses and their function in a network. Now it's time to complete that picture. Networked devices really communicate locally using local mechanisms. Let's assume, for the sake of example, that our local mechanism is an Ethernet network. Figure 10-12 shows a few devices connected via an Ethernet. Two of these devices are hosts that, ostensibly, originate the majority of communications sessions. The other is a server that, at least in theory, is the intended destination of most communications sessions on this LAN.

Each endpoint has a unique IP address assigned to it, so this shouldn't be a problem. At least, that's how it looks. In reality, Ethernet (as is every other LAN protocol) is not IP-based. The reason has everything to do with the concept of logically separated functions. You have probably heard all about the OSI Reference Model and its seven layers. The concept embodied in the reference model is what has enabled open communications and cross-vendor interoperability of networking products.

Figure 10-12 *Although Networked Devices Are Uniquely Identified Via an IP Address, a Physical Address Is Required for Successful Communications*

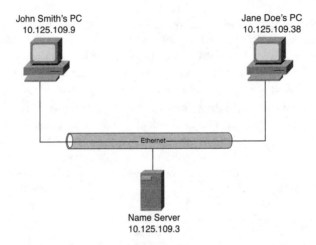

Ethernet and other LAN protocols operate at Layers 1 and 2 of this model. IP and other routed protocols operate at Layer 3. This well-defined separation of functions enables interoperability of IP and Ethernet. But this interoperability takes the form of Ethernet encapsulating IP packets within Ethernet frames for transport through the LAN. Upon reaching its intended destination, the Ethernet frame is stripped off, thereby revealing the IP packet that was embedded in its data field.

This might seem logical enough, but a step is missing. Ethernet and IP are dissimilar protocols. Each has its own addressing system, and those systems are incompatible. Thus, it is necessary to translate IP addresses into MAC addresses for the layered communications session shown in Figure 10-12 to work. This is where ARP comes into the picture.

dress Resolution Protocol

ARP is one of those network protocols you use every day without realizing it. That's because it operates invisibly, without requiring initiative, input, or intervention from individual users. Its function is quite simple: It tracks the correlation between physical MAC addresses and IP addresses for every device attached to the same LAN. So, the step that was missing from the previous example is that ARP "reads" each packet's destination IP address. It then looks in its cache to see if it already knows that IP address. If that IP address appears in the ARP cache, ARP grabs the corresponding MAC address, and that gets used as the destination address in the Ethernet frame.

NOTE   Due to its function as an intermediary between a LAN and the IP suite of protocols, you might be hard-pressed to figure out whether ARP is a LAN protocol or one of the IP protocols. In fact, ARP was originally stipulated in November 1982 in RFC 826. Thus, it is distinctly a native component of IP. RFC 826 positioned ARP as an IP-to-Ethernet mechanism, but it was subsequently extended to all the IEEE's 802 LANs, as well as to FDDI.

Given this role, it becomes clear that ARP must track the correlation between MAC addresses and IP addresses for all devices that lie within the same LAN broadcast domain. This correlation is maintained in a table by each network-attached host. This table is called the *ARP cache*. How that table gets built and is maintained is important in understanding the dynamic and active role that IP plays in a network.

Building the Table

Each host on a LAN builds a table of MAC addresses on its network and maps those addresses to Layer 3 (in this case, IP) addresses. ARP relies on LAN broadcast mechanisms to do this. As you learned in Chapter 9, "IP Multicasting," broadcasting is a technique that lets you transmit a single stream of data for delivery to all the other hosts on your network. Although that chapter dealt with multicasting based on IP addresses, broadcasting is also a native function of every LAN. LAN broadcasting is the capability that forms the foundation of ARP.

Upon startup, each host on a network must begin the arduous task of populating its ARP cache table. To do this, the host uses the LAN's broadcast message to transmit an *ARP request packet*. Such request packets are generated *as needed*. In other words, when a host needs to communicate with another host on behalf of one of its applications, it ultimately needs to convert that destination machine's IP address to a MAC address. An ARP request is generated to look for that specific IP address and is broadcast throughout the LAN. Only the machine whose IP address matches the query is compelled to respond to the request packet.

The response—known as an *ARP reply*—contains the responder's IP address and MAC address. This information lets the querying device build a comprehensive table of devices known to be operating on the same LAN by both their MAC and IP addresses, as needed.

Figures 10-13 and 10-14 better demonstrate this request-and-reply process. Figure 10-13 shows a desktop computer on a LAN broadcasting an ARP request throughout that LAN in an effort to find a MAC address that correlates with IP address 10.125.109.3. Notice that the request is even accepted by the router interface. The router does *not* forward this broadcast. But inasmuch as one of its interfaces is connected to the LAN, it is obligated to accept the MAC broadcasts of that environment just like any other device.

Figure 10-13 *A Desktop Computer Transmits an ARP Request Throughout the LAN to Find a MAC Address for Host 10.125.109.3*

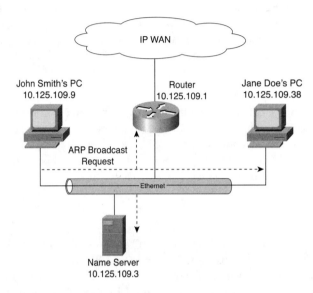

Figure 10-14 shows the device on that LAN with that IP address replying to the ARP request. This reply lets the requesting desktop computer build its ARP cache. Using this approach, the requesting desktop can obtain all the MAC addresses it needs to communicate with its local peers.

Figure 10-14 *Other Devices in the LAN Reply to the ARP Request, Supplying the Requesting Device with Their IP and MAC Address*

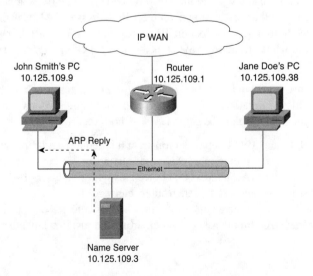

NOTE   At the risk of restating the obvious, machines communicate across a LAN using MAC
addresses. IP addresses are required only when machines communicate between two or
more networks, or if the application requires that protocol. Given the near-complete
dominance of IP, many applications require IP. This can create the misperception that IP
is required to communicate on a LAN.

Keeping the Table Current

Having seen how an ARP cache gets built, you might be wondering how long such a table
can stay current. The answer is "not long." Think about it: Not everyone shows up at work
at the same time. Nor does everyone leave at the same time. Consequently, desktop and
laptop computers are powered up and powered down at staggered intervals in the morning.
If a machine isn't plugged into the network or isn't powered up, it can't respond to a
neighbor's ARP request. So, some means of keeping an ARP cache current is required. Of
course, the notion of desktops and laptops coming online and offline, obsoleting an ARP
cache, implies that peer-to-peer communication is actually used. This might or might not
be the case, but at least you can see why a cache can become outdated.

One common mechanism for maintaining an ARP cache's currency is a simple timer.
System and network administrators alike enjoy the opportunity to establish thresholds for
a timed update of their device's ARP cache. It isn't uncommon to find 4 hours as the time
interval. At the end of that interval, the device flushes its ARP cache and generates a request
that lets it build a new, more up-to-date table.

Although timers provide a nice, automatic means of maintaining the currency of the table's
data, they are far from perfect. The basic ARP mechanisms described up to this point adequately provide a host with a means of building a table. But what happens when a host ceases
functioning, powers down, or otherwise becomes unreachable via the LAN? Given enough
time, the timer of each host would count down to 0 and force an ARP request. But that would
create a period of time in which the contents of the ARP cache could be obsolete. The net
effect would be that a machine would believe that it is reachable locally when it really isn't.

Furthermore, it is highly unlikely that all the timers of all the hosts would elapse simultaneously. Thus, the symptoms of ARP cache obsolescence probably will not be experienced
uniformly throughout a network. This tends to make troubleshooting more interesting. In
cases where, for whatever reason, an ARP cache becomes corrupted or painfully out-of-
date, your best bet is to simply rebuild it.

NOTE   The first time you use ping to test connectivity to an IP address, you will likely see that the
first reply in the sequence of attempts will fail. Subsequent replies will be successful. That's
normal. It demonstrates that the first time around there was no mapping between the IP and
MAC addresses for that destination.

Handling Unknown IP Addresses

Another interesting aspect of ARP is how it handles unknown IP addresses. An IP address can be unknown to ARP for many reasons. For example, it might not be a valid IP address. Excluding that obvious reason, there are at least two other main reasons why ARP wouldn't know about a particular IP address. First, perhaps the IP address belongs to a locally connected device that hasn't connected to the network yet. Alternatively, the IP address could be assigned to a machine that is not on the same LAN. Of course, myriad other possibilities exist too, including that the IP address is invalid, but we'll focus on just those two main reasons.

The process begins when an application passes data to the TCP/IP protocol stack for forwarding to a specific destination (as identified by the destination's IP address). IP engages ARP's services to see if that IP address is known to exist locally. Remember: ARP builds a table that tracks only locally connected machines by their MAC and IP addresses. If the IP address can't be found in the ARP cache, you just can't jump to the conclusion that the device is on a different network.

The next step in figuring out what to do is to poll the local hosts again. Remember, at this point the application has already handed off its data to TCP/IP for encapsulation in an IP packet. That packet must be encapsulated in an Ethernet frame for transmission on the Ethernet LAN. An ARP request packet is generated with its IP address and is broadcast throughout the LAN. The local hosts again check to see if they are the IP address in the request packet. If they are, a reply packet is generated and is sent back to the requesting machine. That requesting machine must do two things: update its ARP cache, and then wrap the IP packet that started this whole process with an Ethernet frame and send it on its way.

However, if no local host replies to the ARP request, it is safe to assume that either

- The host is not local
- The host is local but is not on the network at this time

Either way, the source machine is not off the hook. It still is obligated to find a way to deliver the packet. Let's revisit the previous example of an HTTP session between two desktop computers to see how ARP handles these two scenarios. The way it does this is through the use of a default gateway. A default gateway IP address should be configured every time you configure networked communications on a computer. The LAN's population must use that router interface's IP address (the default gateway) to reach the outside world. ARP correlates that IP address with that router interface's MAC address.

The way this works is relatively simple. The source machine takes the IP packet with its encapsulated application data and places it in an Ethernet frame bearing the destination MAC address of the router's interface. The router accepts that frame (after all, that frame is addressed to it, even if the IP packet contained therein is not) and strips away the frame to reveal the embedded IP packet. This is where the router, functioning as the LAN's default gateway, must make a decision. If the packet bears a destination IP address that belongs to the network from which it was received, it discards the packet as undeliverable. The logic at work here is that it is seldom useful to send a packet out the same interface from which it was received.

NOTE   There was a time when it was never useful to send a packet out the same router interface from which it was received. The introduction of subnetting has changed this. Today, it is not uncommon to find a single router interface that supports two separate IP subnets on the same Ethernet LAN. In such cases, the router may have no choice but to send IP packets (embedded in Ethernet frames, of course) back through the same interface on which they came in.

However, if the destination IP address of that packet is from a different network address, the router sends the packet on its way. This is illustrated in Figure 10-15.

Figure 10-15   *The Router Acts as a Default Gateway and Accepts Ethernet Frames Addressed to Its Interface. Those Frames Contain an Embedded IP Packet Addressed to a Foreign Host.*

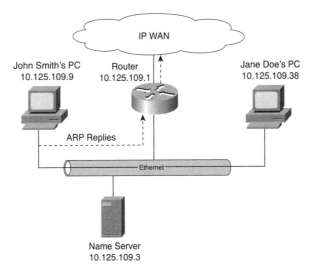

Summary

IP addresses are an integral part of a network: They form a functional link between user-friendly mnemonics and physical or machine addresses. Translation between mnemonics and IP addresses, and between IP addresses and machine addresses, are functions that most people (including network and system administrators) don't think about. That's both good and bad. The good news is that these functions are obviously working and, therefore, remain invisible to the users and administrators. The bad news is that both functions tend to remain misunderstood. Misunderstanding a network-based function is a recipe for disaster, because you can't diagnose and fix what you don't understand.

This chapter was designed not only to round out your appreciation of these functions, but also to show you their operational context in a network. The next chapter takes this a step further by examining how IP addresses work in an internetwork.

Internetworking with IP

Far from being a well-thought-out scheme, the Internet Protocol (IP) has emerged some-what haphazardly over decades. The result is a protocol and addressing scheme that lets internetworks of global proportions be built of distributed networks. The IP address space plays a vital and active role in enabling that scalability. This chapter explores that active role and demonstrates how routers use the IP address space to calculate routes, as well as how network address information is disseminated throughout the Internet.

The Mechanics of Routing

Routing is a complex set of mathematical processes that is embodied in highly specialized *routing protocols*. Routing protocols have numerous functions, including the following:

- Discovery of neighboring routers (those that are directly connected).
- Discovery of destination networks that are accessible via neighboring routers. After discovering destination network addresses, the router has a couple other chores:
  - Comparing different paths (routes) to the same destination network. This is known as *route calculation*.
  - Building a table of known destination networks and the corresponding router interface for each destination. This table is called the *routing table*.

This is a highly simplified explanation of the function of routing protocols and is in no way intended to be comprehensive. An entire book could be written on just one routing protocol. This chapter's goal is much more humble: to help you understand how routing protocols use IP addresses.

It is important to recognize the difference between a routing protocol and a routed protocol. A routing protocol is highly specialized and is limited to router-to-router communications. A routed protocol is much more broadly used. Routed protocols, such as IP and IPX, encapsulate application data for transport across networks. This chapter shows you how routing protocols are absolutely reliant upon the addressing systems of routed protocols.

Discovering Routes

One of the most critical functions of a routing protocol is its capability to discover routes. In other words, a router's protocols communicate with neighboring routers and exchange information about known network addresses and their reachability. In this manner, an iterative process lets all the routers in a network learn about all the network addresses supported within that network. An equally important function of this capability is that it provides a means of identifying—and sharing—news of a change in the network's topology. The network's topology or shape constrains potential paths through the network between any given pair of locations.

Before we delve too deeply into the intricacies of neighboring routers, you might be wondering how a router learns about network addresses. The answer is quite simple: The network administrator configures each interface on a router. Part of this configuration defines that port's communication parameters. Communication parameters can include the speed of the link connected to that interface, the type of network and internetwork protocols supported, and the network address or addresses that are attached via that port. For example, network and internetwork protocols would be the combination of Fast Ethernet and IP. Of course, routers can support a seemingly infinite combination of network and internetwork protocols, so that's just one simple example.

NOTE   Router-to-router communication usually occurs only via neighboring routers. Some routing protocols, such as Open Shortest Path First (OSPF), utilize IP-based multicast mechanisms that enable a richer pattern of interrouter communications. For the most part, sharing routing information is an iterative process facilitated by neighboring routers.

Figure 11-1 depicts the first step in the iterative process of route discovery. In this illustration, backbone Router #2 senses a change in the network's topology and evaluates how that impacts the reachability of destinations in its routing table. More importantly, the protocol begins telling its immediately adjacent neighbors that the topology has changed. Notice that I didn't say the router tells its neighbors that a link is down. The router's job isn't necessarily to troubleshoot the problem and figure out what no longer works. Instead, the routing protocol must figure out what is still accessible. It does so by sharing with its neighbors select pieces of information, including which destination networks are still available via which of their interfaces. Thus, IP addresses are a critical component the underlying mechanics of networking as opposed to being merely a passive means of uniquely identifying machines on a network.

Figure 11-1 *Backbone Router #2 Senses a Change in the Network's Topology*

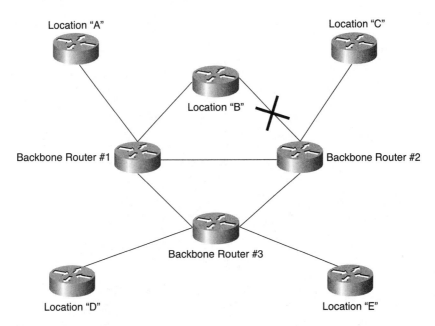

Figure 11-2 illustrates Backbone Router #2's initial attempts at sharing the news of the topology change with its immediately adjacent neighbors. Those immediate neighbors are location C and Backbone Routers #1 and #3. The fact that a link has failed means that routes to destinations that previously relied on that link no longer work. The routers must communicate with each other to learn about what is still accessible (and via which router) in order to ascertain a new set of best paths to all destination networks that remain reachable.

The communication process between these routers is governed by the routing protocol that is used, as well as other highly variable factors such as internal timing mechanisms. This example uses a simplistic model in which information flows fairly evenly throughout the network.

NOTE   The neighbor-to-neighbor communication between adjacent routers that occurs after a change in the topology is called *convergence*. A network in convergence is unstable and can't deliver user packets reliably or effectively. Such instability is a direct function of the loss of consensus about the network's shape. This is normal, and it's a good reason to select a routing protocol that converges efficiently.

A network has converged (emphasis on past tense) when all routers agree on the network's new shape and have updated their routing tables to reflect that new topology. Consequently, the network has returned to a stable, operational state.

Figure 11-2 *Backbone Router #2 Tells Its Neighbors About a Change in the Network's Shape*

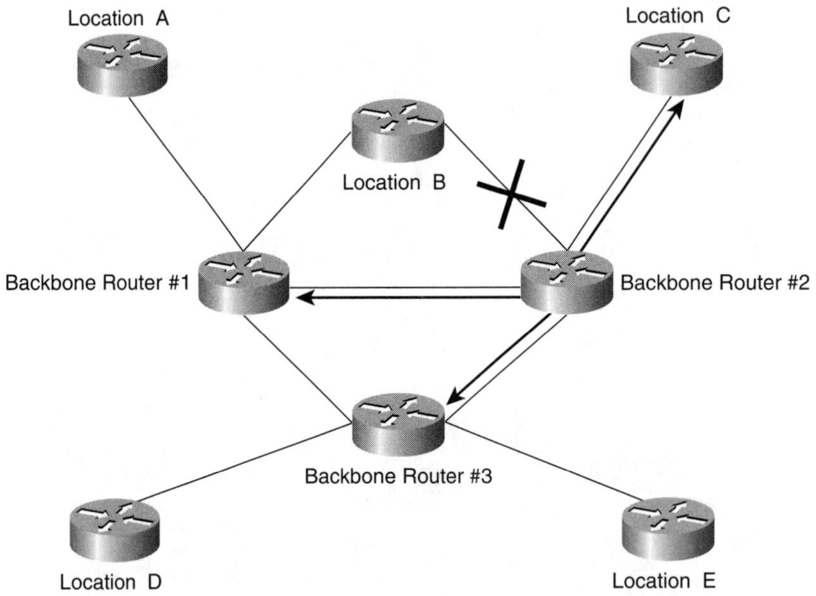

As the routers attempt to develop a new consensus on the network's shape, the neighbors of Backbone Router #2 share the information they have received with their other immediate neighbors. Figure 11-3 shows this step in the iterative process. It is important to recognize that, in Figure 11-3, two routers communicate route information with their immediate neighbors: Backbone Routers #1 and #3. Backbone Router #1 sends that information to locations A and B, as well as to Backbone Router #3. Thus, Backbone Router #3 hears the same story from two different neighbors.

At the conclusion of the communications depicted in Figure 11-3, all routers in the network will have learned about the failure of the link between Backbone Router #2 and Location B. Depending on the complexity of the network's topology and the routing protocol being used, two or more complete iterations of this nature might be required before all the routers reach a consensus. Consensus is a unanimous agreement on which destination network addresses remain reachable, and the best path to use to reach them. The notion of "best path" is applicable only if there are two or more different paths through the network between any given source and destination network pair. The routing protocol would then have the opportunity to mathematically compare the redundant routes and select the one it deems best. Of course, "best" is a relative term, and the outcome of this comparison can change greatly depending on the criteria used in the comparison.

Figure 11-3 *Second Iteration of Neighbor-to-Neighbor Communication*

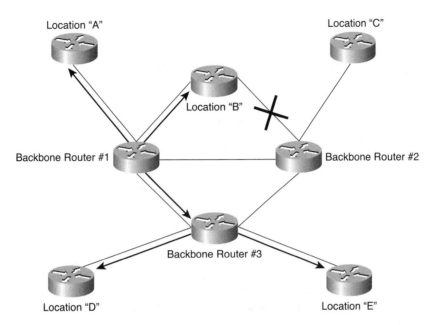

Calculating Routes

One aspect of routing that requires a bit more explanation is how routes are calculated. Yes, that's correct, *calculated*. Remember: This is a mathematical process. Calculating the "distance" to a destination using any given metric lets you make a direct comparison between two different routes to the same destination simply by comparing their respective metrics. Routing metrics are sometimes referred to as a route's *cost*.

There are four very different approaches to calculating a route's cost:

- Distance vector
- Link-state
- Policy-based
- Static

These approaches differ in how they calculate the best route to a destination. The first three are autonomous processes that rely extensively on independent sharing of information between neighboring routers. These three approaches are similar in that they are dynamic routing protocols that make decisions based in part on IP addresses. They differ in that they represent very different approaches to figuring out the best path to each destination network.

The fourth approach, static routing, features a correlation between destination network address and outbound router interface that is hard-coded or preprogrammed by the network administrator.

NOTE   There are times when a router might receive a packet addressed to a network that was previously unknown to that router. In such cases, the packet isn't necessarily discarded as being undeliverable. Instead, a concept known as a default gateway comes in handy. Essentially, you identify an interface on a router as the default gateway. If a packet comes in to an address that isn't in the routing table, it is forwarded out this interface. The concept of a default gateway doesn't guarantee that every packet gets delivered; it just increases the odds.

The concept of a default gateway is one that is universally present in all routing protocols regardless of the route calculation algorithm employed.

Distance Vector Routing

A distance vector routing protocol uses some arbitrary measure of distance to compare different routes to the same destination. The classic distance vector is *hop count*. A hop is a way to count the number of routers in a route. Typically, each router counts as one *hop*. If one path through a network to a specific destination requires passing through five routers, and another requires passing through only three routers, common sense fairly dictates that the three-router path is the better path.

Figure 11-4 shows a small network and how hops are calculated across it. If you look at that figure and think that the hop count should equal 4 instead of 3, you aren't far from the truth: There really are four routers in the path. But if you start counting from 0 instead of 1, the incrementing results in three hops instead of four. That's typical of hop-counting protocols.

Distance vector algorithms date back to the late 1950s. As such, they are mature, stable, and remarkably simple. But time has marched on, and the early distance vector protocols (such as the myriad varieties of Routing Information Protocol [RIP]) are widely perceived as being obsolete due to the simplicity of their route-calculation algorithms.

Link-State Routing

The notion of making routing decisions based on some arbitrary measure of distance is logical. It formed the seminal work in the field of route calculation. In the halcyon days when networks were simple and nascent counting hops made sense, links were remarkably homogeneous. Over time, as networks and networking technologies matured and became more specialized, homogeneity was lost. In simpler terms, it was no longer safe to assume that all the links in an internetwork were T1s. Indeed, some of them could be T3 (with 44.573 Mbps of bandwidth), OC-3 (155.53 Mbps of bandwidth), OC-12 (622.12 Mbps of bandwidth), or even greater. Consequently, the perceived need for more-sophisticated means of route calculation arose.

Figure 11-4   *Counting Hops En Route to a Destination*

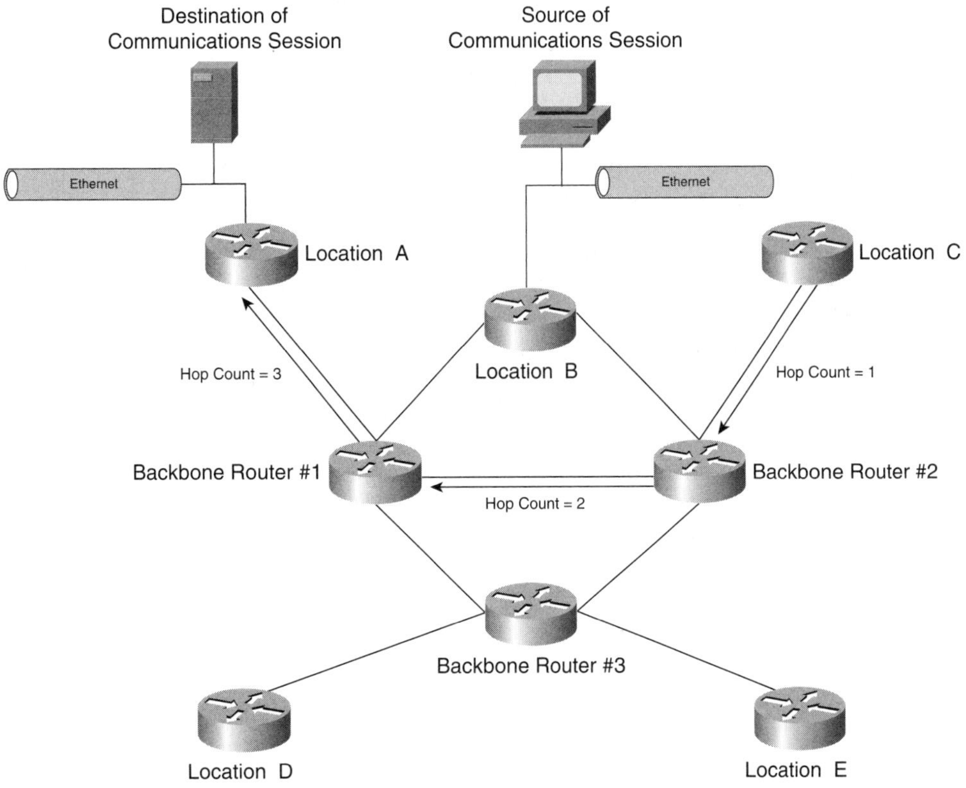

Recognizing the need for a more sophisticated way of calculating routes and figuring out how to do that are two very different things. Depending on what your criteria are, a decision can have multiple "correct" answers. For example, if you were to drive from your home to a nearby mall, you would probably have to choose from several different routes. If you wanted to minimize the amount of traffic you encountered, you might opt for a backroads route that avoided major roads. If you wanted to maximize speed, you might pick a route that put you on the greatest number of streets with the highest speed limits. Alternatively, you might want to minimize the total number of miles you would have to travel, so you would select the shortest path possible. These simple scenarios demonstrate that, unless there is no topological diversity, there can be no single correct answer. So the search for a more sophisticated routing protocol quickly focused on finding appropriate metrics that would be inputs to the route calculation and selection processes.

Over time, consensus developed among network engineers on the need to have routing protocols that could make decisions based on current information on the state of the links in a network. This genre of routing protocol became known generically as *link-state routing protocols*.

Here are some examples of the types of link-state criteria that a routing protocol can use:

- A link's speed
- Delay encountered on a link
- Historical information on a link's reliability (bit error rates)
- Current utilization rates

Routers either have this data configured for their interfaces or can keep track of it. Reading through this short list of potential criteria, the most likely reaction is "Of course! That makes perfect sense!". Why wouldn't you want to base your routing decisions on such detailed information? A decision based on these criteria would enable much more accurate decisions than merely counting hops to a destination—or would it? To better appreciate the logic or illogic of making routing decisions on such criteria, consider the network topology illustrated in Figure 11-5.

Figure 11-5 *Using Link-State Information to Calculate the Best Routes*

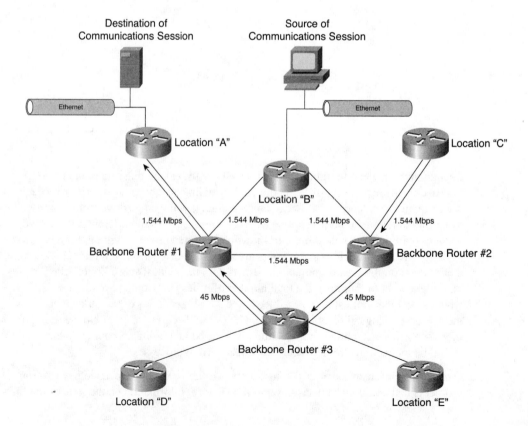

Figure 11-5 shows the same network topology that has been used throughout this chapter. This figure, however, shows the effects of using a link-state routing protocol. The topology shows the bandwidth of each link. All but two of the links are T1s with 1.544 Mbps of bandwidth. Those two links interconnect backbone router #3 with #1 and #2. Given that a link-state routing protocol is used, bandwidth becomes a very important factor in selecting the optimal route—more so than just hop count. You might expect the shortest path to be the best one, but the quality of the links being compared can skew that perception.

Other potential issues with link-state protocols focus on the volatility of the data used to make routing decisions. If the shortest path is actually the lowest-bandwidth, most-congested link in the network, it would make much more sense to take a higher-bandwidth, less-congested path even it if were slightly more circuitous. But this generalization assumes that the information you are basing your routing decisions on is relatively stable. Some measures of a link's state are unstable. Utilization rates, for example, can vary tremendously from one second to the next.

This points out one of the great flaws in the link-state philosophy: A link's state can be highly dynamic. It can change faster than a network's routers can finish sharing routing information. Thus, making routing decisions on highly dynamic information can be counter-productive. Fear not. Many mechanisms have been developed that effectively dampen the volatility of data used to make routing decisions. I just mention this potential shortcoming of link-state routing protocols to help you better appreciate some of the complexity of making good routing decisions.

Policy-Based Routing

A small but very powerful group of routing protocols are geared toward global scalability. These protocols are collectively known as *exterior gateway protocols* (EGPs). EGPs are used only for communicating with, and across, the Internet. Such protocols are designed almost exclusively to provide the scalability that this role requires. They rely on administrator-configured policies and rules to determine what to do with IP packets. This is in stark contrast to both distance vector and link-state protocols, which focus on selecting the best possible route based on some arbitrary metric(s).

Examples of exterior protocols include the archaic Exterior Gateway Protocol (EGP) and the Border Gateway Protocol (BGP). BGP-4 is the routing protocol currently in use across the Internet for communicating routing information between service providers.

Static Routing

Statically configured routes are preprogrammed in a router. No routing protocol is needed, because no routing decisions are left up to the router. The network administrator decides which is the best path to take to reach any given network address, and it hard-codes that path into the router.

The benefit of static routing is that it imposes an absolute minimum of overhead on a router and network. No bandwidth or CPU cycles are consumed in an effort to maintain a current image of the network.

The drawback of static routing is that it is utterly inflexible. If the topology changes, a statically configured route has no way of detecting, or reacting, to such a change. Instead, the network administrator must manually update the statically configured routes to accommodate changes in topology. In lieu of a routing protocol, the network administrator must manually instruct the router what to do with packets destined for each network address. Implicit in this explanation of static routing is the fact that static routes are unidirectional. A network administrator may tell a router how to forward packets that have a particular network address, but that administrator has no control over packets that are inbound. Thus, routing in a statically configured network might well be asymmetric.

Static routing is not exactly a scalable approach to internetworking. This technique is typically found only in very simple networks or is used to secure specific areas within a network.

NOTE   For a much more complete exploration of routing, refer to *IP Routing Fundamentals,* ISBN 1-57870-071-X, published by Cisco Press.

Routing and the Internet

The Internet is a gigantic collection of IP-based networks that are linked to form a ubiquitous global internetwork. Getting past the dizzying scale of the Internet, you can appreciate that the mechanics of routing on the Internet do not vary substantially from the mechanics of routing you encounter in WANs. In fact, the concept of neighbors exchanging routing table information remains remarkably consistent. The routing protocols used are different (they need to be to achieve global scalability), but the fundamentals remain consistent. Neighboring routers continue to exchange routing information within a network. And, at the periphery of a network where two different networks connect to form an internetwork, the neighboring routers actually exchange routing information on behalf of all the routers in their respective networks.

Figure 11-6 builds on the previous example to show how the interconnection between two networks aggregates routing information for each of those networks for sharing externally. The iterative neighbor-to-neighbor communication process occurs both internally (in each of the two networks) and externally (between the two networks via the neighboring routers of each network that form the gateway).

Figure 11-6 *Neighboring Routers in Different Networks Exchange Routing Information*

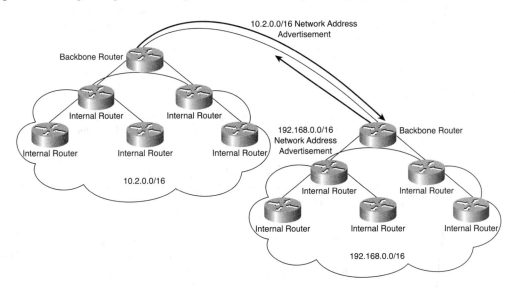

The notion of sharing routing information between networks takes on a whole new meaning
in the context of the Internet. The Internet is intriguing because it is a collaborative yet
highly competitive environment. If you are thinking that you can't collaborate with a
competitor, you aren't far from the truth. In many instances, you wouldn't want to incur
the business risk associated with that activity.

On the Internet, however, collaboration is imperative. No single ISP can operate alone,
simply because not one contains all the Internet's end users and content-bearing hosts.
Instead, the Internet's base of end users and destinations is scattered across thousands of
ISPs around the world. In this environment, competitors must share routing information.
Otherwise, the Internet's global reachability gets compromised. More pragmatically, an ISP
that doesn't interconnect with other ISPs offers limited value to its customers and probably
can't legitimately call itself an ISP.

Please don't get the impression that there is cheerful camaraderie between ISPs. In any commodity-based industry, competition is ruthless. The inter-ISP competition on the Internet, however, takes on an interesting and subtle form that is best described via the accepted tiered designations.

Tiers of Service Providers

Not all ISPs are created equal. Time and competitive market forces have helped the ISP industry coalesce into functional niches as each firm strives to differentiate itself from the competition. Today, there are three tiers of providers:

- **Tier 1** — Tier 1 ISPs are facilities-based. That is, they own their own operating infrastructure, including the telecommunications circuits that interconnect their routers. Typically, a Tier 1 ISP is large enough to be global, but some just span a continent.

  By virtue of its size and reach, a Tier 1 ISP enjoys a certain degree of leverage over its peers (other ISPs). Simply stated, it has a larger market share of end users and/or high-value destination sites than its smaller competitors.

- **Tier 2** — A second-tier service provider might or might not have a national backbone, but it is not facilities-based. Second-tier providers tend to develop specialized niches and enjoy a solid base of high-end customers. Such customers are usually businesses rather than individuals and require high-bandwidth connections.

- **Tier 3** — A third-tier service provider is a small, regional on-ramp to the Internet. Such an ISP might cover a specific geographic region or specialize in certain access technologies (such as any of the myriad flavors of Digital Subscriber Line [DSL]), dialup, or other telecommunications technologies.

How you, as an end user or customer, categorize an ISP is far less important than how ISPs categorize each other. ISPs must interconnect with each other in ways that make economic sense. How ISPs categorize each other can have a tremendous impact on how the costs of interconnectivity between two ISPs get divided. Thus, far from being a semantic discussion, the relationship between ISPs has some very real impacts in terms of economics and service levels to customers.

In very simple terms, no one service provider enjoys a monopoly on the Internet user community. End users and destination websites are scattered across thousands of ISPs around the world. Thus, the ubiquity of the Internet absolutely requires interconnectivity between all ISPs. But ISPs are not created equal, as you have seen in this section.

Tiers Translate into Hierarchy

Reading through the description of the various tiers of ISPs, you might have gotten a sense of the natural leverage that some ISPs enjoy relative to their peers by virtue of their size.

Indeed, the more end users and/or destinations that are connected to an ISP's network, the greater the benefits of establishing a connection directly to that ISP. So, all ISPs are motivated to try and establish a direct link to a Tier 1 ISP.

The converse is also true. The smaller an ISP's customer base, the less reason other ISPs have to establish a direct connection with it. Thus, a Tier 1 ISP has almost no reason to invest in the hardware and facilities required to establish a connection with a Tier 3 ISP. The important concept here is that the negotiating leverage established by the relative sizes of ISPs translates directly into a topological hierarchy within the Internet. This hierarchy, in turn, affects how routing information gets propagated throughout the Internet. The terms used to describe one's relative position in this hierarchy are *upstream* and *downstream*. What flows up and down those virtual streams is not water—it's routing information and IP packets filled with data.

Figure 11-7 demonstrates the concept of upstream and downstream ISPs in the Internet. Although these are highly relative terms, they do make sense when viewed from the perspective of the tiered classification of ISPs. Thus, larger ISPs (such as Tier 1) form the backbone of the Internet. Tier 1 ISPs are, for all intents and purposes, the Internet's backbone. Peering connections between these large providers ensure ubiquitous connectivity for all their downstream customers, including smaller ISPs. The smaller ISPs, such as the Tiers 2 and 3, tend to form the periphery or edge of the Internet.

Figure 11-7 *Upstream Versus Downstream Neighbors*

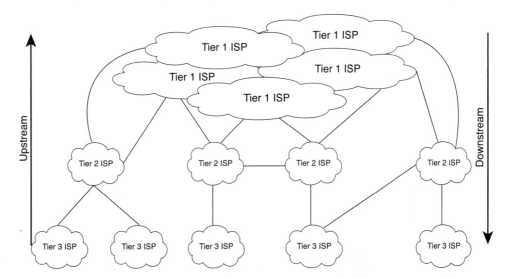

ISPs at the edge of the Internet are sometimes called on-ramp providers. This moniker implies that this is where you enter the Internet. Please don't misconstrue this to mean that you can buy access only from a Tier 3 service provider. Virtually any ISP would be willing to sell you access services. The differentiating factors are price and robustness of interconnectivity with other service provider networks (as indicated by the breadth of peering and transit relationships).

When viewed from the perspective of network address information, the notion of upstream versus downstream takes on greater significance. Essentially, a Tier 3 on-ramp advertises a limited number of network addresses to its upstream neighbors, yet it relies on those upstream neighbors for access to virtually every other network address. For the sake of example, assume that the Tier 3 ISP has a /16 address space (10.2.0.0/16, to be precise). This is the only network address it would advertise to other ISP networks it interconnects with. That ISP would need to be able to deliver its customers' packets to virtually any address on the Internet. Thus, it needs to obtain a full Internet routing table from a much larger ISP. This is illustrated in Figure 11-8.

Figure 11-8 *Advertisement of Network Addresses Upstream Versus Downstream*

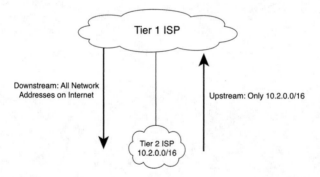

It is important to recognize that a very real danger lurks in the interconnection of different networks. The very act of interconnection means that network address information is shared between networks operated by different entities—competitors. Each trusts the other to share only valid routing information and to operate a stable network that won't generate unnecessary routing updates. Either scenario can adversely affect neighboring networks. This creates the potential for snobbishness on the part of some ISPs when it comes to evaluating other ISPs for establishing interconnection. The result is an interesting trio of interconnection types on the Internet as dictated by the relative leverage of each tier of service provider. The three interconnection types are *public peering, private peering,* and *purchased transit services*.

Peering Versus Transit Services

The Internet is a bit of a misnomer in that it leads you to think it is a single network. As we have discussed throughout this chapter, it is really a patchwork of thousands of IP-based networks. IP and its addressing system let any endpoint connected to the Internet access any other endpoint. But that any-to-any connectivity assumes that physical connectivity exists between those two endpoints. Such connectivity between ISP networks can take one of two basic forms:

- Peering
- Transit

Cumulatively, peering and transit are known as *egress* among ISPs. Egress is a fancy word for exit. In the case of an ISP network, connectivity to other ISP networks extends the reach of an ISP network via the sharing of routing information. But, as you saw in the preceding section, there are great differences between ISPs. For instance, a regional Tier 3 ISP might have a few hundred end users but almost no destinations on its network. Such a provider would benefit far more than a Tier 1 ISP from the interconnection of their two networks. This concept of equality versus inequality forms the basis of differentiating between the two forms of egress.

Peering

Peering is the term applied to a voluntary interconnection between two ISP networks. The ISPs recognize that there are mutual benefits to the interconnection. In theory, peering agreements (both public and private) limit the traffic passing between two networks to just network-to-network traffic. Traffic destined for other networks shouldn't be dumped on a peer's network. Doing so can be a violation of trust and is contrary to the notion of being peers. This type of peered interconnectivity is achieved by sharing just the locally connected network addresses of each network. This limited exchange of network address information precludes packets addressed to other network addresses from using the peering connection. Figure 11-6 demonstrated how peers exchange only their own routing information.

Ostensibly, a peering connection is mutually beneficial to both parties. Consequently, peering partners typically agree to share the costs of their interconnection. Each must invest in the hardware necessary to support the physical interconnection (the router interface port and any equipment that might be required to support the transmission facility). If a leased telecommunications circuit is required, they might opt to share the costs of that circuit. Alternatively, an informal agreement might be made to simply "take turns." Company A buys the first circuit and pays for it entirely. If and when that circuit gets full, Company B springs for the cost of the next circuit. Regardless of how these mutual costs get apportioned, the connection benefits both companies. In other words, they are *peers*. Their private interconnection is known as a *private peering* connection.

Public peering is an interconnection between peers at a specialized facility that is specifically designed to enable large-scale peering among ISPs. Such facilities are known by various names, including *telco hotels* and *exchanges*. The facility's operator creates a data center-like environment complete with physical security, climate control, a "house" network, and electric power that is backed up by both Uninterruptible Power Supplies (UPSs) and a motor-driven generator to ensure that there is no disruption in electricity. Space is then leased to ISPs, and they install routers and other networking gear there. That networking equipment is used to extend the ISP's network into that peering facility and to connect to its operator's house network.

Public peering facilities offer smaller ISPs the opportunity to establish relatively limited-bandwidth connections to a large number of other service providers. The opportunity is borne of proximity to the other ISPs courtesy of the house network.

Although it should be obvious, I'll point out that peering is beneficial because it theoretically represents the shortest possible path between source and destination devices. As a result, peering creates the opportunity to improve network performance through the Internet by allowing ISPs to deliver packets directly to their destination networks.

Transit

Having discussed the importance, if not outright necessity, of interconnecting ISP networks, we need to acknowledge the inadequacies of peering. Public peering requires an ISP to extend its network to a public peering facility. That can require lengthy—and expensive—telecommunications links. Small, regional ISPs that are not located near any public peering facilities might find themselves unable to afford a connection. Such ISPs are equally unlikely to be able to negotiate private peering agreements with any of the Tier 1 or Tier 2 ISPs. The good news is that this doesn't mean they are out of business. For them, there is always the option of purchasing *transit services*.

Virtually every ISP is willing to sell dedicated access to its network via leased telecommunications facilities (also known as *private lines*) to anyone pwho can afford it. If that customer happens to be another, albeit smaller, ISP, the service is called *transit*. The Tier 1 ISP charges the Tier 2 or Tier 3 ISP for the full cost of physically connecting to its network, as well as a variable cost for each megabit of traffic it has to carry for that customer ISP. Included in this traffic quantity might be some inbound traffic destined for the Tier 3 ISP's destinations.

In theory, the Tier 3 ISP should not be charged for these packets. Basis for that statement exists in the world of telecommunications. Telecom is an industry in which the owners of the networks must interconnect to ensure ubiquitous service. Costs are charged back to the customer per minute of use. But seldom does a call begin *and* end within just one carrier network. That means the call's costs are spread across at least two carriers, and the revenues must be shared as well. To facilitate this charge-back, minutes of use must be tracked between the carriers. The carriers then have to "settle up" their bills with each other.

The Internet isn't quite so mature a business environment. Costs are not as uniformly tracked or recovered. All ISPs must interconnect with other ISPs. In the Internet model, an ISP is either a peer (in which case it is exempt from settlement charges) or a transit customer (in which case it is exempt from settlement charges *but* must bear the entire cost of the connection and service).

Summary

Far from being merely a passive means of uniquely identifying computers at the periphery of a network or internetwork, IP addresses play an active role in routing. Routers share IP network addresses that they know about with other routers. That enables any-to-any connectivity within an IP network. Equally important, IP network addresses are also shared between networks to enable internetworks of truly global proportions to be built.

CHAPTER 12

Network Stability

A network's stability is paramount to its operational success. Nobody likes it when a network crashes, or suddenly becomes so overwhelmed that it's temporarily useless. Many factors make up a network's overall stability, including the age and reliability of its hardware, as well as the consistency of its configuration. But the one thing that tends to get overlooked is the network's address space. Fiber cuts and fires tend to grab the headlines, but it is the address space that can either detract from your network's operational stability or be exploited and used to launch attacks.

This chapter helps round our your appreciation of the role of an IP address space relative to a network's stability and security. We'll examine some of the problems that can be caused by operating anomalies that affect a network's address space, as well as attacks made via an address space. We'll also look at some of the solutions to these potential problems and will evaluate their effectiveness in today's Internet environment.

The Problem with "Open" Networking

As you saw in Chapter 11, "Internetworking with IP," the problem with open networking begins with the fact that routers are both intelligent and autonomous. You might be able to influence their decision-making processes, but they ultimately choose the best path to each destination network—unless, of course, you abandon dynamic routing protocols in favor of static routes! That leads us to perhaps the biggest problem with open networking: Routers communicate with their neighbors. Although you could effectively argue that is a feature of networking instead of a flaw (and you'd be correct), the point is that this autonomous communication can sometimes result in the propagation of misinformation.

Within the confines of a single network, the effects of misinformation—or obsolete information—being propagated can be quite painful. But the Internet environment has thousands of hierarchically interconnected IP-based networks. The effects of misinformation leaking out onto the Internet can be absolutely devastating! This is an innate feature/flaw of internetworking. Although the impacts are potentially huge, the nature of the Internet is such that misinformation is seldom leaked deliberately. Such events are almost always caused by human error as opposed to human design.

Human design typically drives attacks on internetworked systems. Although you wouldn't normally attack an address space, you would use IP addresses to propagate attacks. Attacks made directly on an address space can be considered precursors to "real" attacks. For example, a would-be hacker might test an entire block of addresses using a utility such as ping to determine which specific addresses are in use. In this way, information may be gleaned about the inhabitants of any particular IP network. This information would be used to fuel an actual attack on hosts within that network.

The next two sections look at specific problems caused by both human error and human design. This will help prepare you for a deeper look at some of the other challenges that await, as we explore the role of IP addresses in the context of network stability.

Address-Based Vulnerabilities

This section's heading might be a bit misleading; nobody really attacks an IP address space. But, just as IP addresses are the input to the route calculation process, IP addresses are the vector for many network-based attacks. In that sense, IP addresses allow other vulnerabilities to materialize. Some of these vulnerabilities are just the nature of the beast: Having redundant interconnections between multiple networks means that there is more than one path between any given source and destination machine pair. Although that's a key strength of IP internetworking, it also gives rise to some potential weaknesses. Two of the more prominent of these weaknesses are the potential for loops and black holes to occur.

Loops

There is a maxim in routing that is as old as routing itself: It is seldom useful to send a packet out the same interface it came from. But an even older maxim is to build as much redundancy as you can afford. These two truisms appear to conflict, because topological redundancy creates the potential for loops. Figure 12-1 demonstrates this point. It shows a topologically nondiverse network. If any single link or router were to fail, connectivity within this network could be greatly affected. Of course, the impact would vary, depending on what fails.

Figure 12-2 shows how the network can be split by the failure of just one router. Of course, that router would happen to be the one that serves as the backbone for this enterprise network! The net effect is five disparate networks that are incapable of communicating with each other.

Figure 12-1 *A Topologically Nondiverse Network Features All Single Points of Failure*

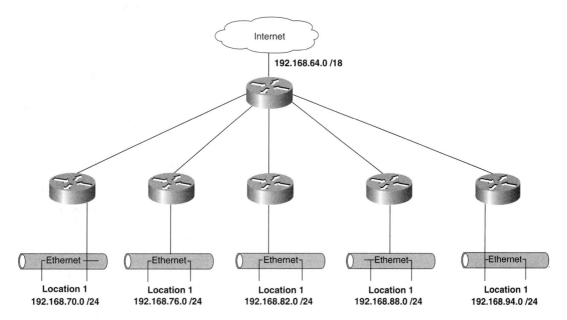

Figure 12-2 *A Failure in a Nondiverse Network Can Split the Network*

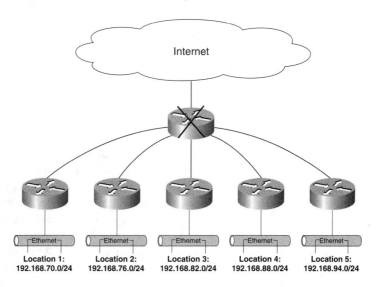

Now, compare the topology shown in Figures 12-1 and 12-2 with the topologically diverse network shown in Figure 12-3. In this scenario, the backbone is a fully meshed ring of routers. If any link fails, the network continues operating unhindered. The only downside is that this creates, topologically, the potential for a routing loop. Look carefully at this network's backbone, and you will see two possible loops. The first exists between the three backbone nodes, and the second is borne of the redundant connections to the Internet.

Figure 12-3 *Topological Diversity Guards Against Failure But Creates the Potential for Loops*

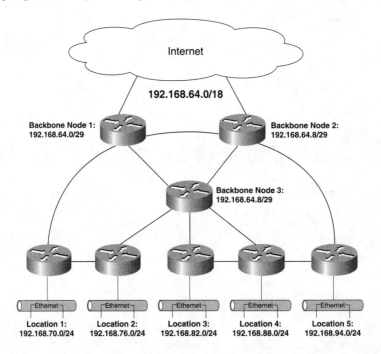

Having a topological loop is a good thing; having a routing loop occur over a topological loop is bad! A routing loop can occur only if the network destabilizes. In other words, something changed the network's topology—a component or link failure, a new circuit's being added, and so on. The network has left its previously steady state, and the routers within that network are actively exchanging information in an attempt to determine the network's new shape. Figure 12-4 shows the sample network with a failure. The failure causes network 192.168.70.0/24 to become *temporarily* unavailable to the rest of the network. It is connected to the backbone via Node 1, and that is the preferred path. All the routers in the network know about 192.168.70.0/24, and they forward IP packets destined for hosts within that network address to Node 1. Thus, one of the backbone routers knows almost immediately that this network has become unreachable, and the other two temporarily persist in the belief that it is still available. This creates the possibility that two of the network routers accept that the other two (which aren't directly connected to 192.168.70.0/24, but they don't know that) still have a valid route to that network.

Figure 12-4 *A Failure Causes Different Routers to Temporarily Have Different Opinions About a Network's Reachability*

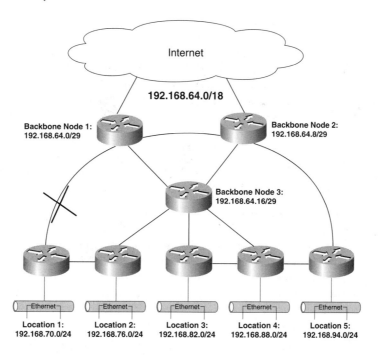

The end result is that packets can be sent in circles because of the imperfect knowledge about the network's topology caused by the router's failure. The routers will eventually figure out that network 192.168.70.0/24 is still accessible via the router at Location 2, but they will have to communicate with each other for a while to figure that out. This process, known as *convergence,* is necessary for networks to dynamically route around problems. However, it also creates a very vulnerable state in which the routers might not be able to deliver packets to known destinations. Worse, until the process ends, the routers can't really know if any particular destination is valid or invalid. And, because it takes time for new information to be fully propagated throughout the network, it is most likely that different routers will have different information about the network. The trick becomes figuring out which information is good, and which is old and obsolete.

Fortunately, looping caused by routers sharing slightly out-of-date information with each other is a well-understood phenomenon. Virtually every routing protocol comes equipped with stability-enhancing mechanisms designed to protect your network from loops. The best approach to preventing routing loops is to trust your routing protocols to do their job properly. That requires you to understand them and configure them carefully. More importantly, you must configure them consistently on each interface within your network. The bottom line is that you *want* loops to exist physically; you just don't want your packets traveling in circles until they die!

Black Holes

Another interesting by-product of building internetworks using intelligent, autonomous devices (routers) is that they can communicate misinformation. Sometimes, misinformation can cause a legitimate route to a legitimate network address to be invalidated. Worse, because routers communicate with each other, the invalidated network address could quickly find itself null and void throughout the Internet. Thus, a perfectly functioning network would be isolated from external communications. This is known as a *black hole* because, from the Internet's perspective, the network has disappeared without a trace!

Network addresses can become blackholed either unintentionally or intentionally for a variety of reasons:

- An ISP can intentionally blackhole a portion of its address space by advertising it to the Internet as a null route. This is a useful tool when you're attempting to reclaim an address block from a former customer that has absconded with it. Alternatively, an ISP can blackhole a customer's network address if that customer is in violation of the ISP's *Acceptable Use Policy (AUP)*. AUP violations can include spamming and hosting illegal content. Advertising a network address as a null route effectively causes that address to become unusable, because the network with that address becomes unreachable.

- A network administrator can blackhole a route within his or her network to prevent users from accessing Web sites or other sources of content that they aren't allowed to access. Such content sites typically support file sharing, but these files can include MP3 files, DivX files, pornographic images, and so on. Although the network administrator might be perfectly correct in blackholing such sites within his or her network, circumstances can exist that would result in the null route's being inadvertently advertised throughout the Internet.

- Anyone gaining control of a router that can advertise routes into the Internet can intentionally blackhole a route as a way of denying service globally to a particular network. That would make a network—and all the devices attached to it—invisible to the Internet. The blackholed network users wouldn't be able to access anything outside their network, nor would any devices outside their network be able to access anything on their network.

The imagination runs wild with various scenarios in which an IP network address is configured as a null route—either intentionally or unintentionally—with far-reaching consequences. Null routes or black holes are a legitimate tool, but their use requires a mastery of internetworking and consistent router configuration. Otherwise, the results can be unintentional and catastrophic. For example, every router in the Internet could refuse to recognize a specific network address block.

Routers can be configured to advertise even statically configured routes to upstream routers. This is particularly useful in an ISP environment, because customer routers are configured to statically route everything that isn't local out of the ISP connection's interface. To the ISP network, the network block assigned to that statically routed customer is known as a static route. Yet the ISP is obligated to let the rest of the Internet know about that customer address. Thus, the ISP might be inclined to advertise even static routes into the Internet.

A problem would occur if that ISP's customer decided to use a null route for a specific network address to prevent its end users from accessing a particular destination. The potential exists for that null route to be communicated to the ISP and for the ISP to recommunicate it to the rest of the Internet. That would be bad. Of course, this isn't how null routes should be used. Additionally, the routers would have to be configured to advertise static routes to external networks in order for this scenario to be a problem. Although this might sound farfetched, it can happen (and it has).

If a network administrator wanted to prevent a Web site from being accessed, routers let you create permissions lists (known more accurately as *access control lists [ACLs]*) that locally constrain accessibility. ACLs are programmed per interface and are not shared with other routers. The point is that null routes can be used inappropriately, and that can have far-reaching and unforeseen consequences. That is why I have listed black holes as a potential vulnerability of the IP address space that can be exploited.

Address-Based Attacks

Although it would be misleading to say that someone can attack your IP address space, there are ways to exploit an address space to launch attacks. In fact, because the address space is *the* way to reach an IP-capable host, the only way to reach that host is to use its address. For this reason, a hacker's first task is to scan an IP address space.

Automated tools exist that let someone test an address space to see which addresses are "live" and which are unassigned. Live addresses warrant further scrutiny. So begins the arduous process of testing for known holes and vulnerabilities to see what has been left unattended and can be exploited. This process is frequently called *port scanning* or, more metaphorically, *knob turning*. Not unlike a thief who wanders up and down a row of homes doing nothing more than turning doorknobs, the hacker is looking for an easy way in.

A hacker who succeeds in this attempt to gain illicit entry to a host has a wealth of options at his or her disposal. First, if there's anything of value on that box, it's gone. The hacker can steal it, delete it, modify it, and so on. Second, it might be possible to learn enough from this compromised host to gain access to other systems. Such secondary damage may be direct (for example, the hacker then logs directly into that new host) or indirect (the hacker uses the compromised machine to gain access to that new host). Exploiting a host in this manner is particularly nefarious, because the attacker appears to be a legitimate user based on the source IP address of the affected IP packets. And it all started with finding an IP address to a host that wasn't secured properly!

NOTE   There are no panaceas with respect to securing a networked computing environment. Instead, security is a function of many different layers that range from a coherent set of methods and procedures to physical security to a dizzying array of both network- and host-based security capabilities. How much damage an attack causes depends on how carefully the overall security of the networked computing environment was crafted. An attack begins with the address space but ends with defenses installed virtually everywhere else.

Other specific attacks that exploit an address space include

- Man-in-the-middle attack
- Session hijacking
- IP address spoofing
- Denial of Service attack
- smurf attack

These attacks directly use IP addresses and are sometimes used in combination to achieve greater impact. We'll look at each one briefly to round out your appreciation of the vulnerability of the IP address space in an open network.

Man in the Middle

The man-in-the-middle attack is a fairly well-known and mature threat. Essentially, some-one inserts a device into a network that grabs packets that are streaming past. Those packets are then modified and placed back on the network for forwarding to their original destina-tion. A quick Net search should lead you to some programs and/or source code that you can use to launch this type of attack—it's really that easy! This form of attack affords the per-petrator the opportunity to steal the data contained in the IP packets lifted off the network.

The worst part of a man-in-the-middle attack is that it can completely defeat even sophisti-cated authentication mechanisms. The attacker can simply wait until after a communication session is established, which means that authentication has been completed, before starting to intercept packets.

The existence of such an attack doesn't directly threaten your network's stability. But it is an exploit that can target a specific destination IP address. A mild form of man in the middle is called *eavesdropping*. Eavesdropping differs only in that the perpetrator just copies IP packets off the network without modifying them in any way. This is tantamount to petty theft, whereas man in the middle more closely resembles vandalism.

Session Hijacking

An interesting twist on the man-in-the-middle attack is *session hijacking*. The name should be self-apparent. Someone gains physical access to the network, initiates a man-in-the-middle attack (ostensibly *after* authentication with a destination host has occurred), and then hijacks that session. In this manner, a hacker can illicitly gain full access to a destination computer by assuming the identity of a legitimate user. The legitimate user sees the login as successful but then is cut off. Subsequent attempts to log back in might be met with an error message that indicates the user ID is already in use.

What a hacker does after hijacking a session depends greatly on that individual. The potential for damage is limited only by the access permissions of the user whose session was hijacked and the hacker's imagination. The hacker can access files for copying to his or her desktop, delete or modify files, or use the session to launch an attack on another host on the same network.

Address Spoofing

Address spoofing is an old game. It entails mimicking someone else's IP address for the sake of perpetrating an attack. The IP address doesn't necessarily have to be a particular person's address. Spoofed addresses are typically selected either at random or to appear to be from a specific entity's network. Using a fictitious source IP address nicely covers the attacker's tracks and makes getting caught less likely. Of course, spoofing an IP address limits the types of attacks you can perpetrate. In simple terms, you have made up an IP address. This IP address gets imprinted in each IP packet you generate as the source IP address. The source IP address is used by the network and the destination machine to route responses back to the correct machine. If that source address is fictitious, there's no way to route responses properly. Response packets are sent to a different host on a different network (the host that is the legitimate possessor of the spoofed address), or they can't be delivered at all! More importantly, it has become quite common for hosts to rely on source address authentication to ensure that the machine they are communicating with really is the one it purports to be.

You might be thinking that address spoofing is obsolete. It isn't. Many a successful hack has been launched using a spoofed address. Remember, the goal of an attack isn't always to establish two-way communication. Some attacks are quite successful using just inbound communications without requiring a response. One such attack is the Denial of Service attack.

Denial of Service

A *Denial of Service (DoS)* attack is a bit more insidious than some other forms of attacks because conventional defenses are powerless to stop it. A particular computer might be targeted, but that computer can remain up and functional yet utterly unreachable to its legitimate user base. In essence, the perpetrator of this attack isn't trying to steal or damage data or do any physical harm. Instead, the perpetrator simply tries to hurt his or her victim by denying that victim's user community the use of one of its assets.

Service can be denied to legitimate users in a variety of ways. For example, a sufficiently large quantity of spurious traffic can be generated in the hopes of overloading either a computer or some portion of the network upstream from that targeted computer. Such attacks would likely require multiple source machines working in concert to attack the target. All those machines could spoof their source address in the hopes of avoiding detection. Another form of DoS attack is to pass illegal communication parameters to a target in the hopes of causing it to crash.

NOTE   A DoS attack that features a simultaneous, coordinated attack from multiple source machines is called a Distributed Denial of Service (DDoS) attack. The best-known example of a DDoS attack is the smurf attack (discussed in the next section).

Either way, the "damage" is transitory, and service can be restored as soon as the spurious traffic ceases or the targeted machine is rebooted. I'm not trying to minimize the potential impact of a DoS attack. Many companies make their living via online services. Thus, you could literally put a company out of business by doing nothing more than preventing its customers from accessing its Web site. Far from being merely an intellectually stimulating what-if scenario, DoS attacks are propagated daily. In recent years, such attacks have put some of the Internet's most prominent Web sites out of service.

smurf Attack

Despite the cute name and the imagery it conjures up, there's nothing funny about a smurf attack. smurf (lowercase letters used intentionally) is a relatively simple, yet highly effective, form of DDoS attack. This attack uses the *Internet Control Message Protocol (ICMP,* a native component of TCP/IP protocol suites). One of the utilities embedded in ICMP is ping (an acronym for packet Internet groper—don't ask me why, though). ping is very commonly used to test the availability of certain destinations. Unto itself, it is benign, and even quite useful. However, smurf can misuse it in a nefarious way.

The way a smurf attack works is quite simple. The hacker installs smurf on a computer. This requires the hacker to somehow gain entry to a computer by guessing passwords, hijacking someone's session, or any one of a seemingly infinite array of possibilities. The hacked machine starts continuously pinging one or more networks—with all their attached hosts—using IP broadcast addresses. Every host that receives the broadcast ping message is obliged to respond with its availability. The result is that the hacked machine gets overwhelmed with inbound ping responses.

The good news is that there are many ways to combat potential smurf attacks. The bad news is that smurf is just one of an ever-expanding collection of DDoS attack mechanisms. The stability of your network requires constant vigilance!

RFC 2267, "Source Address Assurance"

RFC 2267, "Source Address Assurance," was published in January 1998 with the intent of defeating certain types of DoS attacks in IP-based networks. As you learned in the preceding section, DoS attacks are insidious threats to the stability of any network or networked computer. Logically, then, anything you can do to defend against the DoS attack is a good thing. Or is it? In the case of Source Address Assurance, the cure might be worse than the disease. Curiously, many "experts" cite RFC 2267 as the best defense against a DoS attack—distributed or otherwise.

Defending Against DoS

Knowing what a DoS attack is and knowing what to do about it are two very different things. The trick is getting the spurious traffic to stop without causing further harm to the attempts of legitimate users to gain access to the resource being attacked. Discriminating between legitimate users and an attack is a complicated affair, particularly when your attempts to troubleshoot are conducted under duress. Remember, a portion of your networked computing environment is under attack. That attack might well overload either the systems or the network you must use to collect information before diagnosing the problem.

In theory, anyone who intends to cause such a disruption of service on an internetwork likely wants to cover his tracks. In other words, he won't launch an attack from his own desktop, because that would make it easy to trace the attack back to him. So the goal is to obfuscate the source of the attack by using someone else's IP address. Spoofing an IP address is a relatively trivial endeavor. Without going into detail (if I tell you exactly how to do this, all I would accomplish is to make spoofing easier), spoofing an IP address results in a fictitious address being used as the source address of each IP packet generated. Logically, if that source address is fictitious, return packets can't reach their destinations. That too is useful, because it tends to increase the overall amount of traffic generated as the result of an attack.

It's important to recognize that spoofing an address doesn't change an attack's point of origin; it just hides it with a fictitious source IP address. Thus, examining all the packets generated from within a network should reveal an interesting trend. All those packets should bear a source address that was created from the network address assigned to that network. A spoofed address would differ. This is the basis of Source Address Assurance. By examining source IP addresses relative to the network address assigned to a network, you can easily detect a spoofed address. Quite simply, it wouldn't match. Figure 12-5 shows how this works.

Figure 12-5 *A Spoofed IP Address Doesn't Match the Network Address*

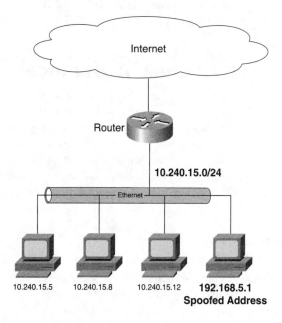

If someone within the customer network shown in Figure 12-5 wanted to launch an attack using a spoofed address, the routers in that network would make their forwarding decisions based on the spoofed packets' *destination* address. No sanity check on the source address would be made. So the packets would be routed to their destination properly despite the obviously mismatched source address relative to the network to which it was connected.

The actual type of attack propagated in this manner almost doesn't matter. The important thing to note is that spoofing lets the attack be carried out with relative anonymity. RFC 2267 was not intended as a panacea against all types of attacks. Instead, Source Address Assurance was a specific tool developed to protect against just those DoS attacks that were initiated by a forged or spoofed source IP address. It worked by preempting the possibility of a spoofed address getting beyond the network from whence it originated.

A Flawed Assumption

It is important to recognize that RFC 2267 was published as an informational RFC. Thus, ISPs were not compelled to enforce its recommendations. Some did, and some didn't. The important thing to recognize is that, because it was just an informational RFC, it didn't attract the attention that a standards-track document would. Consequently, many end-user organizations don't even know it exists and never ask about it when shopping for Internet connectivity.

The ongoing evolution of the Internet, in conjunction with the ever-increasing sophistication of its user community, rendered RFC 2267 obsolete in just four short years. In retrospect, it should be obvious why it was just an informational RFC: Right from the start it was based on a flawed assumption. That assumption was that you could reliably determine a "forged" IP address in a packet by examining the address of the network from which the packet originated.

On the surface, that seems reasonable enough. If an IP packet bears a different address than the network it came from, you should be suspicious of its authenticity—or should you? When RFC 2267 was first published, this assumption was already well on its way to obsolescence! Yet the need for some means of defending against DoS attacks from spoofed addresses was urgent enough that an RFC was put forth. What wasn't mentioned in the RFC, however, was that multihomed customers could be effectively denied service by the recommended filtering!

The Problem with Source Address Assurance

Source Address Assurance, despite the good intentions on which it was founded, quickly became obsolete. The Internet, and its end-user base, matured quickly after its commercialization. Companies in particular quickly realized that billboards on the Net simply weren't of much value. Thus, they developed increasingly sophisticated ways to directly market and sell goods and services and manage customer relationships using the Internet. Many companies emerged with a new business model that relied exclusively on Internet connectivity. With this increased sophistication came a decreased tolerance for the risk of downtime. Consequently, efforts to eliminate single points of failure ultimately led to companies that connected to the Internet via two or more different ISPs.

Although such multihoming nicely solved the problem of single points of failure, it introduced complexities that simply weren't accounted for in RFC 2267. Take a look at Figure 12-6, and you'll see what I mean.

Figure 12-6 shows that the company has attempted to eliminate a single point of failure via dual homing. Unfortunately, this contradicts the logic of RFC 2267. Suddenly, companies upstream of ISP #2 must accept that 10.240.15.0/24 (a network address alien to ISP #2) enjoys a legitimate path through that provider's network. From the perspective of Source Address Assurance, however, it appears to be a spoofed address. In fact, from the perspective of that ISP, there appear to be lots of spoofed addresses! ISPs that implement Source Address Assurance would, by definition, filter out those foreign addresses, thereby rendering moot the benefits of multihomed end-user organizations.

Figure 12-6 *Multihomed Clients Can Defeat the "Logic" of RFC 2267*

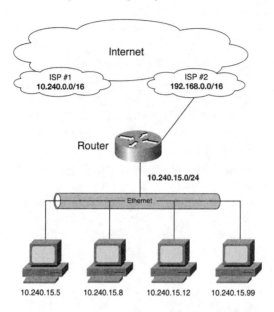

The net effect is demonstrated in Figure 12-7. The heavy dotted line indicates the point at which the 10.240.15.0/24 route is supported through ISP #2's network. The end-user organization believes that it has eliminated a single point of failure, but it doesn't realize that a provider upstream of its provider has effectively limited the reachability of its address space. Without knowing to ask specifically about Source Address Assurance, a dual-homed Internet customer can be paying a lot for the illusion of redundancy. Connectivity tests such as ping or tracert (or traceroute, depending on which operating system you use) to hosts within the 192.168.0.0/16 network will demonstrate that the connection to ISP #2 is working fine, but routing protocols will select the connection through ISP #1 for all destinations outside 192.168.0.0/16.

Therein lies the great debate. Which is the greater good: attempting to ensure network stability by preventing DoS attacks via a spoofed address, or eliminating a single point of failure via multihoming connections to the Internet? The answer depends greatly on your perspective, and how much value you place on customer satisfaction.

Figure 12-7 *The Customer's Reachability Is Limited by an Upstream Provider of The Customer's ISP*

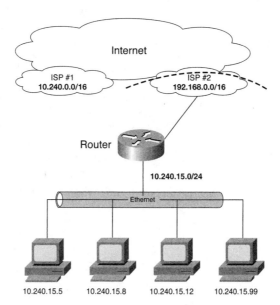

Brand Image Versus Customer Satisfaction

RFC 2267's Source Address Assurance is far from being a topic of only academic interest. As a customer of an ISP, you could find yourself victimized by it. Worse, you could be in jeopardy of this happening without even knowing it!

Multihomed customers who connect to second-tier ISPs must accept the fact that their immediate upstream provider is likely multihomed to other upstream service providers. The net effect is that a first-tier service provider might see a network address being advertised via its downstream and also might see that same network address being advertised via a different service provider. Logic used to dictate that there could be only a single valid route for each network. When faced with multiple routes, which one do you accept as valid? Well, a first-tier service provider that implements RFC 2267 would filter inbound packets and accept only packets from its downstreams that are registered to those downstreams. Any other packets (including legitimate packets of that downstream provider's customers) that bear someone else's network address in their source address field are assumed to be spoofed. As such, they get dropped.

At least one globally recognized telecommunications carrier/ISP relies heavily on RFC 2267 as a means of protecting its brand image. This company has acknowledged that enforcing Source Address Assurance can cause legitimate customer routes to be blackholed, particularly those that are multihomed to two or more ISPs. Yet this company has stubbornly insisted that protecting its brand image is far more important than customer satisfaction.

Although I have gone out of my way to protect the identity of that misguided company, you should be asking your ISP if it, or any of its upstreams, enforces RFC 2267 filtering. If so, it might be time to find another service provider. Ideally, you want to find one that recognizes that brand image is a function of customer satisfaction rather than something that must be defended even at the cost of customer satisfaction. Trust me: When you find a provider that believes in Source Address Assurance, you will have also found a provider that cares a great deal less about your satisfaction as a customer than it does about the stability of its own network.

Address Lending for Network Stability

RFC 2008 was published in October 1996. It foreshadowed RFC 2050/Best Current Practice (BCP) #12, and it remains in effect as Best Current Practice #7. Although it tackles the rather verbose and cumbersome topic of "Implications of Various Address Allocation Policies for Internet Routing," it remains noteworthy for establishing the concept of address lending. More importantly, it clearly documented the benefits of address lending in contrast to address ownership. RFC 2050, in comparison, takes a more limited focus by urging ISPs to provide their customers with an initial address space that should be reclaimed after each customer leaves.

By this point, you should be quite familiar with RFC 1918 addresses, RFC 2050/BCP #12, and NAT. We've looked at them separately a few times. RFC 2008/BCP #7 established the tandem benefits of having end-user organizations "borrow" IP address blocks rather than "own" them. This document was developed as a result of the IETF's experiments with the 39.0.0.0/8 address space (known as the Net 39 Experiments). Those experiments proved unequivocally the benefits of geographic aggregation of address space. Unfortunately, for address space to be aggregatable by region, the entire philosophy of handing out address space would have to be rethought.

No longer did the IETF deem it desirable to just hand out blocks of addresses sequentially to anyone who asked, regardless of geography. The result of that approach was an unwieldy Internet routing table with no hope of aggregating the smaller network blocks. By borrowing a network address block from an ISP, many of the Internet's original addressing problems could be satisfied. Unlike some other RFCs, the benefits of RFC 2008 accrue to both the end-user organization and the Internet at large.

Benefits to End-User Organizations

End-user organizations benefit tremendously by embracing the concept of address lending—they just don't like the idea. During the last two years that I have been employed by AppliedTheory Corporation, I have never ceased to be amazed by the high value and importance that customers place on having their own privately registered address space. It's as if a certain cachet is associated with having your own address space—a sort of credential that announces your seriousness as an Internet user. Discussions about RFCs 2008 and 2050, or even explanations about the ill effects that directly registered address space can have on Internet routing tables, usually produce the same deer-in-headlights stare. It's obvious that they either don't understand what I'm saying, fail to appreciate how it relates to them, or are dumbfounded that I can't appreciate why they need their own address space.

Despite this personal history, I remain convinced of the benefits of end-user organizations. Borrowing an address space all but requires you (as an end user of the Internet) to configure and run NAT. You would use the borrowed address space as your inside global addresses, and you can use any of the reserved RFC 1918 addresses as your inside local addresses. This combination of technologies, as you have seen in this book, affords greater security by hiding internal IP addresses from external networks. More importantly, it enables that end-user organization to change ISPs without the hassle of having to renumber all its internal addresses.

Finally, the combination of NAT and borrowed addresses has the potential to make the IPv4 address space last almost indefinitely, which is of great benefit to anyone not willing to invest in the migration to IPv6. We'll look at IPv6 much more closely in Chapter 15, "IPv6: The Future of IP Addressing." For now, trust me when I say that this is a tremendous benefit! The migration, despite the plethora of transitional devices available in the IPv6 protocol suite, is nontrivial. Thus, I submit that staving off the migration is a huge benefit.

Benefits of the Internet

Although I view the benefits to end-user organizations as very compelling, the concept of address lending offers even greater benefits to the Internet itself in the form of absolutely minimal routing tables. The smaller the Internet's routing table, the more efficiently every IP packet that flows across it can be routed. Thus, the Internet operates more quickly, and end users realize better performance.

Even more importantly, the remaining supply of IPv4 addresses can be deployed in a very logical and efficient manner. Although that's not a lengthy list of benefits, the impact of each one is incalculable. Perhaps that's why RFC 2008/BCP #7 and RFC 2050/BCP #12 remain in effect.

Summary

IP addresses are truly the key to making an IP network useful and usable. The inverse of this statement is that IP addresses are also the means by which networked systems are probed and attacked and the network's operational stability is compromised. Defending against such potential threats to your network's stability begins with an awareness of the pitfalls. This was the modest goal of this chapter. Suffice it to say that maintaining a network's stability starts with a base of good, reliable hardware. On top of that base must be layered great methods and procedures and a solid plan for managing the address space. Chapter 13, "Planning and Managing an Address Space," takes a long, hard look at some of the strategies you can employ when managing an address space.

Planning and Managing an Address Space

Managing an IP address space is a deceptively difficult and complex task. Careful planning and foresight are an absolute requirement but they must be complemented by a keen appreciation of the binary mathematics of the address space itself. Last, but not least, it helps if you understand some of the issues regarding the address space as it relates to the industry you work in.

This chapter looks at the requirements for managing an address space and how those requirements can change with context. In simpler terms, how you would manage an address space for an enterprise differs from how you would manage it for an Internet hosting center or Internet service provider (ISP). Each context has unique operational requirements that must be factored into planning an address space.

The Challenge of Managing an Address Space

On the surface, addressing serves a very logical and necessary function. A network address allows each device connected to a network to be uniquely identified. This is the basis for accurately forwarding data to its intended destination. However critical and necessary this function is, it is not the sole purpose of an addressing system. Addressing also directly affects the efficiency with which a network operates and its potential for scalability.

A network's scalability is also a direct function of how well-designed and -implemented that network's addressing system is. An addressing system that is either poorly designed or poorly implemented has a distinct impact on a network's operating efficiency, as well as its ability to grow.

We'll take a quick look at how you might plan the use of an address space. We'll use the same sample network to show you how the challenges you might face vary depending on whether you are acquiring a new address space or remediating one that's been in use for a while. The responsibility for planning and managing an address space falls on the *hostmaster*.

Role of the Hostmaster

The hostmaster has an utterly thankless, but critical, job: managing an IP address space. Managing an address space involves allocating smaller address blocks carved out of the large block to functions, groups, and so on that need addresses. Their needs can change over time, which directly affects the number of addresses they require. Thus, the hostmaster must satisfy present requirements while carefully husbanding the scarce IP address space to ensure that it will continue to meet requirements long into the future.

Context is everything. The context in which a hostmaster is employed can have a tremendous impact on his operational challenges. His requirements and goals can change dramatically based on whether he is working for an enterprise or an ISP or running an Internet hosting center. Depending on the context, parsing out address space can be interpreted to mean sizing and assigning subnets, managing routable variable-length CIDR prefixes, or even assigning individual IP addresses to endpoints. For now, let's start with the big-picture perspective and drill down to the details.

Developing an Approach

If you ever sneak up on a hostmaster hard at work, you will probably find him staring off into space. Fear not! He is not loafing; he is *thinking!* The role of the hostmaster is probably at least 90% planning. Some of the many things that a hostmaster needs to do include developing an approach to managing an address space. To do that properly, you must hash a thorough appreciation of the binary mathematics of the IPv4 address space against business strategies and goals, including the following:

- Defining goals for the network, which translate into goals for its address space
- Establishing the scope of the network that will be satisfied with specific address spaces
- Identifying the challenges
- Future expectations, including growth projections, *merger and acquisition* (M&A) activity, and any other business plans that will affect the network

Obviously, your approach also depends directly on whether you are starting from scratch with a new address space or just trying to continue the management of an existing network and address space. We'll look at both cases in this chapter. Specific approaches to managing an address space are examined in great detail in the next chapter. Let's move on and round out your appreciation of managing an address space by continuing our big-picture exploration of the process.

You implement an address space strategy via allocations and assignments of IP addresses. The distinction between these two actions is made clear in the next section.

Allocation Versus Assignment

Just as DNS permits you to hierarchically distribute name resolution into zones, a host-master might opt to distribute responsibility for the assignment of IP addresses. Before that can make sense, you need to appreciate the distinction between allocation and assignment of IP addresses. Perhaps the simplest explanation is that you allocate blocks of addresses but you assign addresses individually. It should be obvious that you assign individual addresses out of a block that was previously allocated to a specific purpose or group. Allocations ensure future flexibility by accommodating growth.

More important than future flexibility is keeping a tidy address space. If done properly, allocations help maintain the symmetry of a CIDRized address space. The hostmaster must be ever-mindful of the binary mathematics that are the foundation of the IPv4 address space. As you've seen throughout this book, mistakes are very easy to make but very difficult to correct. The way to avoid mistakes is to take great care when making block allocations. Each block should be crafted with a clear understanding of binary mathematics and the natural CIDR boundaries.

Let's make that more clear with an example. You wouldn't just assign space serially; you would likely be creating idle blocks of addresses that complemented the block allocated. Thus, if you needed to allocate a /25 to a new department, you would begin by searching through your inventory of available blocks to see if you had an unassigned /25 network block. If you did, great! Your search is over. Otherwise, you might look for an available /24. Finding such an address block, you would then have to decide whether to allocate the top half or the bottom half of that block. Table 13-1 demonstrates the two halves of a /24 network block.

Table 13-1   *Upper and Lower Halves of a /24*

Dotted-Quad IP Block	Binary IP Block	Which Half
10.5.1.0 /25	00001010.00000101.00000001.**00000000**	Upper
10.5.1.128 /25	00001010.00000101.00000001.**10000000**	Lower

NOTE   The concept of upper versus lower halves of an address space can be confusing. The example presented in Table 13-1 shows the popular approach to identifying the upper and lower halves. However, if you stop to think about it, you might be tempted to assign the description of "lower" to the block with the lower address numbers. When you chart this out—as hostmasters must do for recording block assignments—the "upper" half of a block is the one you list first. You guessed it: That's the block with the lower numbers.

This symmetry of upper and lower halves progresses even further with each additional bit you add to the network mask. The point is that block allocations are made network masks. The starting point for each allocated CIDR block is readily apparent. However, you won't necessarily see the end of each of those allocated blocks just by looking at the network mask. Thus, by striving to make block allocations by examining the symmetrical relationship between CIDR blocks, you can prevent allocated blocks from unintentionally overlapping. An overlap occurs when one or more IP addresses mathematically fall into two numerically contiguous CIDR blocks.

It should go without saying that the hostmaster must track all address allocations and assignments. Something as simple as an electronic spreadsheet suffices. The actual tool used for tracking is almost unimportant in comparison to the availability of accurate records.

Now that we have briefly examined the role of a hostmaster, the next aspect of managing an address space we need to consider is acquiring an address space.

Acquiring an Address Space

The obvious prerequisite for managing an address space is to actually *have* an address space. Fortunately, there are several good avenues to pursue when it comes time to acquire an IP address space. Of course, there are also one or two really bad ideas! We'll look at all of them so that you can appreciate a bad idea when you see one. Your basic options include the following:

- Obtaining a directly registered IP address space

- "Leasing" one from your ISP

- Implementing one of the address blocks reserved in RFC 1918

- Simply "making up" a network address and hoping it doesn't cause problems

This is far from an exhaustive list, but making it any more complete would require preempting some of the later sections in this chapter. For now, let's assume that this list comprises your basic options for acquiring an address space. This will let us move forward and identify some of the other IP address management issues and challenges that lie ahead.

NOTE   Each of the options for acquiring an address space can be used at any point in a network's life cycle. In other words, none of them are useful only during the prestartup planning stages. They can be equally useful when you're planning for a new network or when you're managing an existing network and address space.

Directly Registered Address Space

The Holy Grail of the Internet's address space is a directly registered network block. Such an address space isn't "owned" by an end-user organization. The entire IP address space (including both IPv4 and IPv6) is owned by IANA. IANA authorizes certain agencies to register other organizations for the exclusive use of portions of this address space. Having a network address block that is directly registered to you lets you continue using that block regardless of which ISP you are using for Internet access.

In return for this exclusivity, the registered organization must agree to pay an annual fee to its regional registrar. Unfortunately for the vast majority of the Internet's user community, the qualifying criteria for obtaining a directly registered address space has become an insurmountable hurdle. This is by design. The tandem goals of this higher hurdle are as follows:

- To ensure that the remaining address space is used wisely by carefully qualifying the stated needs of organizations that apply for such space
- To absolutely minimize the bloating of the Internet's routing tables by encouraging end users to obtain temporary usage rights to an address block from their ISP

"Leasing" an Address Space

RFC 2050 counsels all Internet users to obtain an address space from their current ISP and to regard that space as "leased." When an end-user organization enters into a contract for Internet access with an ISP, that ISP offers the organization the use of a portion of its address space. This address space is what RFC 2050 urges us to regard as being leased. When the contract for service expires, the space must be returned to the ISP. The benefit to the Internet is that each ISP can aggregate all its customers' address blocks into an absolute minimum number of network address blocks that are directly registered to that ISP. Only these high-level address blocks get shared with the Internet's other ISPs and networks.

The problem, from an end-user organization's perspective, is that RFC 2050 could force it to either pick one ISP and stay with that provider forever, or face the undesirable chore of renumbering its network when it needs to change ISPs.

RFC 1918 Reserved Address Spaces

Way back in Chapter 7, "Private Addresses and NAT," you learned about the reserved addresses stipulated in RFC 1918. These reserved private address blocks might be an organization's best option for addressing. No approvals are required, and implementing them does not preclude the future use of any other source of addresses.

In today's Internet environment, the best strategy for an organization that can't get its own directly registered address space is to both lease an address space from an ISP *and* implement RFC 1918. After having explored NAT in Chapter 7, you know that you need to configure *inside local (IL)* addresses (these would be from RFC 1918's reserved ranges) and *inside global (IG)* addresses. The IG addresses would be the globally unique addresses that you "lease" from your current ISP. Changing ISPs results in the relatively minor chore of swapping out the IG block configured on your network address translators.

Just Make It Up!

The last option for acquiring an address space is the least practical, although it might be the easiest approach. Most of the other ways of acquiring an address space require an approval or some other formal agreement. Just making up an address space is as easy as using an RFC 1918 address. No paperwork, review-and-approval process, or anything else is required. You might wonder why anyone would just pick a network address block arbitrarily.

Although I won't pretend to understand the mentality behind such actions, I can tell you that it is done with far more frequency than I care to see! In theory, if the network is isolated from the Internet, it shouldn't matter which network address you use. Based on this fact, some network administrators and/or hostmasters simply exercise a level of professional arrogance by picking a network address block and implementing it. Such actions are extremely shortsighted. You should make every attempt to comply with the Internet's RFCs and Best Current Practices.

Inheriting an Existing Address Space

Inheriting an existing address space might free you from the burden of planning and implementing an address space. But this isn't a free lunch. Instead, you get the dubious distinction of trying to figure out why someone else did things the way they did. Worse, it becomes incumbent upon you to clean things up. Unfortunately, managing an IP space is similar to driving an aircraft carrier: You can't turn either one on a dime!

In very simple terms, it is always easier to start fresh with a new address space and a new network than it is to inherit someone else's mess. If you do find yourself in this position, your approach should be to thoroughly study the existing allocation scheme. Next, define your priorities for the address space, pick a suitable strategy, and look for opportunities to improve over time. The persistent nature of IP assignments means that solving inherited problems takes a lot of time and patience. You have to iterate toward perfection slowly. This means you have to have a very long-term planning horizon and act in a consistent manner over time.

This might sound like simple common sense, but unless you have a solid command of the mathematics of IP addressing, and enough foresight to have a plan, it is impossible to manage an address space well.

The remainder of this chapter focuses on various issues that inevitably accompany the management of an address space. The issues can vary widely based on a number of factors, including where you got your IP address space. Then we can look at those issues in the specific context in which you might find yourself operating—namely, an enterprise organization, an ISP, or an Internet hosting facility.

Address Management Issues for an Enterprise WAN

An end-user enterprise demonstrates some fairly consistent network attributes. For example, an enterprise wide-area network (WAN) should have a fairly secure perimeter. This implies that the borders are well-defined in the first place. The WAN, by virtue of its isolation from other, external networks, affords cocoon-like safety for the networked computing operations. The routers in this network spend much more of their time forwarding IP packets than they do tracking routes, simply because the network's limited scope results in a limited number of internal routes. If there is to be a connection to the Internet, all network addresses that lie outside the network can be treated using the concept of a *default gateway*. As you saw in Chapter 11, "Internetworking with IP," a default gateway is a simplifying logical mechanism. It lets you tell a router which of its interfaces should be used to forward any packets bearing a destination address for which it doesn't have a valid route.

Any specific routes that a router tracks are, by design, for internal addresses. Figure 13-1 shows a typical network topology for an enterprise with five locations and one connection to the Internet. We'll use this topology as our example to reinforce some of the issues unique to an enterprise WAN. Each location is a separate office building that contains its own LAN.

Figure 13-1 *An Enterprise Network Topology*

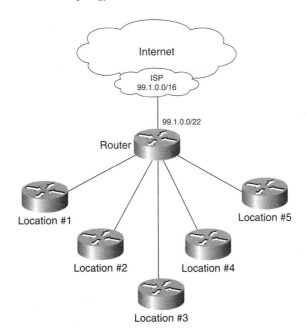

Looking at this figure, you can see that an IP address space is already selected. For the sake of example, we'll assume that the address space was properly obtained and is directly registered to your company. In reality, the address block 99.1.0.0 /22 has not yet been assigned. There might come a day when it is, but for the foreseeable future, it remains reserved by IANA and, ostensibly, available for future use.

This /26 block is advertised *to* your ISP. Thus, at least in theory, the rest of the world can access this network using that network address. The ISP, however, doesn't advertise your /26 network block to the rest of the Internet. Instead, it aggregates that block with the other blocks assigned from its /22 and then just advertises the /22 network block to the Internet.

Hierarchical Allocation

Having acquired an address space, the next priority is figuring out what to do with it. In other words, you need to allocate some addresses to each of the locations. Remembering the distinction between allocation and assignment, it would behoove you to allocate slightly oversized subblocks from your /22 to each of your five locations. The size of each subblock should depend on the size of each location. Obviously, you want to have slightly more than enough addresses at each location as opposed to just enough or not quite enough. Let's assume, for the sake of simplicity, that each location requires no more than 200 addresses. Thus, you need a /24 network for all the various endpoints at each location. Two of your locations, numbers 4 and 5, are only about half the size of the other sites. They can share a /24 with ease. As such, each is given a /25 network.

Besides keeping the example simple, this assumption also allows plenty of room to grow at each location. As explained earlier, this is an allocation of addresses. From the hostmaster's perspective, it is enough to know that a /24 or /25 has been allocated to a specific location. Figure 13-2 shows how you've allocated your CIDR subnet blocks throughout the enterprise network.

The LAN administrators at each location are responsible for assigning addresses to the individual endpoints on their LANs from the allocated /24s. These administrators arc unlikely to just spool out addresses in a serial fashion. Instead, they probably will take advantage of CIDR's flexibility and create subnetworks for groups of related devices.

Grouping Related Devices

Having segmented your /22 into smaller network blocks for each location, the next step is to start grouping related devices at each location. Such grouping might be considered arbitrary. Some people would tell you it's a waste of time. They might even say that you are creating work with no demonstrable benefit. Such folks clearly have never managed an IP address space and are speaking from ignorance.

Figure 13-2 *Address Allocation Within an Enterprise Network*

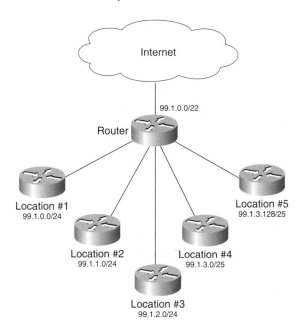

Creating logical groups lets you form subnets more intelligently. Consequently, you can better manage and secure a network. Imagine if all devices in a network were created from the same address block, with no attempt made to logically subnet them. Subnetting can be achieved by picking any one of a number of characteristics, including political boundaries (departments in a company), local geography (floors or wings of a building), or capability (printer, desktop computer, server). There is no right approach; all can be made workable.

However, I can make an argument in favor of subnetting by technical capability. The connectivity patterns of different types of devices can be very distinct. For example, you can count on printers receiving potentially large amounts of traffic but never initiating a communications session. Similarly, client devices can initiate a communications session via a remarkably diverse array of applications, but (hopefully!) they will never be the destination of an inbound request for connectivity. That function is typically reserved for servers. So, the differing communications patterns can serve as a basis for establishing subnets within a LAN. This also makes it easier to enforce some security technologies.

Based on such communication patterns, it is also possible to identify devices that must have a single IP address statically assigned—in other words, an IP address that will remain reliably constant over time. Servers, printers, management ports on hubs and switches, and router interfaces should all have a statically configured IP address. Client endpoints, however, would probably be better served with a dynamic IP address assignment. Several technologies can provide this function, including bootp for UNIX-based computers, and Dynamic Host Configuration Protocol (DHCP). Such technologies work in similar ways: A client machine sends out a broadcast message to find an address server immediately after it boots. This server assigns an IP address to that client machine. These tools were originally part of the massive effort to stave off the Date of Doom, but they have proven themselves far more valuable in saving time by relieving network administrators of the burden of statically configuring IP addresses on client machines.

For the sake of example, you'll carve your /24 CIDR block by function into subnets. You'll use 99.1.1.0/24, which is assigned to Location #2. Table 13-2 shows you the resulting logical groups and the size of their required address blocks. It is important to remember that, because you are using CIDR, the distinction between a subnet and a network address is purely a matter of semantics. All get aggregated up to the /24 block for advertisement to the other routers within the enterprise WAN, and all the /24 networks within that WAN are aggregated back into the /22 for communicating across the Internet.

Table 13-2 *Allocating Blocks Within a /24*

Description of Subnet	Block Size Required	Available Number of Addresses
Base network address	/24	254
DHCP pool for desktops	/25	127
Servers	/28	—
Network interfaces	/29	—
Management ports	/29	—
Printers	/29	—

The next step is figuring out how to carve these required subnet blocks into your /24 address space.

Subnetting the Address Space

After figuring out how much space to allocate to each of your intended subnets, you have to figure out how to subnet the network address space to accommodate these requirements. Table 13-3 shows how the requirements listed in Table 13-2 are accommodated via the subnetting of the 99.1.1.0 /24 network address space.

Table 13-3 *Subnetting the /24*

Description of Subnet	Address Block
Base network address	99.1.1.0 /24
DHCP pool for desktops	99.1.1.0 /25
Servers	99.1.1.128 /28

Table 13-3   *Subnetting the /24 (Continued)*

Description of Subnet	Address Block
Network interfaces	99.1.1.144 /29
Management ports	99.1.1.152 /29
Printers	99.1.1.160 /29
Unassigned	99.1.1.168 /29
Unassigned	99.1.1.176 /28
Unassigned	99.1.1.192 /26

NOTE   Did you notice in Table 13-3 that the unassigned address space was not identified as a single, large group of addresses? Instead, three subnetworks remain unassigned. These subnetworks preserve the symmetry of the CIDR address space and ensure that no boundaries between subnetworks are compromised by future network assignments.

After you have figured out how you will categorize the pool of devices in your network and subnet the network, one last step is left—assigning the IP addresses.

Assigning IP Addresses

The last step in the overall process is to assign unique IP addresses to endpoints. As you saw earlier, "endpoint" is a way to describe virtually anything that lives on or in a network. Desktop computers, networked printers, management ports, and interfaces on network devices, such as switches and routers, servers, and a seemingly infinite list of other types of devices, can all require an IP address.

You know some of these devices will need to be statically configured with an IP address. Such an approach is tantamount to a permanently assigned IP address, but you know that nothing is permanent. Thus, we'll use the term *statically configured* instead of *permanently assigned*. For the endpoints that can be given a dynamic address, a block of addresses is carved from the /24 (in the current example) and is fed to DHCP or a similar tool.

NOTE   It is imperative that you maintain very careful records on any and all statically configured endpoints!

ISP Address Management Issues

An ISP is in an unusual position when it comes to IP address space. Some of its addresses must be used to support internal operations. In this regard, an ISP's networking requirements can resemble an enterprise. However, the vast majority of an ISP's address space is allocated to servicing its customer base. Because we've already looked at address space management issues from an enterprise perspective, there's no need to rehash that here. Instead, let's acknowledge that similarities exist and then focus on the differences.

Whenever an ISP gets a contract to provide Internet access to a new customer, one of the very first considerations that must be attended to is addressing. At this point in time, most end-user organizations have long since migrated to IP for their internal communication needs. Thus, they are likely to already be using IP and some type of IP addressing. The real issue is whether that network address block can also be used for Internet access.

An ISP might find itself having to support IP addressing on behalf of its customers in at least three primary ways:

- An ISP can use its own address space as an inventory of IP addresses for use in satisfying customer needs.

- An ISP can support an address space that is directly registered to, and being used by, a customer.

- An ISP can support an address space that is registered to another ISP but that currently is in use by a customer. Such customers would probably be dual-homed to multiple ISPs, but that's not always the case.

Unfortunately, an ISP can't just arbitrarily select one of these options and use it exclusively. Instead, an ISP is likely to have to support all of these options. The issue of address block ownership can become quite muddled over time. The fact that IETF and IANA have shifted their policies in the past decade with respect to this issue has exacerbated an already unclear issue. We'll look at each approach to address space management for an ISP, as well as their respective implications and consequences.

Assigning Address Space from Inventory

An ISP's business is to provide connectivity to the Internet via IP. Thus, it is essential that an ISP ensure that new customers have a block of IP addresses that they can use to connect to the Internet. One of the means by which this is done is to temporarily assign each new customer a block of addresses carved from a much larger block that is directly registered to the ISP. For example, if the ISP has a /16 network block, it has enough addresses to identify 2 to the 16th (65,535) unique endpoints. Such a block becomes, in effect, part of the ISP's business inventory.

When an ISP grants a customer temporary use of part of its own address space, that space remains registered (in the eyes of the regional registrars, IANA, and so on) to the ISP. Yet there would be great value in being able to identify the party to whom that CIDR block was assigned. The traditional way of discovering to whom an address block is assigned is via the **whois** command. In the case of an ISP's address space, that space would be registered to the ISP, but it can be subassigned to other organizations in small pieces. This is where the Shared WhoIs Project (SWIP) becomes useful.

When an ISP SWIPs an address block to the customer, the ISP remains the only entity that can further modify that SWIP. SWIPing a network address lets an ISP identify to the Internet community which end-user organization is using which CIDR block from its address space. Of course, the other way of looking at this is that SWIPing helps registries ensure that blocks assigned to ISPs are being used correctly.

Assignments from an ISP address block are temporary. The termination date should be set in the service contract that is signed between customer and ISP. The terms and conditions of such contracts likely ensure compliance with RFC 2050. It is imperative that an ISP have procedures in place to ensure that its hostmaster is tightly tied to its service delivery function. This allows the hostmaster to both allocate blocks to new customers as needed and reclaim blocks previously assigned to customers that have left.

RFC 2050

An ISP is awkwardly positioned: It must balance efforts to satisfy customers with operational mandates from the IETF, IANA, and others designed to ensure the viability and stability of the Internet and its address space. Unfortunately, those mandates sometimes are diametrically opposed to what customers want! Stated more simply, an ISP is charged with maintaining an address space's integrity. It uses that address space to provide service to customers. Customers get used to using an address space, and they assume that they "own" it. Such is the life of a hostmaster at an ISP.

We discussed the ramifications of RFC 2050 in Chapter 5, "The Date of Doom." Prior to the publication of that document (which subsequently was embraced as Best Current Practice #12), ISPs were at liberty to regard the address space registered to them as portable. In other words, blocks assigned to specific customers from the ISP's block could be interpreted as being the property of that customer. Thus, when the contract for service ended, customers of some ISPs simply took "their" address block with them. This had the undesirable effect of poking permanent holes in larger blocks. The second problem was that the ex-customer's new ISP had to support its network address, which drove up the number of total routing table entries across the Internet. Thus, address space portability was deemed undesirable.

RFC 2050 effectively ended the mythical claims of portability by declaring that address space registered to ISPs should remain under their charge. ISP customers may be assigned a block of addresses, but both parties should regard that assignment as a lease. When the service contract terminates, the addresses are to be returned to the ISP. This created an interesting problem for ISP customers. Addresses get implemented in a stunning variety of locations: on desktops and laptops, servers, and network interfaces. These are all fairly obvious places for an IP address to be configured. But addresses might also get hard-coded in applications and scripts.

The point is that changing IP addresses is an extremely onerous task. They might get configured on a finite number of devices, but they can get reinforced in a seemingly infinite array of other places. Renumbering is sure to be a costly and risky endeavor. Thus, customers that have made the mistake of directly configuring an address space provided by an ISP will stubbornly resist any and all attempts to force them to renumber!

Supporting Foreign Addresses

A foreign address is one that is not native to a networked environment. There are four scenarios in which a customer can approach an ISP and request that it support a route for its network block even though that block is registered to another ISP:

- The customer organization uses its own directly registered network address space.
- The customer is dual-homed to at least two different ISPs and needs to use just one address block for all connections to the Internet.
- The customer has absconded with an address block from its previous ISP and refuses to renumber its network's endpoints.
- The customer has implemented a block that is unassigned and therefore is not in use.

Each is similar in that an ISP is being asked to support a foreign route. However, the implications of each scenario are remarkably different. Thus, we'll examine them individually.

Using Directly Registered Addresses

Some Internet users are fortunate enough to have their own address space that's directly registered to them. When I say directly registered, I mean just that: They applied for their own address space with their regional registrar. Only directly registered network blocks are considered portable. That is, they are registered to an end-user organization, and that organization may continue to use that network block regardless of which ISP they use for connectivity to and from the Internet.

Although directly registered network addresses might sound like the ideal solution, you should recognize that the Internet's standards and policies are a moving target. What once was considered globally routable may now, in fact, not be! Without going into too much detail about how ISPs set policy regarding how long or short of a network prefix they will support, suffice it to say that any network prefix that isn't a /20 or larger runs the risk of not being supported globally across the Internet. To better appreciate this point, consider Figure 13-3. The dotted lines indicate the limits of the likely reachability of that customer's directly registered network address.

Figure 13-3 *A Customer with a Directly Registered /24 Network Address Block Might Find Its Reachability Limited Across the Internet*

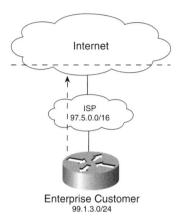

In this figure, a customer with its own /24 network address space purchases Internet access from a second-tier ISP. This ISP ensures that its customers enjoy broad reachability by purchasing transit service from two Tier 1 ISPs. Both of these ISPs, however, are very concerned about the size of their routing tables and refuse to accept any network prefix longer than a /20. This limits the reachability of the customer's /24 to just its immediate upstream ISP.

Thus, an organization with its own directly registered /24 (Class C) network might someday have to accept the fact that its network address isn't being communicated across some ISP networks. When that happens, some tough choices will have to be made. Although this might sound like a far-fetched example, it isn't as outrageous as you might think. Fortunately, most ISPs are willing to discuss exceptions to their policies on a case-by-case basis.

Dual-Homed Customer

A dual-homed ISP customer is one that connects to two different ISPs. Such redundant connectivity affords the customer an added measure of fault tolerance. Figure 13-4 shows the general topology of a dual-homed ISP customer, including the implications of supporting a "foreign" route. The route is considered foreign for two reasons. First, it isn't native to ISP #2. Second, it is part of an address block registered to ISP #1. This puts ISP #2 in the position of having to advertise a valid route for someone else's address space!

Although this practice is becoming increasingly common among end-user organizations that require a fault-tolerant connection to the Internet, it threatens to obsolete many long-standing practices that assume single-connected end-user organizations. We looked at one such practice, known as Source Address Assurance, in Chapter 12, "Network Stability."

Figure 13-4 *A Dual-Homed Internet Customer Requires ISP #2 to Accept a Foreign Route*

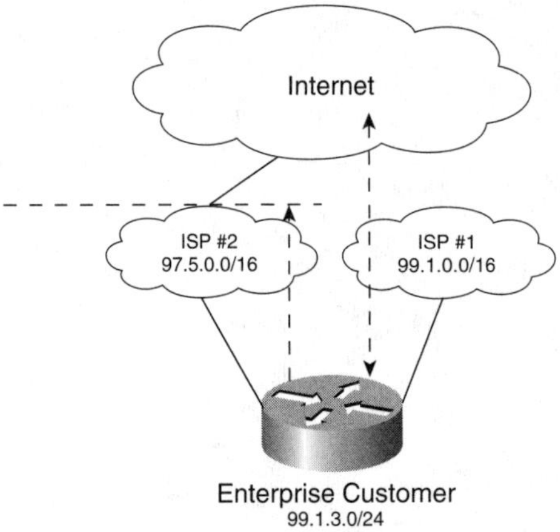

Stolen Address Block

Customers that refuse to part with an address block that was assigned to them by a former ISP sometimes insist that their new ISP accept that block as a precondition to signing a contract with them for service. Although such a precondition seldom makes its way into writing, it isn't uncommon for this to be discussed between customer and sales representative during presale negotiations. Other times, the customer may make no representation other than that it does not need a block of addresses from its new supplier, because it already has one.

Regardless of how it happens, the net effect is the same: The new ISP must accept and advertise a route for a network block created from someone else's address space.

This practice defies aggregation of prefixes, because it is highly likely that the spurious network prefix is not even mathematically close to the ISP's addresses. It also has the undesirable effect of increasing the number of routes that must be supported across the Internet.

"Made-Up" Address Block

Another circumstance can put an ISP in the unenviable position of supporting routes for someone else's address space. Vast portions of the IPv4 address space remain unassigned. Some companies have been known to simply implement a block of addresses from an unassigned range. That would almost make sense if that company required only internal IP connectivity and had no intention of ever connecting to the Internet. Over time, however, requirements can — and do — change. Thus, a company could find itself having to renumber its endpoints if it lacked foresight when it first implemented IP. ISPs should never support an address space that a customer does not have a legitimate claim to use! Although this is a slightly more benign behavior (more ignorant than larcenous), it still results in the same net effect: an ISP's being asked to support a route for an address block that does not rightfully belong to its customer.

The only way for an ISP to ensure that it is not supporting a squatter's rights to an unassigned address block is to query ARIN's (or RIPE or APNIC, depending on geography) whois database before agreeing to support the customer's network block.

What Does It Mean?

The bottom line is that an ISP is likely to have to support routes for an assortment of network addresses. Some of those blocks are created from that ISP's larger blocks, and others are foreign to it. The network blocks it must support tend to be relatively large. The important thing to realize is that the operational issues an ISP faces are just a different aspect of the same challenges facing Internet hosting centers (discussed next) and end-user organizations. Unless you are using IP and you do not connect to the Internet for any reason, you will likely encounter these challenges from one or more perspectives.

Address Management Issues for an Internet Hosting Center

An Internet hosting center is a data center that directly connects to the Internet's backbone. Space within that data center is rented to customers along with Internet connectivity. Such facilities may be owned and operated by an ISP, or they may be ISP-neutral in that they are owned by an organization that does not have its own IP backbone network. Such an organization must either engage in extensive peering relationships with ISPs (which is difficult without a backbone network) or purchase transit services from one or more ISPs. Regardless of how such a facility connects to the Internet, you would be hard-pressed to find any other environment that features as dense or complex a network as an Internet hosting facility. If nothing else, just knowing that the potential exists for hundreds or thousands of different companies to have their Web sites hosted under the same roof should tell you how extensive networking within that location can become.

A couple other attributes make Internet hosting centers worthy of separate examination with respect to managing an IP address space:

- A potentially large quantity of relatively small customer network blocks
- Extreme diversity with respect to types of network and computing products, ownership of those devices, and services supported
- Highly compartmentalized networks that are functionally specialized

Each of these attributes has a direct impact on how a network address space (or spaces) is managed within the data center. We'll take a quick look at each, as well as the peculiar challenges that each holds for a hostmaster.

Lots of "Little" Customers

A typical hosting center customer's presence might consist of half a cabinet of computers and disk drives. Of course, some customers might have several cabinets, or even several rows of cabinets, filled with equipment, but the tendency is toward smaller networks than are seen in an ISP hostmaster's job.

The relatively small size of a hosting center customer's configuration owes to the nature of services provided in such a facility. Many companies appreciate that connecting to the Internet brings a tremendous array of risks. Thus, rather than maintaining their commercial Web site at their own facility, they simply install that site in an Internet hosting center. Connectivity to and from the Internet from the organization's WAN can be made much more secure, because you can better control the inbound attempts to establish contact with hosts on that network.

An Internet hosting center also offers the subtle but significant advantage of placing Web sites right on the Internet's backbone. The alternative is to place the Web site at the edge of the Internet—at the boundary between the customer WAN and the on-ramp to the Net.

The point is that the hostmaster of an Internet hosting facility is likely to be kept busy handing out lots of little address blocks. /28s through /30s are not unusual, even for large computer implementations. Such address blocks are way too small to be supported by an ISP. Consequently, even if a customer had an extra /28 or a similar-sized network, deploying it in an Internet hosting center would be futile.

The CIDR blocks assigned to customer networks would be carved from the hosting facility's larger block. That lets a single CIDR block be advertised to the Internet, as opposed to lots of little network blocks.

Highly Diverse Platforms

Given that a hosting center supports potentially hundreds of customers, you can count on each customer's having a different opinion about which are the best network and computing platforms. This hardware can be owned by the hosting facility or the customer. Customer-owned and operated equipment can be very troublesome. Because the customer is responsible for maintaining the configuration, you can't guarantee that it will subnet correctly, much less follow any of the other stability-promoting guidelines for the IP address space. Thus, you can't count on customer networks to function as expected. Worse, the problems can have an impact on the data center's network, thereby affecting other customers.

Without going into every possible scenario for problems induced by poorly managed customer networks, suffice it to say that the more homogeneous the operating environment, the more stable it can be made. Unfortunately, Internet hosting centers are anything but homogeneous.

Extreme Compartmentalization

Networks within an Internet hosting center are extremely compartmentalized. In simpler terms, there are lots of "little" networks as opposed to one large network that services the entire facility. The extreme complexity of a data center network is caused by the need to separate networks by functionally specialization as well as by ownership. For example, you can safely assume that there is a need for a "house" network that customers use to connect to the Internet. However, there might also be other networks (not connected to the house network) that are used to support backups, administrative duties, clustered computer networks, and possibly even modems or serial connections to customer WANs.

Each customer is also likely to network its own devices to support a variety of functions, including connections back to its own WAN or linking computers in a cluster. Given that each customer could have three or four different networks supporting a single Web site, and multiplying that by the hundreds of customers that could be in a hosting center, you can see how dense and compartmentalized the network environment can be! This creates the potential for confusion, because many of these back-channel networks don't bother using routable IP addresses. Instead, it is standard practice to implement RFC 1918 addresses here. That further ensures the security of such private networks. But statistically it becomes quite possible for two or more of these networks to use the same address space in the same facility. That can make troubleshooting an absolute nightmare. It also makes it absolutely essential to ensure that the back-channel networks do not become interconnected. This is also a very good reason why you should regard RFC 1918 addresses as a finite resource. You can reuse them at will, but treating them as a globally routable address space means that you avoid the confusion of duplicated address blocks on different networks within the same facility.

Summary

This chapter explored some of the challenges of managing an IP address space, including options for obtaining an initial block of addresses. These challenges were further examined in the context of specific business practices. But this chapter stopped short of actually helping you figure out how to carve up and parse out addresses within any given network address block. As you might guess, several approaches can be used. Such address management tactics are explored in Chapter 14, "Address Management Tactics." Together, Chapters 13 and 14 show you how to manage an IP address space.

Address Management Tactics

The previous chapter looked at some of the different network environments and how each environment can affect how you plan for and manage an address space. This chapter expands on this foundation by introducing some of the tactics you can use to manage an address space day-to-day.

When discussing address management with hostmasters, I have yet to find one who described the job as an exact science. In fact, the usual response is an uncomfortable shrug and a sheepish admission that the job is really more of an art than a science. As such, very few universal rules apply. Success in this capacity depends on the hostmaster's innate grasp of binary mathematics vis-à-vis organizational requirements. Given the fluidity of requirements, you can see why I said address management is more art than science.

This chapter examines some of the more common approaches to address space management, explores their strengths and weaknesses, and looks at how each tactic works in a realistic context. This will leave you with ample food for thought should you someday be responsible for managing an address space. The tactics I will show you can be used to create networks within large address spaces or even subnets locally within a network. More important, they can work with all the strategies you saw in Chapter 13, "Planning and Managing an Address Space."

The Challenge of Managing an Address Space

Managing an address space is a deceptively difficult chore, particularly if you are using globally routable addresses. Do you remember the private addresses we looked at in Chapter 5, "The Date of Doom"? These were ranges of regular IP addresses that were arbitrarily reserved by the IETF in RFC 1918 for use in IP-based networks that didn't need Internet connectivity. IP might have been required to support an application base, but the fact that the network was not part of a larger internetwork meant that the addresses didn't have to be globally unique. If they don't have to be globally unique, they can't be routed on the Internet.

NOTE	The private address blocks reserved in RFCs 1597 and 1918 are sometimes described as being nonroutable because they can't be routed across the Internet. Those addresses, however, are perfectly routable within private networks. For that reason, describing them as nonroutable can be misleading. They are more accurately described as *private addresses*.

If you use the private addresses of RFC 1918, your address management chores become greatly simplified. Those addresses, by virtue of not having to be unique globally, aren't a finite resource. Thus, you can assign with almost reckless abandon. Almost. You still need to follow some sort of system to track assignments and manage your network's growth. Because these addresses are not globally unique, you can build in copious room for future growth. However, I caution you to treat whichever address block you implement as if it were a finite resource, regardless of its size. Bad habits are tough to break, so don't get accustomed to sloppy address management practices.

On the other hand, if you are using "real" IP addresses (those that are unique and globally routable), the task of managing that address space carries an extra burden. These addresses are a precious and finite resource. If you squander them, you might have a very difficult time convincing ARIN that you should be entrusted with more addresses. Consequently, it is in your best interest to manage unique IP addresses very carefully. The real art of being a hostmaster lies in balancing address space conservation through careful planning and enabling future growth.

For the purposes of this chapter, we'll walk through some of the inputs to the planning process, but our primary focus will be on the approaches to parsing an address block.

Planning: A Hostmaster's Best Friend

In the simplest of terms, a hostmaster is charged with managing and tracking the consumption of an IP address space. *The decisions you make about how the address space is carved up and distributed can be remarkably persistent.* Thus, it is imperative that you do it right the first time.

Two of the many factors you must consider when planning are long-term growth and technological innovation. Technological innovation is virtually impossible to plan for with any degree of accuracy. You simply never know when the next big innovation will come along. Similarly, an organization's long-term growth can be difficult to plan for simply because each group within the organization grows at different rates. Plus, none of those groups will likely share their strategic future plans with anyone outside their perimeter— even the hostmaster. Either of these contingencies would be difficult to plan for, but trying to plan for both simultaneously can be a nightmare.

Both are sufficiently nebulous as to obviate making decisions with perfect information. In the absence of perfect information, you have to rely on margins for error. In other words, frame out your estimates for future requirements as best you can, and then add in a "fudge factor." The greater the degree of uncertainty in your plans, the larger your fudge factor needs to be. Right about now, you might be thinking that this is an exercise in futility. But when it comes to IP address spaces, you can—and must—plan for ambiguity.

Indeed, a bit of catch-22 logic is in evidence here. If you don't leave adequate room for future expansion, you might find yourself having to repeatedly renumber your users' networks and devices. If you leave too much room for future expansion, you might create even bigger problems when you run out of usable addresses. Quite simply, the room you build in for growth might not prove useful. We'll look at how this paradox works throughout this chapter. Suffice it to say that mismanaging an address space can create unused and unusable IP addresses. The person responsible for charting a course through ambiguity and steering clear of these equally undesirable scenarios is the hostmaster. This leads us to one of the greatest ironies and injustices in the world of IP addressing: Being a hostmaster is a thankless job. If a hostmaster fulfills his duties well, nobody notices. If he doesn't, everybody notices.

The "Classless" Network Engineer Versus the "Class-y" Sys Admin

A system administrator in a data center I managed generated one of the more amusing trouble tickets I have encountered. This person, by virtue of his professional responsibilities, should have had a very firm command of IP addressing—especially as implemented inside that data center. No customers were complaining, and no downtime was being incurred. But there it was: a trouble ticket on a routing problem. Superficial analysis revealed that there was no problem, and that the network was performing as expected. No amount of explanation, it seemed, could dissuade our tenacious system administrator from his belief in the existence of a routing problem. It seemed as if the network engineer and the system administrator were speaking two completely different languages, and no effective communications were possible between them.

When pressed for details, the system administrator explained that two machines, both addressed in the x.168.42.0 network (I've substituted an x for the first octet of the address to protect the guilty), should receive the same Layer 3 broadcasts. But he could prove that, in fact, they were not receiving the same Layer 3 broadcast packets from another host on that network. From a host-level perspective, this indicated a routing problem. The problem was reported and escalated without the benefit of tracing cables or otherwise attempting to discern the network's topology. The only basis for the claim was the commonality of the IP network address.

From the network's perspective, all was in order. The two hosts were on different /28 networks that were separate VLANs connected to the same Layer 2/3 switch. The key piece of information that the system administrator failed to grasp was that both /28 network addresses were carved from the same /24. This system administrator was "class-y" but had no concept of classless IP addresses! The administrator knew that network address blocks were allocated in CIDR blocks as small as /30 inside the data center, yet hadn't grasped the significance of classless addressing.

The only way to get past this conundrum is through planning and the development of a comprehensive address management plan. The basic steps involved in the planning stage are fairly simple:

Step 1   Identify the various user communities, the number of addresses currently needed, and the likelihood and magnitude of future expansion.

Step 2   Evaluate those communities relative to the size of the address space you have to work with. Pay particular attention to the pain factors of underestimating versus overestimating future growth for each community.

Step 3   Determine how many surplus addresses to build in for each community.

After you have completed the planning, the last thing you need to do is implement the plan. This requires you to select a methodology for distributing address spaces to those user communities. Addresses can be allocated manually (in which case records need to be maintained manually) or can be dynamically assigned to specific endpoints using an automated tool such as Dynamic Host Configuration Protocol (DHCP).

Identifying the User Communities

The first step in developing a coherent address management plan is to identify the base of users you need to support. Included in this is some sense of how likely the potential for growth in each group is. This includes not only people, but also the number of IP-addressable peripherals.

Today, a decent planning number for addressing purposes is to allocate two IP addresses for each user. That's not to say each user will need two addresses; some might, and most won't. However, the array of peripheral devices that can be directly connected to the network will only continue to grow. Such devices might be connected to the network to facilitate their shared use (such as printers), or they might only need a connection for their management port (such as LAN switches and PBXs) so that monitoring and/or management software can track them. Each logical group should be considered a community and treated to a separate block assignment.

One of your first steps must be figuring out how large each user community (that is, subnet) is, its propensity to use networked peripherals, and the likelihood of future growth. All these considerations will have an impact on the number of addresses you assign.

Comparing the Pain Factors

The next step in figuring out how to manage your address space is to establish your pain thresholds. Basically, you have to balance the risks of creating address block assignments too close to the required size (that is, leaving little, if any, room for future growth) versus the risks of creating too much room for growth. The best way to assess these risks is to understand how much pain and effort you could incur if you overestimate versus underestimate future expected requirements. This is where there is more art than science in address management.

The negative impact of underestimating growth for any given community is fairly obvious. If the address space they were assigned can't be expanded, you will have to migrate them to a different, larger address space. Each endpoint will have to be reconfigured. If any of them are hosts or destinations that are accessible via host names or domain names, you will have to coordinate DNS changes concurrent with the endpoint reconfiguration. Negotiating with the affected users for scheduled downtime within which you can complete these tasks will be extraordinarily painful. Even worse will be when you have to break the news of the IP renumbering to application developers. It has become a common practice to embed IP addresses directly into custom-developed application software, so renumbering might well translate into rewriting and recompiling software.

Another option might be to simply accommodate growth by using a second range of IP addresses. If the two blocks of IP addresses are not numerically contiguous, you could find yourself having to route between two devices that are essentially on the same network. This approach is far from ideal, but it is much less painful than renumbering.

The impact of overestimating growth is a bit more subtle and tougher to appreciate. On the surface, you could argue that all the negative impacts of a poor address management decision are a direct result of underestimating future requirements. Thus, you could extend your argument that the more excess you build into each network or subnet, the less likely that you will experience any problems. Such an argument is founded on the belief that IP addresses are infinitely available. That's not always the case. In fact, as mentioned at the beginning of this chapter, that is the case only with RFC 1918 addresses.

Overestimating growth in a unique range of IP addresses can result in prematurely exhausting that address space. Today, the watchdogs of the Internet's address space (IANA and ARIN) have really clamped down on giving out address space. Enterprises in particular are routinely turned down when they petition for their own address space. The current philosophy at IANA and ARIN is that, with all the tools currently available (including NAT and RFC 1918 addresses), there is no good reason for a private entity to "own" its own address space. As a direct result of this change in policy, you might not be able to obtain additional IP addresses should you exhaust your existing supply.

NOTE   Nobody really "owns" their IP addresses—not even those that might be registered to them directly. IANA owns the entire Internet address space, but it allocates blocks of addresses to Internet service providers. Those service providers can then assign smaller blocks to their customers for use in accessing, and being accessed from, the Internet. In accordance with RFC 2050 and Internet BCP #12, these assignments are to be regarded as leases. When the contract for service expires, gets canceled, or is not renewed, the customer is expected to return its assigned address block to the issuing service provider.

When you begin evaluating communities of users, it is imperative that you learn to appreciate how resistant to readdressing they would be. That's not to suggest that you do something as ham-fisted as ask them that question directly. Instead, try to figure out the technical and political sources of any potential reluctance to change within their environment. Generally speaking, all users hate change. But some hate it more than others. Those are the ones to identify early in the process.

Building in Growth

You can build in the appropriate amount of growth in a number of ways. Here are the three that I can think of:

- Natural or architectural surplus inherent in the CIDR bit boundaries
- Rounding up to the next-largest bitmask
- Leaving explicit gaps between assigned blocks

These tools for building in growth are not mutually exclusive and can be used in combination.

Natural or architectural surplus is formed almost automatically by the architecture of the binary numbering system. Address blocks and subnets are both are created using powers of 2. Thus, the size of the space you carve out contains 1, 2, 4, 8, 16, 32, 64, 128, 256 (and so on) hosts. Statistically speaking, you will more frequently encounter networks with addressing requirements that fall between these powers of 2 than you will encounter an exact fit. Thus, there is some room for future growth almost automatically when you assign network prefixes or subnets.

Your next option for building in some fluff for future expansion is rounding up. For example, suppose a group requires 13 usable host addresses for its network. You could give them a /28 (or a subnet mask of 255.255.255.240), which yields a total of 16 host addresses.

Subtracting the reserved all-0s and all-1s addresses leaves only 14 usable host addresses. The natural or architectural room for growth in this network would be only one host!

NOTE   When sizing subnets, it is imperative to remember that addresses have to be assigned to nonuser devices, such as LAN switches, router interfaces, network printers, and so on. Thus, as a general rule, you need to overestimate rather than underestimate the number of addresses needed per subnet.

Rounding up that mask to a /27 (a subnet mask of 255.255.255.224) offers 32 total addresses. Subtracting the reserved-value addresses leaves 30 usable host addresses. The surplus for satisfying future growth is 17 addresses (30 − 13). That's a much nicer cushion for supporting future growth than just one address. This is about as much extra as you'd probably want to build into a community of that size. More than that becomes wasteful.

As nice as rounding up masks is for building native capacity for growth, this approach isn't a panacea. It works well for a while, but eventually it results in an inordinate number of surplus addresses. That's just the powers of 2 working against you. For example, rounding up from a /25 to a /24 results in an additional 128 host addresses. Rounding up from a /24 to a /23 generates an additional 256 addresses. Depending on your needs, that's probably a bit more than you really want to allocate. But it is important to recognize this tool for building in growth and to appreciate its abilities and limitations.

The last approach is one we'll look at in a bit more detail throughout the remainder of this chapter. Rather than play games with the binary mathematics of the address space, you can build in room for growth by simply leaving gaps between address spaces you assign. Done properly, two assigned spaces are buffered by a free or unassigned space. That space can then accommodate growth of either of its neighboring address blocks.

After evaluating your users' needs (present and projected) vis-à-vis your address space constraints and the pain of making mistakes, you should be able to make a much more informed decision about which basic tactic(s) you should use to manage your address space.

Basic Tactics

There are four basic address management tactics; each approach has its own strengths and weaknesses. You need to understand each one and then make your own decision about how useful it might be in the context of your job. I wouldn't be surprised if you concluded that the best tactic in any given situation is actually a blend of tactics.

The basic tactics you might find useful are

- Sequential
- Sequential with gaps
- Predefining symmetrical gaps
- Balkanization

Of course, the fifth option is always the random approach. I don't consider that a valid approach for managing an address space. An all-too-familiar scenario is when a new hostmaster comes into an organization, looks at the address allocation records he has just inherited, and concludes that his predecessor assigned blocks at random. I prefer to believe that what initially appears to be a random assignment of address space is nothing more than the entropic effects of constant change being exerted on an address space over time.

We'll examine each of these four basic tactics for managing an address space in the remainder of this chapter. First, I'll describe the approach and how it works. That will help you better appreciate some of the benefits and limitations or drawbacks. Then I'll show you a network diagram and a detailed table to demonstrate how a particular address management tactic would affect address assignment within the context of a specific network.

Sequential Assignment

The most logical approach to use when managing an address space is to assign ranges of host addresses in a sequential fashion. This approach is sometimes referred to as a right-to-left bitwise approach, because you assign blocks from the lowest end of the address range first (using the rightmost bits) and progress in sequence to the higher numbers (moving toward the leftmost bits) in the address space.

Strengths and Weaknesses

There are many benefits to using this simple approach to address assignment. It's eminently logical and easy to follow. Those are important attributes if you inherit someone else's hostmaster responsibilities, or if you hope to someday pass the torch to someone else. Perhaps the greatest benefit of this approach is that it is very easy to see how much of your total address space remains unassigned. It is all numerically contiguous at the high end of your address block. Also, not much effort is required to figure out which block to assign next—it's always the next chunk of available address space.

The single greatest drawback of the sequential approach is that you lock yourself into the size of block you assign. You can plan for growth (architectural and/or bitmask rounding can work well here), but that growth is limited when you assign the next address space. Thus, it is imperative to size these network blocks correctly as you assign them. If you are adhering strictly to a sequential assignment of address space, accommodating growth in excess of the original surplus in any given assigned block of addresses requires you to migrate that user community to a new address space. This isn't likely to improve your customers' satisfaction levels.

You can guard against this by planning for growth with each address block you assign from your network block. But, as we discussed at the beginning of this chapter, trying to plan for growth can have adverse effects. If you build in too much room for growth, you are wasting space. After reviewing the strengths and weaknesses of this approach, it is easy to understand why it is really of most use in situations where little to no future growth is expected.

Realistic Context

Perhaps the best way to solidify the concept of sequential address assignment is to examine what a hostmaster's records might look like in such an environment. Figure 14-1 shows a small network that correlates with a hostmaster's records. This sample network is a /24 block that serves a small business campus. The heart of the campus network is a single device that functions as a Layer 2 and 3 switch. Each of the four individual LANs consists of a single Layer 2 distribution switch, and all are defined as virtual local-area networks (VLANs) on the Layer 2/3 switch. Each VLAN is relatively small (a simplifying assumption) and connects to a single switch dedicated to a single workgroup.

Figure 14-1 *Sample Network for the Sequential Assignment of Addresses*

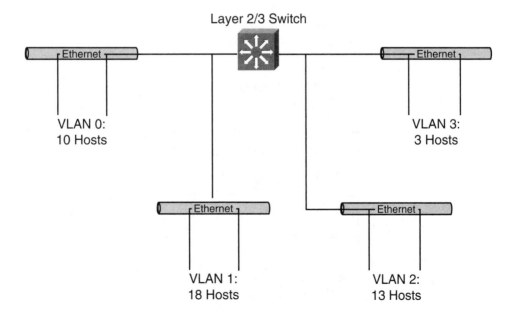

Table 14-1 shows the sequential progression of addresses as you parse address blocks carved out of your network address block. To make it easier for you to see the effects of the CIDR mask (the */number*), the bits in the address that are used to identify the network are bold.

Please note that this example, while not necessarily implemented in the most clever or appropriate way, is quite serviceable. Whether it proves extensible remains to be seen.

Table 14-1   *Sequential Assignments in a 24-Bit Network*

	Binary Network Plus Subnet Address	**Decimal Translation**
Base	**11000000.10101000.01111101**.00000000	192.168.125.0 /24
LAN management ports	**11000000.10101000.01111101.0000**0000	192.168.125.0 /28
LAN management ports	↓	↓
LAN management ports	**11000000.10101000.01111101.0000**1111	192.168.125.15
VLAN 0	**11000000.10101000.01111101.0001**0000	192.168.125.16 /28
VLAN 0	↓	↓
VLAN 0	**11000000.10101000.01111101.0001**1111	192.168.125.31
VLAN 1	**11000000.10101000.01111101.001**00000	192.168.125.32 /27
VLAN 1	↓	↓
VLAN 1	**11000000.10101000.01111101.001**11111	192.168.125.63
VLAN 2	**11000000.10101000.01111101.0100**0000	192.168.125.64 /28
VLAN 2	↓	↓
VLAN 2	**11000000.10101000.01111101.0100**1111	192.168.125.79
VLAN 3	**11000000.10101000.01111101.01010**000	192.168.125.80 /29
VLAN 3	↓	↓
VLAN 3	**11000000.10101000.01111101.01010**111	192.168.125.87
Unassigned	**11000000.10101000.01111101**.01011000	192.168.125.88
Unassigned	↓	↓
Unassigned	**11000000.10101000.01111101**.11111111	192.168.125.255

Our sample network features four VLANs for user communities and another block of addresses used for LAN management ports on the Layer 2/3 switch, as well as the distribution switches. Arguably, the network block assigned for this purpose is oversized. It features a /28 with 14 usable addresses when all that is needed is just four addresses (one for each of the switches). It doesn't seem likely that this network block will be outgrown any time soon, but it is important to recognize the interdependencies between this group of addresses and the other VLANs. Each VLAN currently consists of a single switch, but growth will inevitably require another switch to connect the new users and/or devices. That new switch will require an address for its management port, or you won't be able to monitor it or manage it remotely. Adding new VLANs imposes a similar requirement on this LAN management port group of addresses. Regardless of the reason for adding a switch, each new one that is introduced requires a host address from this group. So, if there were any group you were going to oversize, this would be a good candidate.

The next thing you should notice is the four VLANs themselves (numbered 0 through 3). Table 14-2 summarizes the number of addressed devices in each VLAN, the number of available device addresses (not counting the reserved host address values), and the remainder. A quick look at this table reveals how much (and how little) room for growth really exists.

Table 14-2   *Room for Growth in a Sequentially-Numbered Network*

Community	Net Number of Addresses Available	Number of Addresses Used	Number of Addresses Left Over
LAN management ports (/28)	14	4	10
VLAN 0 (/28)	14	10	4
VLAN 1 (/27)	30	18	12
VLAN 2 (/28)	14	13	1
VLAN 3 (/29)	6	3	3

You can readily see that the network's greatest exposure lies within VLAN 2. This VLAN has only a single available address within its mathematical range. If that community needs to add two more devices, it will have to renumber all its addressed devices to the addresses remaining unassigned in the high end of the address space.

An alternative solution also exists. Because VLAN 3 contains just three devices, it might be easier to migrate those users and their devices to a new address space and simply expand VLAN 2 by changing its mask to a /27. Table 14-3 demonstrates the effects of network address assignments within this network, assuming that you expand VLAN 2 to a /27 network and move VLAN 3 to the next available block of addressing.

Table 14-3   *Post-Change Network Address Assignments*

	Binary Network Plus Subnet Address	Decimal Translation
Base	**11000000.10101000.01111101.**00000000	192.168.125.0 /24
LAN management ports	**11000000.10101000.01111101.0000**0000	192.168.125.0 /28
LAN management ports	↓	↓
LAN management ports	**11000000.10101000.01111101.0000**1111	192.168.125.15
VLAN 0	**11000000.10101000.01111101.0001**0000	192.168.125.16 /28
VLAN 0	↓	↓
VLAN 0	**11000000.10101000.01111101.0001**1111	192.168.125.31
VLAN 1	**11000000.10101000.01111101.001**00000	192.168.125.32 /27
VLAN 1	↓	↓
VLAN 1	**11000000.10101000.01111101.001**11111	192.168.125.63
VLAN 2	**11000000.10101000.01111101.010**00000	192.168.125.64 /27
VLAN 2	↓	↓
VLAN 2	**11000000.10101000.01111101.010**11111	192.168.125.95
VLAN 3	**11000000.10101000.01111101.01100**000	192.168.125.96 /29
VLAN 3	↓	↓
VLAN 3	**11000000.10101000.01111101.01100**111	192.168.125.103
Unassigned	**11000000.10101000.01111101.**01101000	192.168.125.104
Unassigned	↓	↓
Unassigned	**11000000.10101000.01111101.**11111111	192.168.125.255

One of the very subtle, but critical, aspects of this table that you should take the time to appreciate is its symmetry. Remember Chapter 6, "Classless Interdomain Routing (CIDR)," when we looked at the symmetry of subnetting? Essentially, we said that there were two /28s in each /27 and two /27s in each /26. Well, this table maintains this symmetry. The first three network blocks assigned equal a /26 (a /27 plus two /28s). Consequently, all network assignments after this begin on even bit boundaries. Stated differently, there is no encroachment from network to network. Later in this chapter, we'll look at how this example could be butchered through lack of planning and foresight, with potentially catastrophic effects on the user base.

Sequential Assignment with Gaps

A variation on the sequential assignment of addresses is formed by intentionally leaving a gap between blocks. This approach is potentially more practical than a straight sequential assignment. For example, it leaves more room for growth, and it can accommodate growth within any of its component networks without necessarily forcing you to renumber devices. This is particularly beneficial if you know your user communities are likely to grow in the future or if they have demonstrated a tendency to grow either unexpectedly or rapidly in the past.

Here are two key questions you need to answer before implementing this approach to address space management:

- What size gaps should you provide between assigned address blocks? The gap would likely vary across the communities in your user base rather than being a constant size.

- What is the best way to create those gaps? Remember, there are three different ways to create spare capacity: architectural, bitmask rounding, and explicit gaps. Using a sequential approach with gaps means that you will automatically use at least two of these tactics (gaps plus the architectural surplus).

The right answer to the second question might hinge on your answer to the first question. If only a small gap is needed, either architectural surplus or bitmask rounding might well suffice. If a larger margin for expansion is required, an explicitly defined gap is required.

Strengths and Weaknesses

Assigning address spaces sequentially, with intentional gaps between assignments, builds on the strengths of a sequential approach. It lets you see fairly quickly how much address space remains unused at the high end of your address block. More importantly, it does so while avoiding the primary weakness of the strictly sequential assignment method. This weakness is the inflexibility of that approach, which makes it absolutely crucial that you size the network blocks well the first time.

The explicitly defined gaps between assigned network address spaces supplement the natural margin for growth found within each assigned block with a buffer zone between assigned blocks. This free space could be used to satisfy growth within any network that is numerically contiguous to it. Thus, unlike the scenario we discussed earlier, you shouldn't have to renumber subnets except in extreme cases.

The obvious drawback of this approach is that it has the potential to waste address spaces. The larger the explicit gaps, the greater the waste of address spaces. This gets back to the original quandary of having to strike the right balance between current addressing needs and future expected needs. Of course, this approach offers an improvement over just sequential addressing with surpluses built into each network assigned, in that the free space can be shared between either of its two bordering address spaces. That explanation probably still sounds a bit nebulous, so let's look at how explicitly defined gaps in an address space can be beneficial in a realistic context.

Realistic Context

Let's take another look at how you could parse network addresses from within the example illustrated in Figure 14-1. This time, we'll assign our network addresses sequentially but leave gaps explicitly defined between them. This presents a great opportunity to see how a lack of planning can break a network assignment scheme. Table 14-3 maintained some semblance of binary symmetry. The first three network blocks assigned balanced each other out. We started out with two /28 networks (which equals one /27) and a /27 (which, together with the pair of /28s, accounts for a /26 taken out of the top of the address space). So far, the scheme was symmetrical. The last address space carved out for VLAN #3 was a /29. Because it was the last space and is followed only by an unformatted free space, this doesn't pose any problems whatsoever.

This scheme's symmetry can either be extended or broken through the insertion of free spaces. Although those spaces were intended to provide room for growth, they might not be usable, as you shall soon see. More importantly, such spurious blocks can impinge on neighboring blocks. That's not at all obvious when you look at decimal addresses, but it becomes remarkably clear when viewed in binary form. The next two sections show you both the wrong and right ways to manage an address space.

How Not to Manage an Address Space

Table 14-4 deviates from the norm by showing you how *not* to manage an address space. More specifically, it demonstrates the folly of improper planning. In this example, the network and address space used for the previous example remain the same, but I've opted to partition the network assignments with some buffer space. This space, in theory, affords room to grow. That's a good thing—if it is implemented properly.

Take a look a Table 14-4, and then we'll cover the problems inherent within it.

Table 14-4 *How Not to Assign Addresses with Gaps*

	Binary Network Plus Subnet Address	Decimal Translation
Base	**11000000.10101000.01111101**.00000000	192.168.125.0 /24
LAN management ports	**11000000.10101000.01111101.0000**0000	192.168.125.0 /28
LAN management ports	↓	↓

Table 14-4   *How Not to Assign Addresses with Gaps (Continued)*

	Binary Network Plus Subnet Address	**Decimal Translation**
LAN management ports	11000000.10101000.01111101.00001111	192.168.125.15
Intentional gap	11000000.10101000.01111101.00010000	192.168.125.16 /30
Intentional gap	↓	↓
Intentional gap	11000000.10101000.01111101.00010011	192.168.125.19
VLAN 0	11000000.10101000.01111101.00010100	192.168.125.20 /28
VLAN 0	↓	↓
VLAN 0	11000000.10101000.01111101.00011111	192.168.125.31
Intentional gap	11000000.10101000.01111101.00100000	192.168.125.32 /29
Intentional gap	↓	↓
Intentional gap	11000000.10101000.01111101.00100111	192.168.125.39
VLAN 1	11000000.10101000.01111101.00101000	192.168.125.40 /29
VLAN 1	↓	↓
VLAN 1	11000000.10101000.01111101.00101111	192.168.125.47
Intentional gap	11000000.10101000.01111101.00110000	192.168.125.48 /30
Intentional gap	↓	↓
Intentional gap	11000000.10101000.01111101.00110011	192.168.125.51
VLAN 2	11000000.10101000.01111101.00110100	192.168.125.52 /27
VLAN 2	↓	↓
VLAN 2	11000000.10101000.01111101.00111111	192.168.125.63
Intentional gap	11000000.10101000.01111101.01000000	192.168.125.64 /28
Intentional gap	↓	↓
Intentional gap	11000000.10101000.01111101.01001111	192.168.125.79
VLAN 3	11000000.10101000.01111101.01010000	192.168.125.80 /29
VLAN 3	↓	↓
VLAN 3	11000000.10101000.01111101.01100111	192.168.125.103
Unassigned	11000000.10101000.01111101.01101000	192.168.125.104
Unassigned	↓	↓
Unassigned	11000000.10101000.01111101.11111111	192.168.125.255

Table 14-4 shows the interblock gap effect. These gaps are based solely on the sizes of the blocks that are assigned to VLANs. *However, the hostmaster responsible for this mess created the explicit gaps with only superficial thought about the future.* If you consider the *usability* of each of those gaps, you might shake your head and wonder just what the explicit gaps do for you.

The problems begin almost immediately, because a /30 is inserted between a pair of /28s that were assigned to LAN management ports and VLAN 0. This causes VLAN 0 to start at the rather odd host address of .20. As a result, you can see that there are only 12 host addresses in that /28, whereas there should be 16.

NOTE   There's an easy way to avoid having subnets spill over boundaries and into another subnet's range. Simply make sure that the base address of each subnet assigned correlates mathematically to a CIDR boundary. Those boundaries are identified by the decimal value of each bit in the IPv4 address space. Those values—1, 2, 4, 8, 16, 32, 64, and 128—are powers of 2. Any other value is not a power of 2 and requires a mixed pattern of 1s and 0s. That's your clue that you are not starting your subnet on a CIDR boundary. A quick survey of the base IP addresses of the subnets in Table 14-4 vis-à-vis these powers of 2 should quickly identify the problem subnets.

VLAN 2 has the same problem. That is a /27, and its first host address should be 00000. Instead, because a /30 free space was inserted in front of it, it starts at 10100. This has the obvious effect of directly reducing the number of possible host addresses within that subnet. In this particular case, the number of definable host addresses remaining is insufficient for the number of hosts that require addresses in VLAN 2. A /27 should provide 32 possible host addresses; VLAN 2 requires 13, but only 12 are available. This wouldn't make users happy.

A more subtle problem with the way room for growth is provided in this example lies in the arbitrary sizes selected vis-à-vis the architectural limitations of the binary address space. To better illustrate this point, let's look at how we can grow VLAN 2 within the confines of this addressing scheme. VLAN 2 is a /27; it should have 32 total host addresses, but only 12 are available due to the preceding gap cutting into its space. If we increase its bitmask to a /26, we are essentially supernetting it with the next /27. Unfortunately, we didn't think this VLAN would grow much, so we left only a /28 unassigned as a buffer. In other words, we don't have enough room to supernet VLAN 2 with its neighboring free space.

I hope you realize that this is an extreme case designed solely to reinforce the importance of proper planning. This case demonstrates some of the ways an address space can be broken through mismanagement, even if it is well-intentioned. Although I won't go so far as to say that there is any one correct way to manage an address space, there is certainly a lot of room for improvement relative to the last example. The next section looks at one of the possible ways to correctly manage an address space.

In my opinion, this approach is at its best when used in conjunction with RFC 1918 addresses. That way, you have the luxury of up to 16 million IP addresses to play with, and your interblock gaps can be quite generous—preferably even symmetrical. The next section helps you better appreciate the concept of intentional gaps between assigned blocks by showing you the right way to implement this approach.

Predefining with Symmetrical Gaps

The next logical step is to take an address space, presubnet it, and add symmetrical gaps between the preassigned blocks. This is one of the more elegant and sophisticated approaches to managing an address space, but it is difficult to describe. The goal of such an approach is to maintain some semblance of symmetry and order. Scanning back through the tables presented in previous sections, you can see that there's a bit of a "rat's nest" look to the address assignments. In other words, blocks were created as they were needed, and there is no rhyme or reason to the juxtaposition of different block sizes.

One tactic you can use to maintain a more orderly appearance is to preallocate blocks based on prefix size. While I'll admit that neatness might not be something everyone aspires to, it definitely helps keep an address space more manageable and might even prove to be the more efficient approach over time.

This approach is based on the binary mathematics of the IP address space. It should be intuitive by now that in a binary number system, for each numeral you move to the right, you are halving the value of the previous numeral. Conversely, for each numeral you move to the left, you are doubling the value of the previous numeral. Applying this mathematical fact, a /25 network is exactly half of a /24. Thus, there are two /25s in a /24. You can put this concept to use in managing an IP address space by predefining blocks.

If you are managing a large space, such as a /16, you might find it easier to manage space by predefining a pair of /25s whenever you need to create one. That way, a new /25 is ready and waiting should the need arise for a new one. Assigning the lower range of numbers first also creates room for the /25 to grow into a /24. To illustrate this point, consider Table 14-5.

Table 14-5   *Demonstrating Symmetry*

Network Number	CIDR Mask	Base Address
Base	/24	192.168.125.0
1	/25	192.168.125.0
2	/25	192.168.125.128

In Table 14-5, you can see how the /25s neatly cleave the /24 into equal halves. The first one contains host addresses numbered 0 through 127, and the second contains host addresses 128 through 255. Thus, the two /25s are sometimes referred to by their relative values as the "upper half" and the "lower half" of the /24. Should you need to create a network or subnetwork with more than 64 devices but fewer than 128, you would use a /25. To keep things symmetric and enable future growth, you would record both halves being created in your database but assign only one. Ostensibly, you would start with the lower half of the /24. The other would remain free for future use.

Similarly, you can create four /26 networks from within a /24-sized address space. Alternatively, as you can see in Table 14-6, you can take a /24 and carve it into four /26 network blocks. Another neat twist shown in this table is to take one of those /26 blocks and subdivide it into a pair of /27s. The symmetry is apparent even in decimal, because the initial host addresses of each of those smaller blocks starts on a familiar power of 2 or sums of powers of 2.

Table 14-6 *Demonstrating Symmetry*

Network Number	CIDR Mask	Decimal Address Value
Base	/24	192.168.125.0
1	/26	192.168.125.0
2	/26	192.168.125.64
3	/26	192.168.125.128
4	/27	192.168.125.192
5	/27	192.168.125.224

Strengths and Weaknesses

This approach excels in creating a logical and symmetrical framework for the long-term management of your address space. If you maintain your records properly, you can tell at a glance how much address space remains unassigned, and in what size chunks. It is important to remember that you aren't necessarily creating "routes" that your routers will have to track when you predefine address blocks in this manner. A network prefix doesn't become a route until it is implemented. Even then, your network would aggregate network prefixes to deal with the largest block possible without compromising its ability to deliver all datagrams successfully within your network.

Another nice feature of this approach is that you can supernet unused contiguous blocks to create spaces that are larger should the need arise. As you saw in Chapter 6, supernetting absolutely requires numerically contiguous address space. Two or more smaller spaces can be integrated into a single larger space just by virtue of changing a network mask. Predefining address space creates the potential for supernetting in the future.

Perhaps the only weakness in this approach is that the predefined space is inherently idle. However, it isn't necessarily wasted. Remember: This is space that would be idle regardless of how you did your network assignments. Predefining it just puts the available address space into sized blocks that are immediately recognizable and creates room for growth for neighboring networks. If those neighbors don't require growth, the block can be put to another use.

Realistic Context

To better demonstrate the concept of predefined address spaces, consider Table 14-7. In this table, you can see how an address space is parsed across the various departments of a moderate-sized company. The company enjoys a /22 network block, which is equal in size to four Class C networks (1024 total addresses). At a high level, the fictitious company's /22 CIDR block has been sectioned into a pair of /24s and a /23. These blocks are then carved into even smaller blocks for assignment to individual departments within the company.

Table 14-7   *Symmetrical Assignments in a 23-Bit Network*

Network Number	Status	CIDR Mask	Base Address
CIDR block	—	/22	192.168.125.0
Base	—	/23	192.168.125.0
Base	—	/24	192.168.125.0
1	HQ	/25	192.168.125.0
2	**Free**	/25	192.168.125.128
Base	—	/24	192.168.126.0
1	Sales	/26	192.168.126.0
2	Finance	/26	192.168.126.64
3	**Free**	/26	192.168.126.128
4	HR	/27	192.168.126.192
5	Network interfaces	/27	192.168.126.224
Base	**Free**	/23	192.168.127.0

Did you notice that the free spaces were created to maintain symmetry in the address space? We could have taken the /25 free space that immediately follows the HQ space and allocated it to both the Sales and Finance Departments (their two /26s equal a /25), but that would have left three important groups of users landlocked without any way to expand except for renumbering. This isn't a very attractive option. You can expand a subnet in one of two ways. If there's adequate space that is numerically contiguous, you can supernet to create a larger block. Your only other alternative is to move the affected department to a larger space that must be carved from the free /23 space.

In this example, because HQ gets a /25, we retain symmetry by creating a free /25. This effectively consumes the first /24 worth of addresses in our block. The next block of addresses assigned comes from the top of the next /24.

This is perhaps the best way to carve up an address space. Maintaining symmetry through the use of carefully sized and predefined free spaces ensures that you won't run into any problems like the ones you saw earlier in this chapter.

Balkanizing an Address Space

Address space management took on greater urgency with the release of RFC 1917 in February 1996. This RFC was authored as part of the IETF's multifaceted effort to stave off an impending collapse of the Internet's address space and architecture. It didn't define any new technology. It was simply an urgent appeal to the Internet community to return unused address space to IANA for use in satisfying the growing demand for address space.

With the publication of this document, IP address space was viewed as a precious and finite commodity for the first time. Some organizations that had previously "stocked up" on network address space viewed this as justification for their foresight and reinforced the need to maintain their unused address blocks for future use. Their rationale was that if an organization surrendered its unused address blocks to help the Internet meet its surging demand for addresses, it might not be able to get more addresses in the future it they needed them.

One of the less-noble responses to RFC 1917 was the emergence of a new address management strategy: balkanization. Anyone familiar with European geopolitics will recognize the root of this word. The Balkans is a crossroads region of Europe that has long been both a cultural melting pot and a source of conflict. Its location midway between Europe and the Middle East has resulted in its settlement by a remarkable variety of ethnic tribes and religious convictions. The result is a land so divided that it resists integration into a cohesive system of government. In that spirit, balkanization of an IP address space refers to carving it into lots of little pieces so that it can't be taken away. Fragmentation, in theory, could be so complete that nothing remains but unroutable odd-sized blocks between assigned ranges of addresses.

Strengths and Weaknesses

Balkanization is an inherently inefficient practice. In fact, it was specifically intended to be inefficient. This tactic is territorialism at its worst. Its primary benefit is to break a larger address block into many smaller fragments that would be of limited value outside your organization. Attempts to reclaim and reuse otherwise unassigned address space fragments would only result in an increase in the size of Internet routing tables. That's not something that the IANA and ICANN organizations view as good for the Internet in the long term. Thus, balkanization solidifies your claim to a network address space that would otherwise be far too large for your needs.

A subtle benefit of using this address allocation approach is that each block assigned has ample room to grow at both ends of its range of valid addresses. Finally, this approach is rather simple to deploy. Little, if any, forethought and planning are required. In other words, the role of the hostmaster is greatly simplified by virtue of having so much address space to begin with.

The drawbacks of balkanization are few, but noteworthy. Whereas other tactics strive to conserve address space so that the IPv4 address space itself can service an ever-growing population, this approach is strictly selfish. A large amount of otherwise reusable address space is intentionally locked up within one organization.

Another subtle implication is that not every address space is a good candidate for balkanization. This practice is best suited to address blocks that are substantially larger than the networks they are servicing. For example, a /24 with a mere 254 usable host addresses is unlikely to attract the attention of IANA and/or ICANN for reclamation. Thus, it is a poor candidate for balkanization.

I'm not advocating the practice of balkanizing an address space. It is at best a defensive move designed to protect an address space from being reclaimed. Implicit in this is that the space was underutilized to the extent that it should be reclaimed. I mention this approach solely to reinforce the necessity of carefully managing your address space. A random or sloppy approach to managing an address space can have the same net effect as balkanization. Neither is acceptable.

I realize that I have rambled on *ad nauseum* about a somewhat esoteric topic. The next section helps you better appreciate what it means to balkanize an address space.

Realistic Context

Smaller address spaces simply aren't good candidates for balkanization. For one thing, there aren't enough addresses to fragment into smaller blocks. More important, larger blocks afford a greater benefit to the Internet if they can be reclaimed. Consequently, I'll depart from my usual custom of using smaller, more manageable address blocks as examples. The only way to adequately demonstrate balkanization is with a larger block. This example uses a /19 network address block. As you saw in Table 4-1 from Chapter 4, "Variable-Length Subnet Masks," a /19 offers 8192 total host addresses. This is the equivalent of 32 Class C-sized network address spaces.

For the sake of the example, assume that our organization is relatively small. It consists of 600 endpoints scattered across five different geographic locations, with an approximately equal number at each location. A /24 with its 254 usable addresses would more than suffice for each of the five locations. So a /19 is probably way more than we need. In fact, a /22 with its 1024 addresses would probably be just about right. Thus, if we weren't careful, we could find at least half of our /19 in danger of being reclaimed. If that block were reclaimed, we would be left with a /20 (half of a /19), which is still way too big for our needs. But there is a way of scattering our address assignments to make our network appear to require more space than it really does. We can balkanize our network address space.

Because the network belongs to a private enterprise, route aggregation internally is not of concern. There is only a single connection to the Internet, and all addresses assigned (regardless of size) are announced via a single route: the /19. Figure 14-2 shows the basic topology of this sample network. It gives you the context for understanding our hostmaster's records of address assignments within our network. Those assignments are listed in Table 14-8.

Figure 14-2 *Network Topology of the Balkanized Address Space*

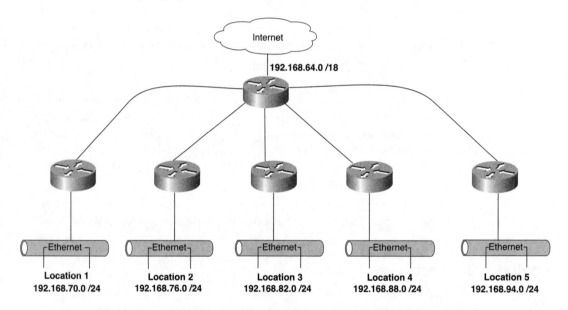

In Figure 14-2, you can see that the hosts at each of the five locations are each treated to a /24 network address block. An additional /24 is allocated to LAN management ports at each of these locations. That brings us up to ten /24 networks allocated out of the 32 that are available in the 192.168.64.0/19 address space. Another one has been allocated for use in identifying network backbone interfaces, which means that 11 are used and 21 are surplus. Table 14-8 shows you how this size block can be fragmented so thoroughly that the remaining free spaces aren't worth using outside the organization.

Table 14-8   *Balkanizing a 19-Bit Network*

	Binary Network Plus Subnet Address	Decimal Translation
Base	**11000000.10101000.01**000000.00000000	192.168.64.0/19
Backbone interfaces	11000000.10101000.01000000.00000000	192.168.64.0 /24
Backbone interfaces	↓	↓
Backbone interfaces	11000000.10101000.01000000.11111111	192.168.64.255
Unassigned	11000000.10101000.01000001.00000000	192.168.65.0 /24
Unassigned	↓	↓
Unassigned	**11000000.10101000.01000001.**11111111	192.168.65.255
Unassigned	11000000.10101000.01000010.00000000	192.168.66.0 /24
Unassigned	↓	↓
Unassigned	**11000000.10101000.01000010.**11111111	192.168.66.255
Location 1 LAN management ports	**11000000.10101000.01000011.**00000000	192.168.67.0 /24
Location 1 LAN management ports	↓	↓
Location 1 LAN management ports	**11000000.10101000.01000011.**11111111	192.168.67.255
Unassigned	**11000000.10101000.0100010**0.00000000	192.168.68.0 /23
Unassigned	↓	↓
Unassigned	**11000000.10101000.0100010**1.11111111	192.168.69.255
Location 1 hosts	**11000000.10101000.01000110.**00000000	192.168.70.0 /24
Location 1 hosts	↓	↓
Location 1 hosts	**11000000.10101000.01000110.**11111111	192.168.70.255
Unassigned	**11000000.10101000.01000111.**00000000	192.168.71.0 /24
Unassigned	↓	↓
Unassigned	**11000000.10101000.01000111.**11111111	192.168.71.255

continues

Table 14-8   *Balkanizing a 19-Bit Network (Continued)*

	Binary Network Plus Subnet Address	Decimal Translation
Unassigned	**11000000.10101000.01001000.**00000000	192.168.72.0 /24
Unassigned	↓	↓
Unassigned	**11000000.10101000.01001000.**11111111	192.168.72.255
Location 2 LAN management ports	**11000000.10101000.01001001.**00000000	192.168.73.0 /24
Location 2 LAN management ports	↓	↓
Location 2 LAN management ports	**11000000.10101000.01001001.**11111111	192.168.73.255
Unassigned	**11000000.10101000.01001010.**00000000	192.168.74.0 /23
Unassigned	↓	↓
Unassigned	**11000000.10101000.01001011.**11111111	192.168.75.255
Location 2 hosts	**11000000.10101000.01001100.**00000000	192.168.76.0 /24
Location 2 hosts	↓	↓
Location 2 hosts	**11000000.10101000.01001100.**11111111	192.168.76.255
Unassigned	**11000000.10101000.01001101.**00000000	192.168.77.0 /24
Unassigned	↓	↓
Unassigned	**11000000.10101000.01001101.**11111111	192.168.77.255
Unassigned	**11000000.10101000.01001110.**00000000	192.168.78.0 /24
Unassigned	↓	↓
Unassigned	**11000000.10101000.01001110.**11111111	192.168.78.255
Location 3 LAN management ports	**11000000.10101000.01001111.**00000000	192.168.79.0 /24
Location 3 LAN management ports	↓	↓
Location 3 LAN management ports	**11000000.10101000.**01001111.11111111	192.168.79.255
Unassigned	**11000000.10101000.01010000.**00000000	192.168.80.0 /23

Table 14-8 *Balkanizing a 19-Bit Network (Continued)*

	Binary Network Plus Subnet Address	Decimal Translation
Unassigned	↓	↓
Unassigned	**11000000.10101000.0101000**1.11111111	192.168.81.255
Location 3 hosts	**11000000.10101000.01010010.**00000000	192.168.82.0 /24
Location 3 hosts	↓	↓
Location 3 hosts	**11000000.10101000.01010010.**11111111	192.168.82.255
Unassigned	**11000000.10101000.01010011.**00000000	192.168.83.0 /24
Unassigned	↓	↓
Unassigned	**11000000.10101000.01010011.**11111111	192.168.83.255
Unassigned	**11000000.10101000.01010100.**00000000	192.168.84.0 /24
Unassigned	↓	↓
Unassigned	**11000000.10101000.01010100.**11111111	192.168.84.255
Location 4 LAN management ports	**11000000.10101000.01010101.**00000000	192.168.85.0 /24
Location 4 LAN management ports	↓	↓
Location 4 LAN management ports	**11000000.10101000.01010101.**11111111	192.168.85.255
Unassigned	**11000000.10101000.0101011**0.00000000	192.168.86.0 /23
Unassigned	↓	↓
Unassigned	**11000000.10101000.0101011**1.11111111	192.168.87.255
Location 4 hosts	**11000000.10101000.01011000.**00000000	192.168.88.0 /24
Location 4 hosts	↓	↓
Location 4 hosts	**11000000.10101000.01011000.**11111111	192.168.88.255
Unassigned	**11000000.10101000.01011001.**00000000	192.168.89.0 /24
Unassigned	↓	↓
Unassigned	**11000000.10101000.01011001.**11111111	192.168.89.255
Unassigned	**11000000.10101000.01011010.**00000000	192.168.90.0 /24
Unassigned	↓	↓

continues

Table 14-8 *Balkanizing a 19-Bit Network (Continued)*

	Binary Network Plus Subnet Address	Decimal Translation
Unassigned	11000000.10101000.01011010.11111111	192.168.90.255
Location 5 LAN management ports	11000000.10101000.01011011.00000000	192.168.91.0 /24
Location 5 LAN management ports	↓	↓
Location 5 LAN management ports	11000000.10101000.01011011.11111111	192.168.91.255
Unassigned	11000000.10101000.01011100.00000000	192.168.92.0 /23
Unassigned	↓	↓
Unassigned	11000000.10101000.01011101.11111111	192.168.93.255
Location 5 hosts	11000000.10101000.01011110.00000000	192.168.94.0 /24
Location 5 hosts	↓	↓
Location 5 hosts	11000000.10101000.01011110.11111111	192.168.94.255
Unassigned	11000000.10101000.01011111.00000000	192.168.95.0 /24

This example bears the earmarks of an insightful, maybe even insidious, hostmaster. Did you notice that all the backbone router interfaces are assigned IP addresses from the same /24 block? Similarly, LAN management ports are assigned numbers from other ranges of numbers. Each location has been treated to a /24 just for this purpose. Although this lets each location grow to a maximum of 254 LAN switches, it seems highly unlikely that this number is needed. Instead, it seems more likely that a /29 or /30 address block would serve this purpose marvelously.

You might be wondering why such networking devices would be given their own IP blocks. The answer is simple, and it isn't to facilitate routing. This practice greatly simplifies data collection for network monitoring, management, and trend-analysis tools. Generally speaking, it is always preferable to separate the addresses of infrastructure devices from hosts that function as destination and/or origination points of a communication session.

The combination of overallocating blocks achieves the goal of balkanization. It makes the network look as if it requires 11 Class C-sized networks (/24s). The fact that those 11 /24s are scattered across the entire /19 range effectively fragments the remaining free space into discontiguous blocks. If they were numerically contiguous, a reasonable argument could be made for their return to IANA and ICANN for reallocation to another Internet user community. In their current form, any attempt to reclaim them would only result in a bloating of the Internet's address routing tables, because they defy effective aggregation.

Summary

The tactics you employ for managing an address space are absolutely critical in the successful long-term management of an address space. As I constantly remind my graduate students, there are precious few absolutes in internetworking. Picking the "right" approach requires that you have a solid command not only of the technology but also the context in which you are applying and managing it. The approaches described throughout this chapter are not the only ways to manage an address space. Other approaches exist that are highly implementation-specific. For example, you could allocate blocks by departments within a company, by floor in an office building, or even by region. Recognize that each of these approaches still requires you to select a tactic for parsing address space within whatever arbitrary scheme you have selected.

This chapter concluded our exploration of the IPv4 address space by looking at ways to manage network address spaces. These approaches are generic enough that they can probably be used with virtually any number-based network address. For the time being, that is IPv4. However, IPv6 continues to loom on the horizon. It might well become tomorrow's de facto standard protocol for internetworking. The next chapter concludes this book by looking at this emerging protocol.

PART V

The Future of the Internet Protocol

CHAPTER 15

IPv6: The Future of IP Addressing

The current version of the Internet Protocol, IPv4, dates back more than 20 years. Technically, only its roots go back that far; many of its components and functions are much newer. It has been updated and renovated extensively over time to keep pace with the Internet's evolution. Despite some of the turmoil, consolidation, price-based competition, and other fallout from the dot-com bust of 2000–2001, I think it's quite safe to say that the Internet isn't going away. In fact, its future is all but assured. What's not so certain is the future of IP.

There are two schools of thought concerning the future of the Internet Protocol. One camp claims that IPv6 is inevitable and wrings its collective hands trying to figure out how to convince the rest of the world. The other camp, a somewhat more-pragmatic lot, sees no compelling reason for the "upgrade." They are perfectly content to see IPv4 soldier on and benefit from continued retrofitting with new features and functions.

Without touching off a pseudo religious war (this argument revolves around what you *believe* as opposed to what you *know*), it's necessary to more closely examine the capabilities of IPv6. In this chapter, you will see both sides of the great debate: the technical reasons why an upgrade is needed, as well as why so many in the industry don't believe a migration is warranted. This discussion sets the stage for an examination of IPv6, including some of the features that make it dramatically different from its predecessor. Then you can decide for yourself what the future holds.

The Need for More

Chapter 5, "The Date of Doom," looked at many of the reasons that motivated the development of IPv6 and the incredibly successful stopgap tools. Remember, these stopgaps were intended solely to buy enough time for the IPv4 address space for IPv6 to be developed. The motivating factor was the impending depletion of the Class B address space. A "Date of Doom" was projected—the date on which the Internet would no longer be able to service the needs of many of its users because its address architecture proved to be less scalable than the Internet itself. The good news is that the scare tactic worked: The Internet's technical and engineering communities rallied and drew up a two-pronged battle plan. One group would be dedicated to solving the problem long-term. Another would focus on short-term tactical efforts to shore up the old protocol, buying some time for the long-term solution to be developed and implemented.

You have already seen some of the fruits of this labor. CIDR, DHCP, private addresses, and NAT are just some of the more-familiar patches applied to IPv4 to buy time for IPv6 to take shape. Other efforts included mundane things such as more-prudent husbandry of the remaining unallocated address spaces. Together, these stopgap efforts were so successful that the need for IPv6 has become the subject of great debate! However, fairness requires that we examine the progress made by the long-term teams rather than just summarizing the successes of the stopgap efforts.

When reviewing this brief summary, remember that IPv4 grew out of a relatively simple protocol suite that was designed for much simpler days. Its problems were the direct result of exponential growth in both scope and the number and types of applications that were designed specifically for use in IP networks. You shouldn't be surprised that IPv4 is showing its age; rather, you should be delighted at how well it has held up in the face of the Internet's explosive growth.

Solving the Long-Term Problem

The engineers focused on the long-term problem called their team IPng for *IP, next generation.* I guess there were a few Trekkies on the team! These engineers realized that they were given a golden opportunity. By taking a broader view of the problem, they could solve all of IPv4's shortcomings rather than just finding a way to build a more-scalable address architecture for the existing Internet Protocol suite.

The perceived problems with IPv4 included the following:

- A limited address hierarchy, which had an increasingly negative effect on routing efficiency and the size of the Internet's routing tables.

- A relatively small address size, compounded by a grossly inefficient (but mathematically logical) size-based classification system. Although the overall size of the IPv4 address space might have been large enough to service the world's connectivity needs indefinitely, the way it was carved up, allocated, and used actually wasted large numbers of addresses. Thus, the general perception is that the IPv4 address space was too small.

- Numerous functional limitations, including lack of native support for mobility, and performance requirements of specific applications. Mobile computing was starting to mature, as were applications that were highly sensitive to network delays—none of which IPv4 could easily support.

The crew that developed all of IPv6's myriad components thought through every shortcoming and saw to it that the new protocol was the answer to all their problems and concerns.

NOTE   As you read through this chapter, you'll notice that the proposed replacement to IPv4 was IPv6. You might wonder whatever happened to IPv5. The answer is not at all obvious. IPv5 was assigned by the IETF to an experimental streaming protocol known as ST-II. ST-II never really got off the ground, and the IETF decided to simply retire the IPv5 designation rather than creating potential for confusion by reusing it to describe another protocol.

Barriers to Acceptance

Having established both the motives and the need for updating the Internet Protocol, it is imperative that we look at what might be slowing its acceptance. Because IPv6 is so radically different from IPv4, upgrading requires far more than just loading a software patch snarfed from the Net. The upgrade process can only be described as a migration, because many different elements must be moved, and that movement might take months or years to complete.

Technological migration of any sort must be worth the pain and effort required. Otherwise, the market has demonstrated time and again that the migration won't be undertaken. Examples within the narrow and specific field of telecommunications and data networking yield a plethora of evidence to back up this claim. For example, ISDN simmered for years—a classic example of a solution in search of a need. Similarly, ATM as a local-area network technology enjoyed tremendous publicity in trade magazines and the like, but ultimately it failed because backward compatibility was a joke, and the market decided that migrating didn't bring enough reward to warrant the cost and risk.

The architects of IPv6 understood this implicitly. It is very easy to see how they bent over backward to make the new protocol as backward-compatible as possible. They took even greater pains to ensure that an entire suite of transition tools was available that would mitigate the difficulties of migrating from IPv4 to IPv6. As we examine IPv6's address hierarchy, special attention will be paid to the mechanisms specifically designed to mitigate the pain of migration.

Overview of IPv6

IPv6 was spelled out in a series of RFCs published in the summer of 1995. Quite a few focus on the minute details of a new protocol, such as extensions to existing routing protocols to support the new address size and architecture. Rather than subjecting you to an exhaustive review of these RFCs, a more focused look at some of the more salient points (as they relate to IP addressing) should suffice.

Address Architecture

The addressing architecture for IPv6 was originally stipulated in RFC 1884, published in December 1995. This RFC was updated and obsoleted by RFC 2373 in July 1998. The revolutionary nature of the next generation of IP was evident in this document. Specifically, the proposed address space was enormous, and the way it was carved up demonstrated the sophistication that comes only with decades of experience with a technology set. The new protocol was everything a network engineer could have hoped for. More importantly, it appeared poised to solve all the long-standing "problems" with IPv4, and great pains were obviously taken to ensure ease of migration. Much of this was accomplished just within the address architecture.

128-Bit Address

The most significant aspect of the new Internet Protocol is the sheer size of its address space. At 128 bits in length, the new address space is 4 times the size of the IPv4 address space if you count the number of bits in the address. Mathematically, this works out to 340,282,366,920,938,463,463,374,607,431,768,211,456 possible addresses, which is obviously more than 4 times the number of available addresses IPv4 offers. In fact, that's such a huge number, I don't know of any mnemonics for some of the groupings. There are millions, billions, trillions, and quadrillions, but after that, things get fuzzy. Those mnemonics represent just under half of the total number. In other words, the address space is so large that it is beyond the scale most people are familiar with.

Base16 Address Notation

This new address space is also treated to a new notation format. Instead of addresses being referenced in a four-part dotted-decimal format, IPv6 addresses are expressed using a hexa-decimal notation with colons. For ease of use, the 128-bit address is broken into eight groups of 16 bits, which are separated by colons. For example, FF01:0:0:0:0:0:0:101 is a valid, but reserved, IPv6 address.

Each of the eight 16-bit fields can have a maximum value of 1111111111111111 in Base2, which translates into 65,535 in Base10 and FFFF in Base16. The Base10 is included just for your edification; it is not used in IPv6 address notation. The Scientific Calculator included in every Microsoft desktop operating system lets you practice converting any symbolic string between Base2, Base10, and even Base16. A little practice might make the IPv6 addressing scheme seem a bit less daunting.

NOTE   The technical update of IP with version 6 is so complete that even IPv4's reserved loopback address has been replaced with a much simpler and technically elegant mechanism in IPv6. The IPv6 loopback address is 0:0:0:0:0:0:0:1.

It is important to note that, even though the address space has been defined, not all of it is usable. Only about 15% of the total address space is currently defined well enough to be used. The remainder is unallocated and will provide ample room for growth after the protocol reaches widespread usage. The fact that so much of the space is unutilized creates the opportunity for some keystroke-saving shorthand. IPv6 permits you to truncate a repetitive string of 0s by substituting a double colon. For example, FF01::101 is an acceptable shorthand for FF01:0:0:0:0:0:0:101. Despite the convenience of this shorthand, the bottom line is that, with IPv6, DNS becomes an absolute necessity!

Be careful not to mistake binary for decimal or hexadecimal numbers. Up to this point, we really haven't discussed the Base16 number system. You should be intimately familiar with Base10 and we've looked at Base2 so many times throughout this book that it, too, should be familiar. Base16, also known as *hexadecimal* or just plain *hex,* is just another number system. This one uses 16 symbols to represent numeric values. Table 15-1 demonstrates the relationship between Base2, Base10, and Base16.

Table 15-1   *Comparing Binary, Decimal, and Hex*

Binary	Decimal	Hex
0	0	0
1	1	1
10	2	2
11	3	3
100	4	4
101	5	5
110	6	6
111	7	7
1000	8	8
1001	9	9
1010	10	A
1011	11	B
1100	12	C
1101	13	D
1110	14	E
1111	15	F
10000	16	10
10001	17	11

Did you notice in the table that the symbols 0 and 1 (as well as their myriad combinations) represent legitimate numbers in all three of these number systems? For example, the symbolic string 10 is valid in all three, but it represents different values in each system. In Base2, it translates to a decimal 2. In Base10, it's obviously a ten. In Base16, it represents one group of 16 and no 1s. That's where the potential for confusion comes in. Some of those symbols are also used in both Base2 and Base10. This raises the potential for confusion if the number system being used isn't explicitly identified.

Ordinarily this wouldn't be a problem. Mathematicians tend to be well-disciplined enough that they explicitly identify the number system they are using, especially when it isn't Base10. Unfortunately, the RFCs that stipulate the address architecture often identify the contents of reserved fields. These fields are of many different sizes, and that often means two or more fields lie within a single 16-bit address group! Fields used as flags with reserved values that are less than 16 bits in length are explicitly identified using binary bit-string values, even though the address itself is expressed in hex. I'll point those out as we come to them.

Address Types

Getting beyond the dramatic change in the size of the IPv6 address space, you can't help but be struck by the equally dramatic change in how address space is used. Rather than arbitrary allocations between block sizes, the IETF sought to carve the new address space into functional categories, each of which would enable more-efficient routing through a more-sophisticated hierarchy. These functional categories are known as anycast, unicast, and multicast. Noticeably absent was the broadcast address type. IPv6 doesn't use broadcast addresses, but it satisfies that function through the multicast address type.

Throughout this book, we've looked at how IPv4's addressing system works. Implicit was that there were two types of addresses: those that get assigned to individual hosts to uniquely identify them and those that are used to forward data to multiple hosts (multicast). Well, IPv6 gives a name to the first type of address: unicast. IPv6 also preserves the concept of multicasting, albeit in a slightly different way. These two concepts (unicast and multicast) should be familiar enough by this point in the book that we don't need to rehash them here.

Anycasting, however, is a completely new concept that is unique to IPv6. The need for anycast addresses became apparent after the successful commercialization of the Internet. Often-visited Web sites needed to be geographically dispersed to better service their user community without causing congestion in any one part of the Internet. That gave rise to the problem of how to address geographically dispersed but functionally equivalent hosts. The answer, anycasting, doesn't impose some of the delays of a DNS-based solution. It simply routes packets to the "nearest" host that has that address, as determined by whichever metrics the routing protocol uses to calculate routes to destination networks.

Anycast

An anycast address is created simply: You assign the same unicast address to two or more IPv6 hosts. In theory, such hosts are functionally equivalent, and you would want to route packets to the "nearest" host. This works well in applications such as distributed Web sites.

There is a tremendous variety of unicast address types. Anycast addresses can be created from any of them. Consequently, anycast addresses are numerically indistinguishable from unicast addresses. This necessitates a safeguard. Otherwise, anycast groups could be created by accident and could wreak havoc in the form of intermittent failures of specific hosts (those with the same address) within your network.

The safeguard is that anycasting must be explicitly enabled on your router's interface(s). I would gladly provide you with the syntax required to accomplish this, but as of Cisco IOS Release 12.2(2)T, support for this feature has yet to be developed by Cisco Systems. Support has been promised for an as-yet unspecified future release. I have included coverage of anycasting in this chapter because it is a powerful and intriguing innovation. The fact that support for it has yet to appear in the IOS should tell you just how raw IPv6 is as a product, despite years of hype and development.

Multicast

Support for multicasting, however, is better defined and implemented. Much like its IPv4-based counterpart, the IPv6 multicast address is an identifier that correlates to a list of unicast addresses that are logically linked for the purposes of receiving streams of multicasted information.

All IPv6 multicast addresses begin with the binary prefix 11111111, or FF in hex. This prefix flags the entire address as being a multicast address. The complete structure of the IPv6 multicast address is as follows:

- An 8-bit *multicast flag* set to 11111111.
- A 4-bit *lifetime* indicator set to 000x, where x can be either 0 or 1. 0 indicates a permanent multicast group (similar in concept to a well-known port number), and 1 flags a temporary group.
- A 4-bit *scope* indicator that limits the group's scope. Scope describes the reach of a multicast group within a network, autonomous system, or internetwork.
- A 112-bit *group* identifier.

NOTE   The Cisco Systems documentation on IPv6 multicasting uses the terminology "lifetime" for the 4-bit field that immediately follows the 8-bit multicast flag. If you check RFC 2373, you will see that this field is identified somewhat generically as "flags." Both are used for the same purpose, and Cisco adheres to the published format and use of this field. Just the terminology differs. This benign example demonstrates the potential for differences of interpretation that can exist between published specifications and product documentation.

The notion of scope is interesting in that not all multicast codes are automatically assumed to be global. Rather, they can be limited in scope much the same way that unicast addresses are limited. That's something we'll look at in the next section. The scopes of multicast codes are listed in Table 15-2. Mathematically valid values not listed in the table are unassigned.

Table 15-2   *Scope Values and Limits*

Binary Value	Hex Value	Scope
0001	1	Node-local
0010	2	Link-local
0101	5	Site-local
1000	8	Organizational-local
1110	E	Global

These scopes let you multicast to a predefined group of hosts on the same node, the same local-area network, within the same site, within the same private network, or anywhere in the Internet. You might question the logic behind having such limits for multicasting purposes, and you'd probably be right! However, these scopes make much more sense when you realize that broadcasting has been eliminated in IPv6. Instead of a discrete broadcasting mechanism, IPv6 uses reserved multicast addresses to broadcast to all hosts within specific scopes. The reserved all-nodes multicast addresses are listed in Table 15-3.

Table 15-3   *Use of Scopes for Broadcasting*

Scope	Multicast Address
All IPv6 node addresses within scope 1 (node-local)	FF01:0:0:0:0:0:0:1
All IPv6 router addresses within scope 1 (node-local)	FF01:0:0:0:0:0:0:2
All IPv6 node addresses within scope 2 (link-local)	FF02:0:0:0:0:0:0:1
All IPv6 router addresses within scope 2 (link-local)	FF02:0:0:0:0:0:0:2
All IPv6 router addresses within scope 5 (site-local)	FF05:0:0:0:0:0:0:2

Unicast Address Architectures

The unicast address type is remarkably specialized and warrants closer scrutiny. IPv4 featured an address architecture that differed only in the sizes of the routable portion of the address. In other words, the various classes and later classless blocks of network addresses all enjoyed the same functionality. This is no longer true in IPv6.

IPv6 was designed with an eye toward functionality. Thus, no fewer than five distinct types of unicast address architectures were developed:

- Aggregatable global unicast address
- Link-local-use unicast
- Site-local-use unicast
- IPv4-compatible IPv6 unicast
- IPv4-mapped IPv6 unicast

The following sections further describe these architectures in terms of their functionality and specific structure. Each one introduces several more hierarchical layers than can be found in IPv4. The purpose and benefits of these layers will be explained as we come to them.

NOTE   You might encounter references to other types of IPv6 unicast addresses that aren't listed here. Those addresses either are completely tangential to the content of this book (such as NSAP-compatible IPv6 unicast addresses) or are still being evaluated for possible development (such as IPX-compatible IPv6 unicast addresses). Others might have slipped into obsolescence and are no longer part of the protocol. One particular type to note is the former *ISP unicast* address. This type has been obsoleted. Its functionality has been both supplanted and augmented by the aggregatable global unicast address.

Aggregatable Global Unicast

Created in RFC 2374, published in July 1998, the *aggregatable global unicast* address type was specifically designed to enable very efficient routing through the Internet. Of particular concern to the architects of this new protocol was the potential effect on routers and the Internet's routing efficiency. Let's face it: When you increase the length of an address by 400%, you probably also increase the memory consumption of routers that have to keep track of those addresses by the same percentage—that is, of course, unless you fundamentally change the nature of the address.

This new type of address is far more hierarchical than the IPv4 address space. Its hierarchy contains several new fields that enable a tremendous improvement in routing efficiency. After we look at the structure of this new address type, it should be a bit clearer why routing efficiency improves despite the four-fold increase in the size of the addresses. The aggregatable global address contains the following data structures:

- A 3-bit *format prefix* that must be set to the binary value 001. This bit string value identifies the address as being an aggregatable global unicast address.
- A 13-bit *Top-Level Aggregation ID* (TLA) field.
- An 8-bit *Reserved* and unused field.
- A 24-bit *Next-Level Aggregation ID* (NLA) field.
- A 16-bit *Site-Level Aggregation ID* (SLA) field.
- A 64-bit *Interface ID* field.

Looking over the structure of this unicast address type, you can see the logic behind the hierarchy. It is not unlike a postal address, except that in this address the specificity increases, whereas a postal address decreases in specificity as you advance through the hierarchy of the fields. In simpler terms, a postal address first identifies the specific recipient, then that recipient's street address, then the town in which that street is located, and then the state in which that town is located.

The aggregatable global unicast address follows the same logic but inverts the pattern. It offers two fields (a total of 40 bits) for differing levels of hierarchy that directly facilitate the aggregation of routes into larger-sized address blocks. This tends to reduce the size of routing tables by eliminating specificity until it is needed.

To make this seem a bit more real, imagine the TLA (Top-Level Aggregator) being used to identify a large corporation, such as the Acme Manufacturing Company. Acme is spread over several states and enjoys an extensive internal *wide-area network (WAN)*. But it connects to the Internet at only one location. Acme has extended its network to an Internet exchange (MAE-West, for example). The world's Internet users can route to Acme using just its TLA field. That gets you inside its WAN, where the NLA (Next-Level Aggregator) is used to route traffic. The NLA could be used in a virtually unlimited number of ways, but for the sake of simplicity, let's assume that Acme uses the NLA to identify states within the U.S. Its WAN can then route traffic based on just the TLA and NLA. Once inside each state, traffic is routed to the specific destination site using the Site-Level Aggregation (SLA) identifier. The most specific portion of the address, the interface identifier, isn't used until after the traffic reaches the correct site.

Aggregatable global addresses also offer benefits to those who choose to connect to the Internet via an ISP. Ostensibly, such customers use addresses that bear the ISP's identifier in the TLA rather than their own. The world's Internet users could have their traffic routed to any of that ISP's customers by using just that ISP's TLA. Today, individual address blocks must be tracked, which can get quite onerous. Thus, there is the potential for a tremendous reduction in the size of the Internet's routing tables.

Link-Local-Use Unicast

A concept first proposed way back in RFC 1597, and later updated in RFC 1918, was the notion of private IP addresses. We looked at these RFCs in Chapter 5. You saw that three distinct blocks of addresses were reserved for use in private networks. Ostensibly, this arrangement conserved address spaces by creating addresses that didn't have to be globally unique! You didn't need permission to use them; you just couldn't route them over the Internet. TCP/IP, as a protocol suite, was maturing, and it rapidly became a global de facto standard for network-based communications. But not everyone who needed TCP/IP to support an application also required access to the Internet. For those people and organizations, private addressing was perfect. It was a graceful way of making an existing protocol and address space go a little further with an absolute minimum of effort.

IPv6 embraced the motivation behind these RFCs but solved the problem in a different way. The solution was termed the *link-local-use anycast* address. This ungainly name belies a simple concept: Use an endpoint's physical address (a *Media Access Control [MAC] address*) as the basis for a unique IP address that is valid only for *local* communications. MAC addresses are each globally unique, but they aren't a good basis for a routable internetwork address because of their relatively flat hierarchy. A MAC address contains only two components—a hexadecimal serial number and a manufacturer identifier— neither of which lends itself to routability in a network.

The IPv6 link-local-use address contains three components:

- A 10-bit *local-use flag* that must be set to the binary value 1111111010
- A 54-bit *reserved,* but unused, field that must be set to the binary value 0
- A 64-bit *Interface Identifier* field

The Interface Identifier can be based on an endpoint's MAC address (MAC addresses aren't 118 bits in length), but it doesn't have to be. The only requirement stipulated in RFC 2373 is that the Identifier must be unique on *that link*. Routers are not allowed to forward packets bearing this type of address in either their source or destination address fields. This limits the use of this address type to just a single LAN environment. Consequently, there is no requirement for global uniqueness with this address architecture, but addresses must be unique per link.

This approach theoretically allows a conservation of address space by reserving a range of addresses (all starting with the binary string 1111111010) that can be used only for communications on a LAN. Please note that this string is just the prefix to the first 16-bit group of the IPv6 address (remember, IPv6 addresses are broken into eight 16-bit groups separated by a colon). Because this string is just 10 bits in length, the last 5 bits of the first 16-bit address group determine the Base16 symbol used to represent the total value of those bits.

A potentially contravening argument can be made against the intent behind the purported benefit of this address type. The address space represented with this binary prefix is huge!

RFC 2373 tries to mitigate the perception of overkill by stating that only 1/1024 of the IPv6 address space is allocated to link-local-use addresses, but a small percentage of a gigantic number is still a huge number. There is no escaping the basic fact that you don't need 118 bits to create a unique address within a LAN. You could probably accomplish that universally with less than 20 bits. Remember, the entire Internet is currently being serviced with just 32 bits of addressing. So 118 address bits for LAN addresses is ludicrously excessive! I'm reminded of the mind-set that existed when the IPv4 address space was first being allocated. The prevailing philosophy was that the address space was so huge relative to demand that it would never be depleted. With this simple philosophy, many an inefficient solution was rationalized and accepted. Only time will tell if history will repeat itself in this arena.

Site-Local-Use Unicast

An alternative to the ISP unicast address type is the site-local-use unicast address. This type of address is specifically designed for organizations and/or enterprises that require IP and IP addresses for internal communications but that do not need to access the Internet. Ostensibly, a private but routable address type would keep routing very efficient across the Internet by reducing the number of addresses (routes) that routers in the Internet would have to track and maintain.

Implicit in this description is the fact that the site-local-use unicast address is valid for use within only a single site. The question is, what constitutes a site?

The site-local-use unicast address contains the following structure:

- A 10-bit *local-use flag* that must be set to the binary value 1111111011
- A 38-bit *reserved,* but unused, field that must be set to the binary value 0
- A 16-bit *Subnet ID* field
- A 64-bit *Interface ID* field

The functionality of this address type differs slightly from the link-local-use unicast in that routers may forward packets that bear either a source or destination address of this type. The caveat is that they cannot forward them out of the site! Figure 15-1 demonstrates the routability of this type of address.

Figure 15-1 *Routability of the Site-Local-Use IPv6 Unicast Addresses*

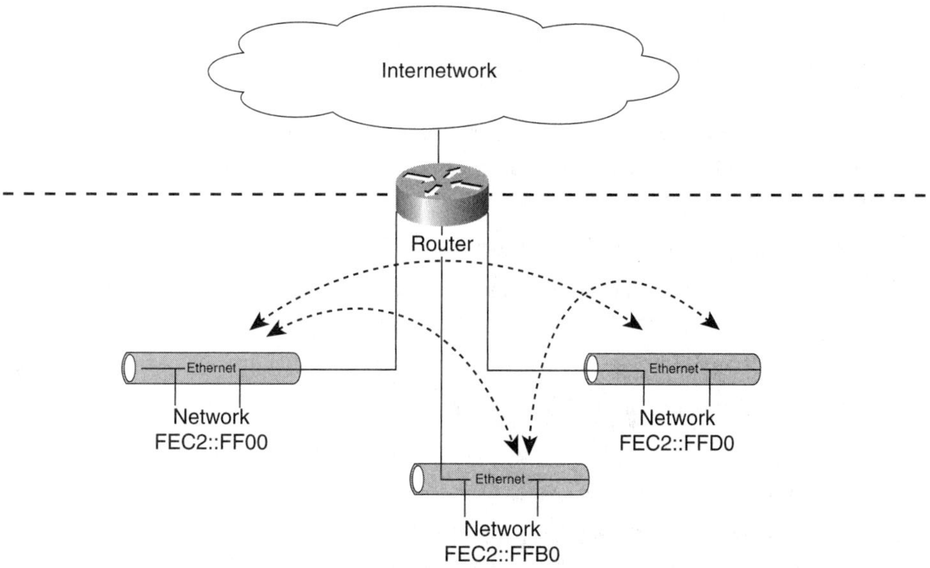

You probably want to know what would happen if someone using this local-use address type later needed to connect to the Internet. Would he have to completely renumber? Would he have to set up an address translator? Well, I'm happy to tell you the IPng team has already thought through this dilemma. Site-local-use unicasts can be "upgraded" to a routable address by replacing the 10-bit local-use prefix with a routable ISP prefix. In theory, this makes for a very graceful migration path. I say "in theory" because I have yet to find anyone who has actually performed this upgrade. Still, it's reassuring to know that a complete renumbering isn't in store when you want to migrate from a site-local-use unicast to a globally routable address type.

IPv4-Compatible IPv6 Unicast

One of the mechanisms established specifically to facilitate migration from IPv4 to IPv6 is the IPv4-compatible IPv6 unicast address. This type of address permits backward compatibility with any IPv4 addresses that might linger during or after a migration to IPv6. The way this address type works is quite simple, but it makes the most sense when you view its structure. This address type has three fields:

- An 80-bit field (conveniently equivalent to five of the 16-bit IPv6 address fields!) is reserved and is set to 0

- A 16-bit field is also reserved and is set to 0

- The last 32 bits of IPv6 address contains the "old" IPv4 address

This address type is brilliant in its simplicity. The architects of IPv6 realized that one of the barriers to migration was the logistical nightmare of redesigning (and then implementing!) a new addressing scheme. This unicast address obviates the need to do that by allowing you to keep your existing IPv4 addressing scheme. Migration is made possible by prefacing an existing IPv4 address with 96 bits of 0s. In this manner, a barrier to migration is removed.

It is important to notice that this type of IPv6 address doesn't spare you from the burden of renumbering. You still have to "renumber" each endpoint, but the logistics of renumbering become different. Typically, renumbering requires several steps:

- Obtaining or identifying a suitable address space
- Figuring out how to use that space (either in terms of subnetting schemes or allocations of smaller, routable blocks created from the original address space)
- Identifying the universe of devices that have an IP address
- Identifying migration options for each of the devices to be renumbered
- Building a migration plan by selecting the optimal migration option for each device
- Implementing the new address space

Much of the work involved in implementing a new address space can be automated through a tool such as DHCP. Of course, some devices require static addresses or lack the intelligence to be able to use dynamic configuration tools. Thus, such tools are useful but not panaceas. Despite this caveat, it is easy to see that the vast majority of the effort in any renumbering process is expended up front in the planning stages. So, having a type of address that would greatly reduce the up-front planning requirements was seen as a real boon.

IPv4-Mapped IPv6 Unicast

Another very interesting address type that was specifically designed to mitigate the pain of migration is the IPv4-mapped IPv6 unicast address. Despite a name similar to IPv4-compatible addresses (and an extremely similar data structure), this type of address is radically different. In fact, network administrators can't assign this type of address to endpoints! Instead, this address type provides backward compatibility with IPv4 addresses by enabling automatic tunneling of IPv4 packets through IPv6 network regions.

This address type has the following structure:

- An 80-bit field is reserved and is set to 0
- A 16-bit field is reserved and is set to high values (FFFF in hex and 1111111111111111 in binary)
- 32 bits of IPv6 address contains the "old" IPv4 address

If you missed it, the only structural difference between IPv4-mapped and IPv4-compatible unicast addresses are the values set to the 16-bit field. This unnamed field is set to high values (hexadecimal F) in the IPv4-mapped address and low values (hexadecimal 0) in the IPv4-

compatible address. Otherwise, both address types feature a reserved and unused 80-bit field set to 0s, and both preserve the integrity of the original, premigration IPv4 address.

The IPv4-mapped IPv6 unicast address differs functionally in that it is not assigned to endpoints in the network. Rather, it is constructed and used by routers that can communicate in both IPv4 and IPv6 as a means of transporting IPv4 packets (generated by IPv4-only endpoints) through an IPv6 network. How this works is illustrated in the next section.

Comparing IPv4-Compatible and IPv4-Mapped Addresses

IPv4-compatible and IPv4-mapped IPv6 addresses share a pair of commonalities:

- Both contain embedded IPv4 addresses.
- Both were explicitly designed to help ease the pain of migrating to IPv6.

Superficially, it might appear as if they are more similar than different. Their differences, however, are profound and lie in how they are used.

IPv4-compatible addresses facilitate a migration by letting you "retain" your existing IPv4 addresses and addressing scheme by embedding them within an IPv6 superstructure. These are assigned to specific IPv6 hosts, which are then connected to an IPv6-capable network. Figure 15-2 demonstrates how this looks in a typical, but tiny, network.

Figure 15-2 *Using IPv4-Compatible IPv6 Addresses*

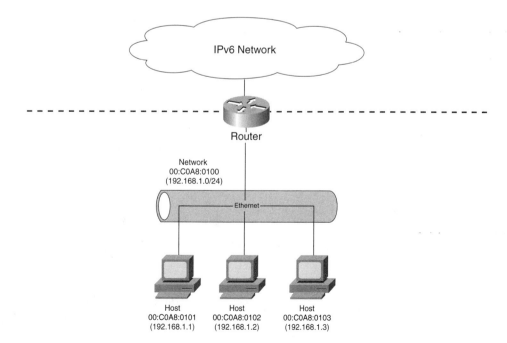

Contrarily, IPv4-mapped unicast addresses can't be assigned to hosts, yet they play a vital role during the transition from IPv4 to IPv6. Given the nature of this type of migration, as well as the stubbornness of some types of addresses, it is highly probable that a migration will be quite lengthy and protracted. For example, you might never be able to "upgrade" the IP address on the management port of an older local-area network hub or switch. You are almost forced into accepting a dual-address environment for a long time. Thus, it was imperative for IPv6 to contain mechanisms to minimize the trauma of an extended migration. The IPv4-compatible IPv6 address is one such device.

IPv4-mapped unicast addresses are constructed, as needed, by IPv4/IPv6 routers. In essence, the dual-protocol routers function as gateways between IPv4 and IPv6 network regions. They wrap an IPv4 address with an IPv6 packet and an address for transport through IPv6 networks en route to its IPv4 destination. Upon arrival at the far edge of the IPv6 network region, ostensibly at another router that is both IPv4- and IPv6-capable, the v6 portion of the address is stripped, and the original IPv4 addressing and packet structure are launched on the way to the address's final destination.

A topological example of how this could work is illustrated in Figure 15-3.

Figure 15-3 *Using IPv4-Mapped IPv6 Addresses*

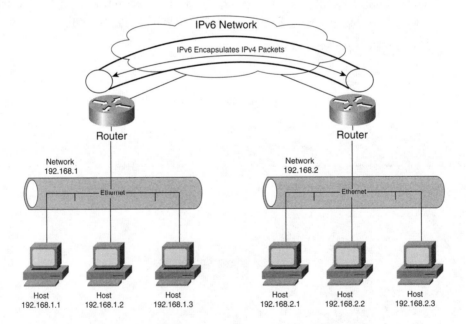

This buys you the opportunity to upgrade your network in stages. First you could upgrade the backbone to IPv6, configure your routers to support the creation of IPv4-mapped unicast addresses, and then take the time to carefully plan the migration of the rest of your network. Such a migration might or might not feature the use of IPv4-compatible IPv6 addresses for the hosts at the edges of the network.

More Migration Tools

In addition to the IPv4-embedded IPv6 unicast addresses, a series of other tools and techniques can be used to facilitate a migration. These tools are native to the IPv6 protocol suite and include the following:

- Product support for running dual protocol stacks (IPv4 and IPv6)
- IPv6 tunneling through IPv4 core networks
- Translation gateways (Network Address Translation-Protocol Translation [NAT-PT])

Each of these is worth exploring in a bit more detail, although NAT-PT is not yet supported as of Cisco IOS Software Release 12.2(2)T.

Dual Protocol Stacks

A classic technique for migration is to run in a parallel environment. In other words, you establish the new environment in parallel with the old. Both coexist long enough for a graceful and unhurried migration to be completed. Although such a dual mode is more expensive, it is inherently less risky than a flash-cut. In the case of IPv6, a flash-cut is probably not even feasible. Quite simply, too many devices with IP addresses need to be cut over. The quick list might include hosts and servers, but don't forget that management ports on hubs and switches, printers, and countless other devices all use IP and IP addresses. Only the smallest of environments can realistically contemplate a flash-cut to IPv6.

For all other networks, product support has been and is being developed that lets a device run both protocol stacks simultaneously. From a client computer's perspective, this affords older applications the opportunity to continue using the IPv4 protocol, while newer applications can be configured to use IPv6. In theory, both would use the same connection to the local-area network.

Virtually any device that can be configured to use an IP stack can be configured to support dual stacks. However, routers are particularly useful in this capacity. Such routers function as gateways between IPv4 and IPv6 network regions and can accommodate traffic in either format. To configure a router interface as a dual-stack interface on your Cisco router, start from global configuration mode and use the commands shown in Table 15-4.

Table 15-4   *Syntax to Configure Dual Stacks on the Cisco Router Interface*

Command	Function
Router(config)#**ipv6 unicast-routing**	Enables the forwarding of datagrams with IPv6 unicast addresses.
Router(config)#**interface** *interface-type number*	Specifies the type and number of the interface being configured. This command also places the router in interface configuration mode.
Router(config-if)#**ipv6 address** *ipv6-prefix/prefix-length* [*eui-64*]	Specifies the IPv6 network address prefix assigned to the interface. This command also lets the interface process IPv6 packets.
Router(config-if)#**ip address** *ip-address mask* [**secondary**]	Specifies a primary or secondary IPv4 address for the interface. This command completes the configuration of a dual-stack interface.

IPv6 Tunnels Through IPv4 Networks

It is possible to encapsulate IPv6 packets with an IPv4 packet for transport through an IPv4 network en route to an IPv6 destination. This is sometimes called *overlay tunneling*. This moniker derives from the fact that the one protocol is overlaid on the other protocol. Overlay tunneling can be achieved in three ways:

- Manually configured tunnels
- Automatically configured tunnels
- 6-to-4 tunnels

The distinctions between these tunnel types are subtle, but they revolve around how source and destination addresses are formed for the IPv4 packets (which encapsulate the IPv6 datagram) forwarded through the tunnel. Remember, IPv4 doesn't recognize IPv6 addresses, so when you encapsulate an IPv6 datagram with an IPv4 packet structure, you can't use the source address of that IPv6 datagram. It simply won't work in the IPv4 network. So the addresses have to come from somewhere else!

Three different mechanisms have been developed to solve this problem, albeit in different ways. All three can be configured only on dual-protocol routers. They are examined a bit more closely in the next three sections. Before perusing those sections, look at Figure 15-4. It demonstrates the typical topology seen in a tunneling scenario. It gives you a picture that might make it easier to understand some of the subtle distinctions between the three types of IPv6-over-IPv4 tunnels.

Figure 15-4 *Tunneling IPv6 Through an IPv4 Network*

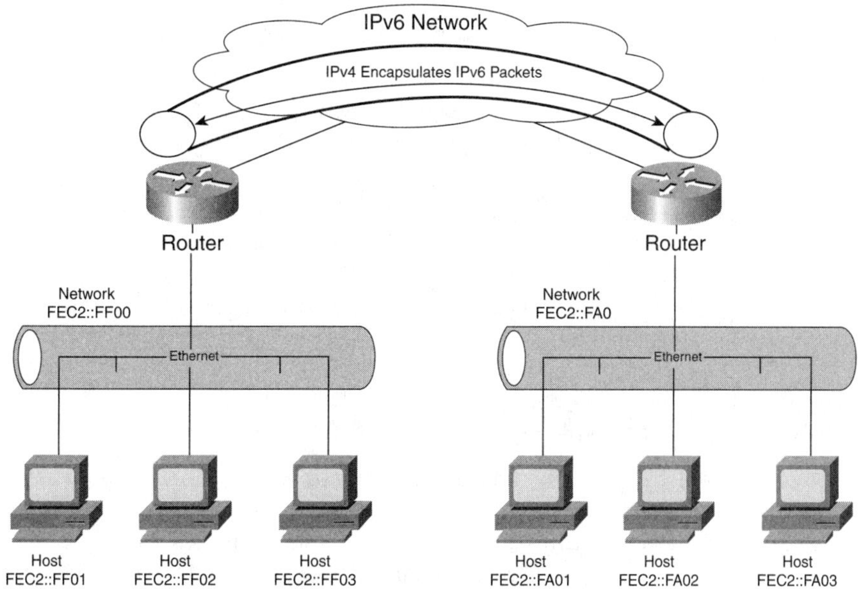

Manually Configured Tunnels

Manually configured tunnels are just what their name implies. An IPv6 address is manually configured on a tunnel interface. IPv4 addresses are then also manually assigned for use as the tunnel's source and destination addresses. That is, IPv6 datagrams passing through the tunnel are wrapped with an IPv4 packet, and the IPv4 source and destination addresses that were manually configured on the tunnel's interface are used as the source and destination addresses of those newly-created datagrams.

To help make this a bit more real for you, Table 15-5 contains the syntax required to configure a manual tunnel on a Cisco router interface.

Table 15-5 *Syntax to Configure Manual Tunneling on the Cisco Router Interface*

Command	Function
Router(config)#**interface tunnel** *tunnel number*	Specifies the tunnel interface and logical identification number. This command also places the router in interface configuration mode.
Router(config-if)#**ipv6 address** *ipv6-prefix/prefix-length*	Specifies the IPv6 network assigned to the interface. Also enables the processing of IPv6 packets on that interface.

continues

Table 15-5 *Syntax to Configure Manual Tunneling on the Cisco Router Interface (Continued)*

Command	Function
Router(config-if)#**ip address** *ip-address mask* [**secondary**]	Provides a primary or secondary IPv4 address for the interface.
Router(config-if)#**tunnel source** {*ip-address* | *interface-type interface-number*}	Specifies the source IPv4 address *or* the interface type and number to be used on the tunnel interface.
Router(config-if)#**tunnel destination** *ip-address*	Stipulates the IPv4 address to be used as a destination address in the IPv4 packets traversing the tunnel.
Router(config-if)#**tunnel mode ipv6ip**	Completes the definition of the manual IPv6 tunnel.

Automatically Configured Tunnels

Automatic tunneling, as you can probably surmise after reading the preceding section on manually configured tunnels, does not rely on statically configured IPv4 addresses to be used as source and destination addresses for the tunnel traffic. Rather, source and destination addresses are dynamically fabricated using IPv4-compatible IPv6 addresses. Of course, this implies that you are actually using IPv4-compatible IPv6 addresses in your IPv6 network. Otherwise, this approach just isn't right for you.

The low-order 32 bits of the IPv4-compatible IPv6 address (those to the right of the numeric address) are used to generate the source and destination addresses for use in the tunnel. Configuring this type of tunnel is much simpler, because many steps are omitted—notably, those that manually configure the IPv4 addresses. Table 15-6 outlines the syntax and sequence to configure an automatic tunnel.

Table 15-6 *Syntax to Configure Automatic Tunneling on the Cisco Router Interface*

Command	Function
Router(config)#**interface tunnel** *tunnel number*	Specifies the tunnel interface and logical identification number. This command also places the router in interface configuration mode.
Router(config-if)#**tunnel source** *interface-type interface-number*	Specifies the source interface type, as well as the number for the tunnel interface. It is important to remember that you must have configured the interface you are specifying in this command with both an IPv4 address and an IPv6 address!
Router(config-if)#**tunnel mode ipv6ip auto-tunnel**	Completes the definition of the automatic tunnel using an IPv4-compatible IPv6 address.

In theory, the IPv4 packets created via the IPv6 automatic tunneling mechanism can be routed by whichever route is deemed least costly in the IPv4 network. Only the origin and terminus of the tunnels are fixed, and they are referenced by routable IP addresses.

6-to-4 Tunnels

A 6-to-4 tunnel is a variation of an automatic IPv6 tunnel in that the addresses used in the tunnel are automatically fabricated. However, this tunnel type requires you to create a static IPv6 route over the tunnel's interface. This type of tunnel is useful when either you aren't using IPv4-compatible IPv6 addresses or you are interconnecting two IPv6 networks that each have only a single egress point to the same IPv4 network (in which case a static route is the most efficient solution).

Table 15-7 outlines the configuration syntax for the 6-to-4 tunnel type.

Table 15-7   *Syntax to Configure Manual Tunneling on the Cisco Router Interface*

Command	Function
Router(config)#**interface tunnel** *tunnel number*	Specifies the tunnel interface and logical identification number. This command also places the router in interface configuration mode.
Router(config-if)#**ipv6 unnumbered** *interface-type interface-number*	Enables the processing of IPv6 packets on this interface without having first assigned an IPv6 address to the tunnel's interface.
	The *interface-type* and *interface-number* fields specify the global IPv6 source address that the unnumbered interface should use on all IPv6 packets it creates.
Router(config-if)#**tunnel source** *interface-type interface-number*	Specifies the source interface type and number for the tunnel.
	The interface being used must have been configured with both an IPv6 address and an IPv4 address!
Router(config-if)#**tunnel mode ipv6ip 6to4**	Stipulates an IPv6 automatic tunnel using a 6-to-4 address.
Router(config-if)#**exit**	Exits interface configuration mode and returns to global configuration mode.
Router(config)#**ipv6 route 2002::/16 tunnel** *tunnel-number*	Completes the definition of the 6-to-4 tunnel by establishing an IPv6 static route to the tunnel interface.
	The tunnel number specified here should be the same one used in the **interface tunnel** command.
	Also, note that the 2002 is hexadecimal, not decimal!

The fact that the last step in the configuration of this tunnel type is a static IPv6 route should tell you that the IPv6 source and destination addresses play no role in the manufacture of the addresses to be used across the tunnel.

This concludes our review of the various transition mechanisms developed for IPv6. The fact that so many tools are expressly designed to facilitate a migration, yet so few people are migrating, is quite revealing: Tools to assist a migration are of value only *after* you decide to migrate. So, the logical question is...

What Are We Waiting For?

A good reason to migrate! Sorry. I didn't mean to yell, but this is one of those points that I strive to make sure all my graduate students at Syracuse University's School of Information Studies understand completely. A technically elegant and brilliant solution to a nonexistent problem will not gain acceptance in the market. Conversely, a cheap and nasty product might gain broad commercial acceptance so long as it is sufficiently reliable and offers demonstrable value relative to the present method of operation. Just look at Ethernet.

Simply stated, the marketplace is predominated by commercial entities. The mission of these entities is to make money for their owners and/or stockholders. They are not in the business of chasing technology to enhance the satisfaction levels of their technical person- nel. A new technology is embraced *only* when it offers value that enhances a company's ability to succeed.

IPv6 has been languishing for several years. Much ado was raised early on, and the new protocol was widely publicized and acclaimed. This publicity was largely driven by a sense of urgency that rivaled the later Y2K bug hysteria. The Internet was going to stop working because we were running out of addresses! Well, that made the value proposition clear. Companies had become so accustomed to using the Internet in support of their commercial operations that they couldn't just let it die.

With this motivation, the IETF set about developing the next generation of the Internet Protocol. Simultaneously, they chartered a number of teams to buy time by propping up IPv4 with stopgap mechanisms solely intended to make the existing address space last a little longer. These stopgap mechanisms, as you have seen throughout this book, have had a profound impact on the Internet address space. More importantly, these mechanisms offered long-term relief from the address shortage. The unintended result was that the motivation for migrating to IPv6 disappeared! Again, the market embraces a new technology only when doing so is in the market's best financial interest.

IPv6 Niches

The vast majority of North America seems content to just continue using IPv4, updating it as needed. IPv6, however, might find a receptive market in some regions of the world where the local allotment of IPv4 addresses is nearing depletion. For countries unable to obtain new address spaces, migrating to IPv6 might be the only solution.

Other nascent industries, too, might find IPv6 a better fit for their needs than IPv4. Wireless service providers might find some of the features of IPv6 perfect for their needs. Similarly, the *Internet 2* is already up and running on IPv6. Of course, that's not a "production" network, and it can afford downtime and the less-than-perfect performance that often accompanies migrating to a "new" technology. However, you cannot deny that IPv6 is starting to diffuse throughout the world's base of internetworks.

Summary

IPv6 is a network engineer's dream protocol. It was meant to be. Despite this, IPv6 has continued to languish; products with native IPv6 support have been slow to emerge, and users have been even slower to migrate. Examining this phenomenon reveals the delicious irony of this entire saga. IPv6 was conceived as the ultimate solution to a less-than-gracefully-aging IPv4's myriad problems. Emergency efforts to keep IPv4 alive proved more successful than anyone could have imagined, and the incentive to migrate disappeared, leaving IPv6 out in the cold—a brilliant solution to a now-nonexistent problem.

The fates of the two protocols remained intertwined, but IPv6 will see broad acceptance only if IPv4 falters and experiences another short-term crisis with its addressing system. The crisis will have to be with its addressing, because we have seen time and again how readily the basic IPv4 protocol suite can be extended to encompass other functions. Thus, no "killer application" is waiting to be discovered that will drive the market's acceptance of IPv6.

In the interim, market acceptance will be limited to specialty network owners and providers, and other niches where IPv6 is the only practical solution.

INDEX

Numerics

128-bit addresses, 306
16-bit network addresses, 57–59
172.16 reserved space, 122
192.168 reserved spaces, 123
20-bit addresses, 122
24-bit addresses, 122
24-bit network addresses
    subnets, 47–54, 56–59
    VLSM, 73–78
2-bit masks, 49–51
3-bit masks, 51–53, 312
4-bit masks, 53–54
5-bit masks, 54, 56
6-bit masks, 56–57
6-to-4 tunnels, 323

A

Acceptable Use Policy (AUP), 238
accessing MAC addresses, 313
ACLs (access control lists), 239
acquisition of address space, 256–257
adding subnets, 75
addresses
    128-bit, 306
    16-bit, 57–59
    20-bit, 122
    24-bit, 47–54, 56–5, 122
    anycast, 309
    base 16 notations, 306–308
    blocks, 29
        made-up, 268
        preserving, 92–93, 95–99
        stolen, 268
    broadcasting, 172
    CIDR, 110–113, 115–117
    Class B, 83–86
    class-based, 37
    foreign support, 266, 268–269
    global, 176
    GLOP, 176–178
    hijacking, 98

host, 60, 71
IP, 21–28, 239–243
    assigning, 263
    FLSM inefficiencies, 69–73
    hierarchies, 28–29, 31–37
    multicasting, 175–179
    translating MAC addresses, 205–211
    vulnerabilities, 234, 236, 238–239
IPv4, 22
IPv6
    architecture, 306–308
    comparing to IPv4 of, 317–318
    migration tools, 319–324
    types of, 308–313, 315–317
limited-scope, 176
MAC, 313
managing, 253, 273–274
    acquiring, 256–257
    Balkanizing, 292–298
    enterprise WANs, 259–263
    hostmasters, 254–256
    inheriting, 258
    Internet hosting centers, 269–271
    ISP, 264–267, 269
    planning, 274–279
    sequential assignment, 280–288
    symmetrical gaps, 289–290, 292
    tactics, 279–280
mapping, 50
multicast, 309–310
NAT. *See* NAT
nonreportable, 96
nonroutable, 122
private spaces, 121–124
rationing, 97
reserved, 178–179
security, 233
    lending, 248–249
    open networking, 233–243
    RFC 2267, 243–248
spoofing, 241
subnets, 60
subnetting, 39–43, 45–47, 262
subsets, 135
third tiers, 40–41

F

File Transfer Protocol. *See* FTP
files, host.txt, 148–150
first assignable addresses, 48
Fixed-Length Subnet Masking. *See* FLSM
flatness, hosts.txt file, 149–150
flexible subnet masks, 66
FLSMs (fixed-length subnetwork masks), 39
    inefficiencies of, 60–61, 69–70
    sizing, 45
foreign addresses, support of, 266–269
formatting
    IP
        addresses, 21–28
        converting numbers, 23–24
        hierarchies, 28–37
        names, 148–150
FQDN (Fully Qualified Domain Name), 151
fragmentation, 93
    aggregation, 93
    preventing, 96
FTP (File Transfer Protocol), 148–150
Fully Qualified Domain Name (FQDN, 151
functions, IP routing protocols, 215
FYI documents, 15

G

gaps
    sequential assignment, 285–288
    symmetrical, 289–292
gateways, protocols, 223
generic TLDs, 153
global addresses, 176
global expansion of TLDs, 154
GLOP addresses, 176–178
groups
    devices, 261
    joining, 182
    leaving, 182
    multicast, 181–183
growth, planning IP addresses, 278

H

handling unknown IP addresses, 210
hexidecimal numbers, 307
hierarchies
    DNS, 150
        ccTLDs, 163
        namespaces, 151–152
        obtaining namespaces, 163–164
        TLDs, 152–163
    enterprise WANs, 260–263
    IP addresses, 28–37
    ISP tiers, 226, 228
hijacking
    address spaces. 98
    sessions, 241
histories, CIDR, 101–102
hop counts, 220
host.txt files, 148–150
hostmasters, 254–256
hosts, 173
    addresses, 60, 71
    IP addresses, 29
    mathematical trade-offs, 67, 69
    platforms, 270
    unicasting, 170
human-friendly, creating IP addresses, 23–24

I

IAB (Internet Activities Board), 8
IANA (Internet Assigned Numbers Authority), 8, 97
ICANN (Internet Corporation for Assigned Names and Numbers), 8, 155
ICMP (Internet Control Message Protocol), 242
identification of users in communities, 276
IESG (Internet Engineering Steering Group), 10
IETF (Internet Engineering Task Force), 5–11, 22
    Date of Doom, 83–86
        interim solutions, 86–89
        Net 39 experiment, 89–90
        preserving address blocks, 92–93, 95–99
        unused addresses, 90–92
    working groups, 11
IGMP (Internet Group Management Protocol), 181
IGMPv1, 182

Cisco Press
Learning is serious business.
Invest wisely.

Cisco Press Solutions

High Availability Network Fundamentals

Chris Oggerino
1-58713-017-3 • **Available Now**

High Availability Network Fundamentals discusses the need for and the mathematics of availability, then moves on to cover the issues affecting availability, including hardware, software, design strategies, human error, and environmental considerations. After setting up the range of common problems, it then delves into the details of how to design networks for fault tolerance and provides sample calculations for specific systems. Also included is a complete, end-to-end example showing availability calculations for a sample network.

Performance and Fault Management

Paul Della Maggiora, Kent Phelps, Christopher Elliott,
James Thompson, Robert Pavone
1-57870-180-5 • **Available Now**

Performance and Fault Management is a comprehensive guide to designing and implementing effective strategies for monitoring performance levels and correctng problems in Cisco networks. It provides an overview of router and LAN switch operations to help you understand how to manage such devices, as well as guidance on the essential MIBs, traps, syslog messages, and show commands for managing Cisco routers and switches.

IP Routing Fundamentals

Mark Sportack
1-57870-071-X • **Available Now**

Approach your introduction to routing in IP networks with this definitive book that explores the mechanics of routers, routing protocols, network interfaces, and operating systems. This reference provides essential background information for network professionals who are deploying and maintaining LANs and WANs, as well as IT managers who are seeking information on how evolving technology will affect future networks.

E-Support

Andrew Connan and Vincent Russell
1-58720-052-X • **Available Now**

Learn what eSupport is and how it can help your business. This book consists of non-technical, conversational, and easy-to-read interviews with the experts. Setting up an eSupport system isn't cheap or simple, but you can use this book's information as a guide to setting up a successful eSupport system, or improving the one you've got.

CCNA Certifications

Interconnecting Cisco Network Devices

Edited by Steve McQuerry
1-57870-111-2 • **Available Now**

Interconnecting Cisco Network Devices teaches you how to configure Cisco switches and routers in multiprotocol internetworks. If you are pursuing CCNA certification, this book is an excellent starting point for your self-study.

Cisco CCNA Exam #640-607 Certification Guide

Wendell Odom
1-58720-055-4 • **Available Now**

Although it's the first step in the Cisco Career Certifications, the Cisco Certified Network Associate (CCNA) exam is a difficult test. The recent additions of performance-based questions have made it even more challenging. Your first attempt at becoming Cisco certified requires a lot of study and confidence in your networking knowledge. When you're ready to test your skills, complete your knowledge of exam topics, and prepare for exam day, you need the preparation tools found in *Cisco CCNA Exam #640-607 Certification Guide* from Cisco Press.

Cisco CCNA Exam #640-607 Flash Card Practice Kit

Eric Rivard
1-58720-048-1 • **Available Now**

CCNA test time is rapidly approaching. You've learned the concepts, you have the experience to put them into real-world use, and now you want to practice, practice, practice until exam time. *Cisco CCNA Exam #640-607 Flash Card Practice Kit* gives you three methods of proven late-stage CCNA exam preparation in one package: more than 350 flash cards, 550+ practice exam questions, 54 study sheets

The CD-ROM contains 350+ flash cards and more than 550 practice test questions. Flash cards are downloadable to Palm OS and Pocket PC handheld devices.

CCNA Practical Studies

Gary Heap, Lynn Maynes
1-58720-046-5 • **Available Now**

CCNA Practical Studies is a guide for students and instructors alike to gaining essential hands-on experience in networking lab environments. An equally effective supplement to concept-based study guides or as a stand-alone reference for applying CCNA knowledge, this text provides lab-executable scenarios that cover the entire range of CCNA topics. Starting at the physical layer of the OSI model, your students are presented with a layered approach to learning how to build a small network. Each chapter tackles a major subject area such as router configuration, routing protocols, bridging and switching, ISDN, access lists, and IPX. Each subject presents a mini-lab, walking them through the lab scenario and explaining in detail the commands used, why the authors chose the specific commands, and the resulting configurations.

Cisco Press Solutions

Managing Cisco Network Security

Mike Wenstrom
1-57870-103-1 • **Available Now**

Managing Cisco Network Security focuses on implementing IP network security and contains a wealth of case study material, configuration examples, command summaries, helpful tables and diagrams, and chapter-ending review questions, making this book an effective preparation tool for the MCNSportion of the Cisco Security Specialist certification, part of the new Cisco Qualified Specialist certification track.

Cisco Secure PIX Firewalls

David Chapman and Andy Fox
1-58705-035-8 • **Available Now**

Whether you are preparing for the Cisco Security Specialist 1 certification or simply want to understand and make the most efficient use of PIX Firewalls, *Cisco Secure PIX Firewalls* provides you with a complete solution for planning, deploying, and managing PIX Firewall protected networks.

Cisco Secure Virtual Private Networks

Andrew Mason
1-58705-033-1 • **Available Now**

Cisco Secure Virtual Private Networks provides you with the knowledge to plan, administer, and maintain a virtual private network (VPN). Learn how to reduce network cost, enable network scalability, and increase remote access efficiency by deploying Cisco-based VPNs. You will also learn how to configure and test IPSec in Cisco IOS Software and PIX Firewalls; secure remote access connections to corporate networks with IPSec; create a secure tunnel to a Cisco VPN Concentrator and PIX Firewall; and configure the Cisco VPN Concentrator, Cisco router, and PIX Firewall for interoperability.

Cisco Secure Intrustion Detection System

Earl Carter
1-58705-034-X • **Available Now**

Cisco Secure Intrusion Detection Systems provides a clear explanation of why network security is crucial in today's converged networking environment, how the Cisco Secure Intrusion Detection System (CSIDS) improves the security on a network, and how to install and configure CSIDS. The CSIDS is a real-time, network-based IDS designed to detect, report, and terminate unauthorized activity throughout a network. The industry's first and now the market-leading IDS, CSIDS is the dynamic security component of Cisco's end-to-end security product line.

CCNP

CCNP Remote Access Exam Certification Guide

Brian Morgan, CCIE #4865, and Craig Dennis, CCSI
1-58720-003-1 • **Available Now**

Prepare for the Remote Access exam with this comprehensive late-stage preparation tool. Designed to enhance your knowledge of how to design, configure, maintain, and scale a remote access network using Cisco products, *CCNP Remote Access Exam Certification Guide* incorporates an in-depth reference of key topics, practical scenarios, chapter review questions, and a test simulator on CD-ROM to focus your learning.

CCNP Support Exam Certification Guide

Amir S. Ranjbar, CCSI
0-7357-0995-5 • **Available Now**

Get prepared for the CCNP Support exam with this feature-rich troubleshooting resource. With coverage of the concepts involved in diagnosing, isolating, and correcting network problems, *CCNP Support Exam Certification Guide* provides a comprehensive review of all CCNP Support exam objectives. Elements like pre- and post-chapter tests, practical scenarios, and a 200+ question test simulator on CD-ROM assess your readiness for the exam and identify areas that require further preparation.

CCNP Routing Exam Certification Guide

Clare Gough, CCIE #2893
1-58720-001-5 • **Available Now**

Prepare for the Routing exam with this late-stage study resource. Explore access lists, queuing, scalable routing protocols, route redistribution and summarization, dial-on-demand routing, dial backup, and the integration of bridging with a routed network. With in-depth reference of exam objectives, practical scenarios, review questions, and a test simulator on CD-ROM, *CCNP Routing Exam Certification Guide* helps you achieve mastery of all exam topics.

CCNP Switching Exam Certification Guide

David Hucaby, CCIE #4594, and Tim Boyles
1-58720-000-7 • **Available Now**

Ready yourself for the CCNP Switching exam with this feature-rich late-stage preparation resource. Pre- and post-chapter tests, practical scenarios, and the test simulator on CD-ROM are just a few of the elements of *CCNP Switching Exam Certification Guide* that focus your learning. Enhance your knowledge of deploying Cisco products and services that enable multilayer switching connectivity and transport while preparing for the CCNP #640-604 test.